The AMERICAN MEADOW GARDEN

The AMERICAN MEADOW GARDEN

Creating a Natural Alternative
to the Traditional Lawn

JOHN GREENLEE

Photography by SAXON HOLT

TIMBER PRESS
Portland | London

Photographs copyright © 2009 by Saxon Holt.

Published in 2009 by Timber Press, Inc.

The Haseltine Building
133 S.W. Second Avenue, Suite 450
Portland, Oregon 97204-3527
www.timberpress.com

2 The Quadrant
135 Salusbury Road
London NW6 6RJ
www.timberpress.co.uk

ISBN-13: 978-0-88192-871-6

Printed in China

Library of Congress Cataloging-in-Publication Data

Greenlee, John.
  The American meadow garden : creating a natural alternative to the traditional lawn / John
Greenlee ; photography by Saxon Holt. — 1st ed.
      p. cm.
  Includes bibliographical references and index.
  ISBN 978-0-88192-871-6
  1. Meadow gardening—United States. 2. Grasses—United States. 3. Natural landscaping—
United States. I. Holt, Saxon. II. Title.
  SB439.G737 2009
  635.9'64—dc22   2009019438

A catalog record for this book is also available from the British Library.

CONTENTS

PREFACE

WHY CREATE MEADOWS? For me, the reasons are many. Meadows are far more satisfying than either a lawn or traditional border, combining the best attributes of both: like a lawn, a calming place for the eye to rest, yet with the richness and complexity of a border. Unlike lawns, meadows are better for the environment, a safe habitat for beneficial insects and pollinators, a place where native ecology can thrive. Meadows, by attracting a diversity of "life," are animated, alive with rhythmic movement, catching both wind and light. No lawn can do that. And—properly designed—meadows require less maintenance and consume significantly less resources than lawn or border.

I hope this book explains my passion for meadows and persuades readers to make meadow gardens of their own. I cannot tell you when, exactly, in my adult life I became

This was my first meadow garden. It was an urban southern California oasis—you'd never know you were surrounded by concrete and three million people.

Kurt Bluemel's poolside garden. Kurt was a great inspiration to me—he really got the grass movement going in America.

aware of my love for meadows; I can tell you that my love for these special spaces continues as strong as ever. You see, I've been growing grasses as a nurseryman for more than two decades, yet it seems like only yesterday that my affair with them began. I say "affair" because a meadow is like a seductive mistress. Grasses are sensual. You can smell them, and hear them, and watch them move. Meadows are sexy, just like lovers—they never stop changing, never ceasing to surprise. My love affair with meadows has become my life's work. Now I make meadow gardens for a living.

Looking at where I grew up—the most sterile, "natureless" surroundings you could imagine—you might wonder how I ever wound up being called the Grass Guru. Our house was a '60s cookie-cutter tract home in Fullerton, California—Orange County before it was the O.C. In those days, developers were busy building Everyman's vision of the American Dream. They couldn't cut down orange groves fast enough. Each L-shaped house had its own patch of lawn and a lollipop tree newly planted in the front. This was before "planned communities," with few parks and no real nature, at least from a kid's standpoint, as far as the eye could see. No tree was taller than an 8-foot stake, and no leaf ever turned a fall color that matched our third-grade reader. Remember your winding childhood creek? Ours was turned into a straight concrete storm drain. Our natural streams were literally paved into gutters.

But. On the edge of the development, on a phase not yet built, was what we called "The Field." It was our favorite play spot: there the street ended, and the gutter just spilled water out, making what seemed like a natural stream cutting through a seasonal meadow of grass. The field was bordered by a row of big old eucalyptus trees, a classic California windbreak for the remaining citrus groves. They made that field seem a thousand miles away from the new houses they hid. Some scientists say that we humans all have "The Savannah Syndrome," a DNA chip passed on by our African ancestors, who began on the savannahs, that draws us to the grasslands. But I think our instinctive love of grass happens when, as a child, you're just as tall as the grass. I'll never forget being flat on my back in that field, almost hypnotised by the swaying back and forth of grasses and staring at the clouds moving overhead. The wind, noisy in the eucalyptus trees and whispering in the grasses, is a song that still plays in my head. Late afternoons, catching the light, the grasses just seemed to glow. In the rainy season, we could pull up clumps of grass with small chunks of moist earth and lob them at each other. My brothers and I would play hide and seek, make trails and forts, and just enjoy being in the tall grass. I also remember the meadowlarks, and that indescribable liquid trill they make. You only find meadowlarks where you find grass; they make their nests on the ground, in the grass. I stumbled upon their sky-blue speckled eggs and wondered, why were they there? In that field, I think, is where meadows got under my skin.

The first "real" nature I encountered came through summers spent at our Boy Scout Camp in the nearby San Bernardino Mountains. My favorite hike ended at a meadow opening in a Jeffrey pine forest. Jeffrey pines smell like vanilla on a hot summer's day, and I vividly recall sitting there, out of sight in an old tree stump, watching hummingbirds fight over the nectar of the native scarlet columbines and purple penstemons that were sprinkled throughout this golden, scented meadow. I'd watch their acrobatics until it was time to head back to camp.

At summer's end it was back down the mountain to the smoggy suburbs below. I cut lawns on Saturdays and after school, and pulled weeds in people's yards for money. I hated lawn mowers—for some reason, I never learned to love machines. I'd rather have been in that mountain meadow than chopping nature into oblivion. Half the "weeds" I pulled looked prettier than the gardens around them.

The first Earth Day ever was during my senior year of high school. The environmental movement was just beginning, and my ecological awareness was beginning to clash with my declared college major—ornamental horticulture, at Cal Poly, Pomona. Most of my friends were majoring in turf grass management, but turf grass and I just never

A whimsical piece by the garden artist Simple. This gate leads to a sunken garden, surrounded by bamboo to cool and screen me from the surrounding concrete jungle. I think Simple was making fun of my always being trapped on L.A. freeways.

hit it off. To me, turf management classes seemed to be about "controlling" nature, a better living through chemistry approach—as if horticulture spelled danger and always required protective gear. But from where I stood, horticulture opened me up to the amazing world of plants.

Remember, I grew up near Los Angeles—the Cuyahoga River may have caught fire but the Los Angeles River was paved! Today, most of Los Angeles bears little resemblance to the ecology it once was. Much of southern California was originally oak savannah—grassland dotted with oaks. They say ships at sea could find the port of Los Angeles from 50 miles away, by seeing the poppy fields of Altadena blazing 30 miles inland. Poppies grow in grass. Los Angeles used to be grass. As a horticulture student, for the first time I began to understand the eclectic urban ecology around me. I also began to understand the world of gardening. Sure, lawns look great, but at what cost to the environment? My better living through chemistry college degree didn't jibe with my growing awareness of the natural world. As a student, I put lawns in for clients, but what I really wanted to do was to fill their gardens with plants. Why plant a boring lawn bordered by unimaginative shrubs when you could fill a garden with flowers and create garden spaces with birds and butterflies—just like nature? I began to learn about plants, of all types—bulbs and perennials and palms and succulents. I fancied myself quite the plantsman when I got out of school. I thought I knew my plants. As it turned out, I had a lot more to learn.

My epiphany came in 1984 at Kurt Bluemel's nursery near Baltimore, Maryland. There—for the first time in a nursery—were the plants I'd played in, in "The Field." The grasses. How I remember feeling cheated by my college plant ID professors! Where were those grasses from? How could they have hidden from me for so long? There in front of me were hundreds of varieties, row after row of grasses, waving in the wind. I remember saying to myself, "This is it." That day in Kurt's nursery, my love affair with meadows was sealed. Since no one on the West Coast was then growing these plants, I decided to do so myself. I made my first grass garden with my business partner at the time, Mike Sullivan, in San Marino, California. Greenlee Nursery was founded in 1987 and continues to this day, the oldest specialty grass nursery on the West Coast.

I've continued to make meadow gardens ever since, and I suppose I will till my dying day. I've never lost my sense of wonder and affection for meadows. I've created them in Florida, St. Louis, British Columbia, and Hawaii. I've made them on dune sand in Malibu and in the desert at Death Valley. Wherever you travel, if you look hard enough, you'll find meadow grasses growing. Wherever you garden, there will be grasses that thrive and bring you joy. I've spent a good deal of my life making meadows. Let me help you make one.

ACKNOWLEDGMENTS

Every grass, every meadow, and all the gardens and plant people I've met—especially since writing my first book, *The Encyclopedia of Ornamental Grasses* (Rodale 1992)—are, in part, responsible for the book you hold in your hands. Still, certain people should be credited for their overwhelming influence and support.

First and foremost, my grateful thanks to my friend and colleague Ruth Chivers, without whom this book would never have been. To Neil Diboll, who insisted that I "plant" my book before writing it. Thanks also to Saxon Holt and Tom Fischer and everyone at Timber Press. And lastly, to my wife, Leesa, and our son, Sedgie, who gave me the time to get this book down on paper (yes, using an H2 pencil, a lot of them).

I could not have done it without you all.

—JG

As soon as I finished *Grasses* (Storey 2002), I wanted to do a meadows book. I am grateful that John Greenlee was ready to do this book, for he opened my eyes to what a garden meadow can be. Thanks, as John has already done, must go to Ruth Chivers, whose steady support kept us on track. And, of course: thanks, Flora!

I also wish to acknowledge a network of friends and colleagues who share a passion for gardening and selflessly share information and locations. I cannot possibly name you all but certainly must thank all the people who graciously allowed me into their gardens: Dave Fross, Luanne Wells, Ellen Hoffs, Chuck Stopherd, Peter Bergmann, Joann Driggers, Nan Derryberry, Richard McPherson, Paul and Kay Fireman, Ron Lutsko, Donald Hess, Carole Marks, Katherine Greenberg, Stephanie and David Mills, Jack Chandler, Matt Moynihan, Scott Ogden and Lauren Springer Ogden, Panayoti Kelaidis, Susan Sanders, Andrea Delong-Amaya, R. J. Brandes, Thaya Dubois, Hillary Green-Pae, Sandy Hill, Cynthia Tanyan, Rosemary Chang, Jack and Kay Keohane, Kelly McLeod, Roger Raiche, Virginia and Sander Vanocur, Gary Matus and Dan Sheehan, Jill and Rich Carter, Mark and Donna Gormel, Gary Campbell, Nancy Ondra, David Ellis, Kurt Bluemel, Nancy Beaubaire, Tom and Diane Peace, Randy and Karen Woods, Margaret Wilfey, Judith Phillips, Jan Wiste, Tom Steiner, Jim Spiegel and Dinorah Gutierrez, Wes Brittenham, Gail Haggard, Neil Diboll (big shout out to Neil's blackened catfish recipe), Dick and Carole Cline, and Roy Diblik.

—SH

CHAPTER 1

THE LURE
OF THE
MEADOW

The meadow garden at River Farm, headquarters of the American Horticultural Society.
No other group of plants quite catches light like the grasses. When the light passes
through their leaves, grasses glow in late or early light.

Snapper Prairie State Natural Area, Wisconsin. Immense in area, Snapper Prairie is often likened to an ocean. Whereas meadows seem safe and enclosed, prairies are often more exposed to wind, sun, and rain.

THE OBVIOUS PLACE FOR A MEADOW GARDEN is most likely the space currently planted with lawn. Do you really need a lawn? In most suburban gardens, lawns serve little or no purpose; they are seldom used and are way too small for competitive sports. "Silly lawns," my friend, landscape architect Wolfgang Oehme, calls them. Sure, they get walked on occasionally, but there are meadow grasses that will let you do the same thing, with less mowing and with far less consequence to the environment. In the three-county Los Angeles Basin alone, mowers, blowers, and edgers create 22 tons of air pollution a day. Worst of all are the chemicals used by gardeners in their quest for a "healthy" green sward. The amount of fertilizers, weed killers, and insecticides put on the average lawn is staggering. These chemicals—more often abused by untrained

Mt. Tamalpais State Park, California. Water has a special relationship to meadows. It adds sound and a sense of life. Slow water adds reflective surfaces that change color as the light changes.

amateurs, not professional lawn services—are poisoning our environment at an unprecedented rate. Fertilizers are dissolved salts; fungicides usually contain heavy metals; and insecticides are insidious, killing the good bugs along with the bad. Despite the alert given by Rachel Carson in her *Silent Spring* (1962), we almost lost the bald eagle and the California condor, and biologists still worry about decreasing amphibian populations in an increasingly warmer and drier world. All these concerns should be real to every gardener because we all share this one planet. There is a better way, as this book will show you.

At base, all meadows are grasslands. In various times and on various continents, these grass ecologies have been described as meads, pastures, savannahs, sods, and lawns; some of the world's most famous grass ecologies are the South American pampas, South African veldt, the steppes of Russia, and the great North American prairie. These ecologies are characterized by vast, largely treeless grass-covered landscape. Although they vary greatly in their components, they are broadly similar in their nature and look.

Meadows are generally acknowledged to be grassy openings in landscapes with trees, often associated with streams or creeks. Meadows can be composed of indigenous spe-

Short-grass ecologies, like the one shown here, are getting increasingly rare. Thankfully, more and more nurseries are growing the plants that inhabit these meadows. Florissant Fossil Beds National Monument, Colorado.

cies, or they can be mixes of both native and introduced or exotic species. Rightly or wrongly, we may also refer to pastures as meadows. More often, pastures, especially those with a long history of grazing by horses, cattle, or sheep, are altered native ecologies, with very little or no native components.

Meadows, although dominated by grasses, are also a madcap of many other broadleaf plants, something that is like no other plant community. A meadow is a symphony of color, light, and texture. Any one small plot of meadow may look amorphous or anonymous, but actually it is rich in plant species with bulbs, annual grasses, sedges, rushes, mosses, and lichens interwoven to make a living cloth—the hair of the earth, as the great German horticulturalist Karl Foerster put it in his book, *Einzug der Gräser und Farne in die Gärten* (Introducing grasses and ferns into gardens). Like icebergs in the ocean, there's as much, if not more, going on beneath the soil in meadows, out of sight, than there is visible above the ground. And because they are filled with a diversity of plants, they support a diversity of life: from the crucial microbial level to birds, bees, and butterflies, all kinds of creatures are found in meadow ecologies.

For me, meadows have always meant grassy places that were enclosed or framed by the natural features surrounding them. By the sea, you will find grasses adapted to sand, salt, and the wind of the dunes. Meadows on ridge tops, often called balds or portreros, are populated by grasses and other plants adapted to survive the extreme conditions

The movement of birds, bees, and butterflies adds animation to grass ecologies. Blue Ridge Parkway, Virginia.

I believe it is human nature to be drawn to the light that filters through the openings among trees. Meadows gain from the sense of safety and shelter offered by nearby trees. Rocky Mountain National Park, Colorado.

Alpine meadows are intoxicating, maybe in part because they sparkle under the intense, clear mountain sky. Holy Cross Wilderness, Colorado.

found in these locations. In parts of the Midwest, the term "glade," an opening among trees, is interchangeable with "meadow." For many people the word meadow is synonymous with the phrase "mountain meadow." Indeed, after one reaches an altitude of 8,000 to 9,000 feet, the forest trees give way to grassy, flowering meadows, no matter where such conditions are found in the world. Meadows can show up anywhere. For the sake of this book, we will define meadows as grassy spaces that are not mowed and maintained like conventional lawns.

The beauty of meadows

Just as there is no real scientific definition of meadow, if you talk to different people, chances are, you will get differing opinions of what makes a meadow, and that really says it right there. Meadows can be whatever you want them to be, but they are always a place of destination, and a particular magnet for children. Prairies, beautiful in their ocean-like vastness of endless waves, have almost infinite horizons, but the meadows I design all have a backdrop: sometimes trees, sometimes hills and mountains, more often the disguised boundaries of the gardens they are in, or the rest of larger areas, where people are lucky enough to have the luxury of such space. There is usually a door—a portal, if you will—where you step from forest into the light and the grass. For me, the beauty of meadows is all about the relief of a sunny opening after the dark drama of trees.

Moving from light to dark spaces brings a sense of drama to the garden.

Grasses have an almost magical ability to catch and reflect light.

Outdoor furniture, whether fancy or simple, can make the experience of a meadow more inviting and pleasurable.

(next page top) Rushing water adds the sensory experience of sound to a meadow. In this scene, the grasses on the water's edge are seasonally flooded. Big Thompson River, Colorado.

(bottom) Meadows can be especially valuable in marrying the house to the site when the development is on the edge of a natural area.

Meadows are about sky and light; each is an open invitation to lie back in the grass and watch the clouds overhead. Watch the light change, and watch the grasses changing with it: no other plants catch light quite like grasses. In early and late light, the translucent leaves of grass even take on the dramatic colored light shows of dawn and sunset. Clouds and fog are part of the meadow, too. Beads of dew and shadows of moving clouds on waving grasses are all part of the meadow. For me, meadows are all about being in them—you can design them with well-planned paths that meander through lush growth. Or plan enclosed sitting and meeting spaces so that you don't have to stretch out on the ground to appreciate them fully. Unless you really want to, that is!

Grasses and water are a good combination (both are liquid and have movement) and, as it turns out, a natural one as well: meadows are often found by water, near a creek or river, along the seashore, or by a lake. Meadows can be secret spaces, tucked away in

Settlers heading west often chose meadows for their homesteads. Meadows provided food for livestock and allowed the settlers to see who was coming and going.

dense woodland or steep canyon; such damp, shaded, ferny meadows have a special feeling all their own. Alpine meadows are places to rest, draw your breath, and admire the beauty and grandeur of nature all around you.

Meadows do not have to be expansive—they can be small, like prefect little jewels, tucked behind a hedge, fence, or wall in town and suburban gardens. Simple meadows with just a few components can be a place for the eye to rest. Meadows are beautiful transitions between a garden and the wider landscape. On rural sites, meadow plantings can bring the landscape beyond the boundaries into the garden, smudging the garden's end into the natural landscape.

Most meadows are sunny open fields with good, fertile soil and plenty of water. That's precisely what makes them so desirable, and across the country, most meadows were the first areas to be inhabited by settlers pushing the frontier westward. It's no wonder so few native meadows are left: meadows were the first places to be plowed and built on. But even deserts have meadows: Las Vegas literally means "the meadows" in Spanish. Often good desert ecology has a component of grass, especially along desert arroyos or canyons. In desert light, grasses can be at their most stunning. Grasses soften the harshness of arid soil and rock, rendering them more human and habitable. Their fine-textured softness belies the toughness of desert grasses.

A dry garden in Santa Fe, New Mexico, with Mexican feather grass (*Nassella tenuissima*), New Mexico privet (*Forestiera neomexicana*), and upright prairie coneflower (*Ratibida columnifera*). This garden is stunningly golden. It glows in the moonlight.

One of the main drawbacks of a conventional lawn is the constant mowing it requires.

GRASSES FOR NATURAL LAWNS

Here are some of my favorite grasses to walk on. Follow me now. Take off your shoes and feel your grass. Satin, velour, corduroy, denim, silk, cotton—the fabric of grass has to be experienced in its diversity and entirety. On second thought, forget walking—when was the last time you lay down in grass?

Acorus

Agrostis hallii

Agrostis pallens

Anthoxanthum odoratum

Bouteloua gracilis

Buchloe dactyloides

Distichlis spicata

Festuca

Poa arachnifera

Poa compressa

Natural or meadow lawns: a better alternative

By definition, lawns are areas of finely mown grass. A lawn is usually composed of grass species that lend themselves to regular mowing to maintain shorter height. The most common turf grasses in the United States are blues, ryes, bents, fescues, Bermuda, zoysia, centipede, St. Augustine, and paspalums. Few are native. The turf grass industry has focused primarily on these species; they have been selected and extensively hybridized to withstand close cutting by machine and regular foot traffic. Rarely do they resemble their original species: they've been treated with radiation, doused with hormones, crossed and crossed again—all so that they can be kept low and tight. Most conventional lawn grasses need 30 to 40 mowings a year to maintain their manicured appearance. And constant cutting requires constant watering and feeding. Now there is new research into splicing genes in turf grasses to make them chemically resistant to weed killers. Is this a good thing? I wonder. I think we may be creating super weeds.

Yet every region in this great country of ours has its own native sods, which—with very little mowing or cutting—grow naturally as a turf. In recent years, the increasing awareness of the ecologies that once predominated has brought to light native grasses and sedges that make natural or meadow lawns, naturally. These native plants, found in nature before urbanization and modern development, are short by nature, reducing the amount of mowing required for them to stay low. Natural lawns (lawns of nonconventional turf grasses) are adapted to their regional rainfalls, soil types, and climatic conditions.

A natural lawn (from 2 to 6 inches in height, depending on the variety of grass planted), while lawn-like, is quite different from a conventional lawn. If you want a crisp clean look, natural lawns may not be for you. But natural lawns can truly function as conventional turf; they can do what lawn does. From a strictly design perspective, a lawn is a cool green place for the eye to the rest, a place of calm apart from the busyness of a mixed border. Natural lawns can perform this function as well as mowed turf does. And, as they do not require mowing or edging in the conventional sense, there is the additional possibility of flowers and bulbs. Less noise, less water, less labor-intensive. Maybe a natural lawn is right for you.

Most property sizes have shrunk in America. Lawns have gotten smaller and less "useful" in a very real sense. Now, in many older neighborhoods, the urban forest has matured, making our suburban spaces shadier, and increasingly our garden understory is affected by tree roots. In some gardens, it's just too shady to grow a good lawn. Or perhaps the children have grown up and are no longer playing on the lawn. Maybe it's time for a change.

In addition to grasses, each region of the country has its own native sedges that will make these natural lawns. Sedges are a group of grasslike plants belonging to the family Cyperaceae. Most people are familiar only with wetland and weedy species, but in fact

Kelly and Steve McLeod opted to have a lawn of California dune sedge (*Carex pansa*) in front of their Los Angeles home rather than a conventional lawn. Their choice is much better for the environment.

Neil Diboll's No-Mow fescue lawn, at his Wisconsin nursery, makes a fine understory for his orchard and blends well with the surrounding prairie.

many of our best candidates for natural lawns are sedges. They vary in color, height, leaf width, softness, and flowering habit. Some are evergreen, carrying some green through most of the winter; others go dormant with the first hard freeze. Some are best in full sun; others can take deep shade. Some are sand-loving; others can tolerate the heaviest clays.

Meadow sedges that are useful for natural lawns are a particular interest of mine. I have found them from coast to coast, in almost every climate, both in nature and in sub-urban ecologies. Many vary only slightly from one another, and identifying them can be difficult, even for botanical experts. At our nursery in California, we offer regional clones from throughout the United States, most with great potential in garden settings.

A lush sedge lawn of European meadow sedge (*Carex remota*). The compact habit and fine foliage of European meadow sedge make it a particularly sturdy lawn substitute.

(previous page) This small sedge lawn, in the Austin, Texas, garden of Scott Ogden and Lauren Springer Ogden, is a much smarter choice than a lawn that needs constant mowing. Composed mainly of *Carex retroflexa*, it is also chock-full of rain lilies (*Zephyranthes*), waiting for the right time to produce their surprising flowers.

Conventional lawns are water-hungry monsters.

SEDGES FOR NATURAL LAWNS

Carex albolutescens
Carex appalachica
Carex 'Beatlemania'
Carex eburnia
Carex filifolia
Carex flacca
Carex pansa
Carex pensylvanica
Carex perdentata
Carex praegracilis
Carex retroflexa
Carex texensis

Specialty grass nurseries are the best source for local genetic material, and many native plant nurseries grow local clones. When creating natural lawns, it's OK to use a mix of sedges as well as using them in singular masses and sweeps.

The amazing adaptability of these plants has somehow been lost on the turf grass industry. Maybe they don't want a lawn that does not need mowing, watering, and fertilizing like a regular lawn. As more people become aware of the many native sedges that can be utilized as lawns, I'm sure more species and varieties will show up in mainstream nurseries.

Meadows as a solution

Meadows offer a solution to the madness of lawn culture. Many of us just don't want to put precious time into the all-consuming project that is the reality of a good-looking conventional lawn. The alternative—paying for a lawn service—is hardly more attractive in this economy. And think of it: it's not only the energy consumed by mowers; you must also factor in the gas and oil for mowing crews to drive to the site the required 35 times annually, on average. The pollution from the vehicles, mowers, and edgers is in addition to the methane created by the dumping of lawn cuttings. Once on site, noisy lawn care machinery annoys humans and scares wildlife out of your garden. Birds flee, butterflies and bees fly away—until the screeching and whining has ceased. And water is a finite resource that in many regions of the country will never be more plentiful or cheaper. In many areas, aquifers are not being replenished by rainfall, and water is increasingly scarce. There is no longer enough of it to supply lawns. Growing populations and dwindling supply is our scary future, and our landscapes must change with the times.

Native or not, designed or not, meadows are an excellent alternative to the traditional lawn. If you're lucky enough to start with a rich, native patch of plants, you can give nature her head, and let her do the design work while you take the role of managing and editing the plants without adding any outsiders. But, again, such opportunities are rare these days—in fact, that's why some of my clients call me in, to recreate a vision of what might have existed in past times in their gardens. What *is* imperative is that meadow components be eco-friendly, rather than just native for native's sake. Create meadows using grasses and ornamental plants that suit the environment and conditions of your site, be they tropical, wet, rooftop, coastal, hot desert, shady woodland, exposed hilltop, or whatever. Why keep a bad lawn when you could plant a good meadow?

A designed meadow can be exquisitely layered with plants, just as nature is, and as horticulturally sophisticated as any fussy perennial border. Grass is the glue that holds it all together.

CHAPTER 2

HOW AND WHERE GRASSES GROW

A sedge meadow in the Sierra Nevada, California. Native sedges can be found throughout North America. Look hard enough, and you'll find sedges that will thrive in your climate.

ONE OF THE FIRST STEPS in creating a meadow garden is to understand not just how grasses grow, but how grasses grow in different parts of the country. Most books about grass begin with definitions of warm-season and cool-season grasses. This is fine, but what they don't say is that cool-season and warm-season grasses can grow differently in different parts of the country. Creating a beautiful meadow does not require a degree in botany, but it does require that you understand the basics of grass ecology. In this chapter, we'll cover these basics.

Grasses and grasslike plants

First things first: when we talk about grasses in meadow making, we're talking not just about true grasses, from the family Poaceae, but a host of grasslike plants too numerous to mention, in other families. Sedges, rushes, restios—in essence, any grasslike plant can be considered a "grass." There are more similarities than differences among them; still, an old nursery school botanical rhyme sums up some of their distinguishing characteristics like this: "Sedges have edges / Rushes are round / And grasses have nodes from the tip to the ground."

Most rushes are wetland natives (some capable of growing in several inches of water), and it is true that most have cylindrical, hollow stems. The restios (Restionaceae) as well as many members of the lily (Liliaceae) and amaryllis (Amaryllidaceae) families have lance-linear leaves that look like grass. When these bloom, it is a surprise: flowers float above what seems to be grass. Botanists need to distinguish among these botanical allies; meadow gardeners just need to know that they are all closely related and that they can fill many of the same roles in the garden. Many people get overwhelmed, thinking they need to tell a restio from a rush, but what it really comes down to is knowing the characteristics of the plant itself, not the structure of its sexual parts. It is more important to know that there are runners and clumpers, long-lived and short-lived, evergreen and deciduous, water-lovers and drought-takers, sun-lovers and shade-lovers among all these groups. Leave botany to the botanists, and get into gardening.

Warm- and cool-season grasses

Warm-season grasses tend to be dormant and dried in the winter; they begin to grow in the spring and usually flower in summer or fall. In the Southwest, many go drought dormant between scarce summer rains. Many warm-season grasses display fall foliage color, as temperatures cool and day length shortens. Their autumn palette, as with trees and shrubs, ranges from hot reds and rich rusts through to glowing embers of oranges, warm tans, and bright yellows. Although some warm-season grasses hold this color into winter, most will dry to browns and parchment colors as they senesce. In wet winters or under a snow load, last season's foliage begins to melt away. New shoots will emerge through the old leaves as spring comes around. Many warm-season grasses are confused in warm climates; in the mild Mediterranean West or subtropical South, their dormancy is short and fall color, too, is fleeting.

Cool-season grasses tend to be evergreen year-round. Most begin to grow in late winter or spring; some begin to grow in the fall and actively grow in the winter,

This New Mexico lawn of buffalo grass (*Buchloe dactyloides*), edged with little bluestem grass (*Schizachyrium scoparium*), will tolerate extremes of heat and drought. Summer rains will green it up seemingly overnight. One inch of water per week will keep it green throughout the summer.

Often confused with *Eragrostis chloromelas*, *E. elliottii* is a love grass native to Florida. Its winter color is stunning when backlit.

(left) In winter and spring, the grasses on this California hillside are a brilliant emerald. Later, as the heat of summer sets in and the rains stop, these grass ecologies go brown and dormant. Finding native grasses that will stay green with a little additional water is key to meadow gardening in a Mediterranean climate.

(right) Texas bluegrass (*Poa arachnifera*) and evening primrose (*Oenothera berlandieri*) blend in a drought tolerant Malibu garden. Among drought tolerant grasses, Texas bluegrass has exceptionally dark green foliage.

depending upon temperatures and rainfall. Many cool-season grasses on the West Coast, however, are green only when the rain falls, from November to April, turning beige and brown—sometimes we prefer to say golden—when they are dormant in the summer. And in high altitudes, cold winter temperatures can blast even cool-season grasses, turning them dormant. Depending upon latitude and temperatures, these grasses tend to bloom in early spring and early summer and into the fall. Many have showy emergent colors, with new foliage tinged pink or shiny bright green; these often fade as the season progresses. Without a winter chill, many of these grasses will never grow and thrive. Like certain fruits, they must have their vernalization in order to grow and thrive.

While meadows can be made of warm-season grasses, it is the cool-season grasses that tend to make meadows look like meadows. A somewhat indefinable quality makes cool-season grasses more "meadowy."

Annual or perennial?

Grasses are generally separated into annuals (completing a full life cycle in one growing season) and perennials (persisting for more than one year). Some grasses are strongly perennial, enduring ten years or more; others are weakly perennial, living perhaps two or three years before they die. Meadows are best made with a strong foundation of long-lived perennial grasses; those consisting of entirely annual grasses can make interesting and exciting grass ecologies, but it is easy for weeds to invade them. Fleeting as they are, annual grasses are often good as accents or for seasonal effects. Short-lived peren-

The No-Mow fescue in the foreground thrives in the dry shade of the trees, while the little bluestem (*Schizachyrium scoparium*) thrives in the sunny opening.

Large, clump-forming grasses aren't easy to walk on; a path is the best way through them.

Aggressively spreading grasses are worth your attention. These are very "successful" plants; some, even natives, can completely overwhelm your plantings. Some creep and spread; others reseed themselves, casting thousands of potential plants to the wind and into the surrounding ecology. In many situations, you may *never* be able to eliminate these plants from your garden. Every region of our country has its own set of aggressive spreaders. It is of the utmost importance that you know which ones can affect your garden and meadow. Check out "The Wicked Ones" in Chapter 7 to learn about the worst offenders.

nial grasses can also be used in a meadow as accents, but it is unwise to use short-lived grasses where long-lived species better suit the site conditions. It is important to know which grasses are long-lived in your region; some grasses that are long-lived perennials in northern tier states (blue fescue, for example) are winter annuals in low deserts or hot humid southern climates.

Clumping or creeping?

Most grasses grow either in tight clumps (these are said to be cespitose), or they creep and spread to form a colony. With clumping grasses, the rhizomes do not spread, and the grass grows as a mound of foliage. Some clumping grasses can be walked on because they lie flat, like a mat. Others form clumps so dense they are not easily trod upon: one can walk "through" them, but not "on" them. Growth patterns must be considered when designing meadows, in order to avoid one grass becoming overly dominant in any one area.

Of the grasses that spread by creeping, some creep slowly and are easy to use in a meadow. Others can be wickedly aggressive and have the potential to take over an entire site—and even encroach into your neighbors' lots. Grasses that creep can do so in two ways: from aboveground stems, called stolons, and from underground stems, known as rhizomes. Creeping grasses tend to be easiest of all to walk on because they form a uniform colony.

Grass flowers

It's amazing how many people think grasses do not have flowers. We have become so disconnected from our natural world that most people know grass only as lawn. Stop mowing and you begin to see the incredible array of grass flowers. Besides variety of form and color, they also bloom at various times of the year. Sophisticated meadow gardens can have grasses blooming over a long period of time, from late winter through spring and into fall.

Grasses are flowering plants, and grass flowers, and the seedheads they produce, are key to successful meadow making. Grasses vary greatly in their tendency to spread from seed. Some grasses are wicked reseeders and spread aggressively from seed. Others rarely or never set viable seed and are well mannered in a garden setting. As all keen gardeners know, the ability to spread easily from seed can be a blessing or a curse in a garden. Non-native or exotic species can pose not only a threat to your garden but to nearby native ecologies as well. Seeds don't stop at garden boundaries, so it is not surprising that many weedy grasses, which are unfit for meadow making, have already spread throughout many suburban garden settings. Every ecology, from Hawaii to Maine, Seattle to Miami, has non-native weedy grasses in their local ecology. Successful meadow making depends on controlling or managing equally well both the good grasses and the not so good. The best meadow grasses, native or non-native, are what I like to call good garden citizens; they are well-behaved components and stay where you put them.

Flowering grasses like hairy melic (*Melica ciliata*) rival flowering perennials for drama.

Grass flowers are technically an inflorescence, a group of flowers. Some are showy and cover the plant so that the foliage is totally hidden beneath the flowers. Other grasses have flowers that are insignificant, held down inside the foliage and barely noticed. Whether inconspicuous or not, grass flowers are arranged in many different ways. Some are slender see-through spikes; others are billowy, silky, or cottony puffs. Most showy flowering grasses display two colors: the first, the color of the emerging flower; the second, the color of the fading flower, as the seedheads mature and ripen. Newly emerging grass flowers are often white, pink, black, purple, and red; seedheads become the glorious tawny shades of late summer and fall. Purple muhly (*Muhlenbergia capillaris*) has cloudlike flowers that emerge purplish and later become golden. Panicum blooms are flushed with the most incredible silver-blushed red before assuming their bleached autumn russets and browns.

(left) The diaphanous flowers of *Muhlenbergia capillaris* 'White Cloud', a white form of the popular purple muhly and one of the last grasses to bloom in autumn.

(right) Smooth brome (*Bromus inermis*), an invasive species that can nevertheless be managed to make a successful meadow. However, if you are given the choice, there are native grasses that can do the job just as well, if not better.

(left) Eastern gamagrass (*Tripsacum dactyloides*) has small but richly colored, downward-hanging flowers. While showy in a conventional sense, they are also fascinating up close. As with many grasses, the ripe seeds are an important food source for wildlife.

(right) Purple muhly (*Muhlenbergia capillaris*). This species has two forms in the U.S. nursery trade: Florida plants are taller, with greener foliage, while Texas clones are shorter, with grayer foliage.

Some showy grass flowers are like many prized flowers of other garden plants: fabulous but fleeting. These grasses create special moments that may last only a week or so and then are gone. Texas bluegrass, *Poa arachnifera*, is one such grass: its emerging flowers are like spider webs with fine silky threads, and then, like many of the best moments in life, or in the garden, they fade. With careful planning, such ephemeral shows can be enjoyed throughout the year: simply plant early, mid, and late season flowering grasses. Pampas grass (*Cortaderia selloana*) is perhaps the best example of a grass that has an iconic flower; its flower says exotic, Victorian. But the majority of grass flowers are neutral and blend well with almost any gardening style. That most people are not familiar with them only adds to their wonder.

Native grasslands

The North American continent is a vast and varied part of the planet, spanning more than 3,000 miles east to west, four time zones, and latitudes from the southernmost tip of the Florida Keys at 25°N to the northernmost point of Alaska at 72°N. And in all this expanse, from tropical southern climates to snowy arctic tundra, grasses and sedges will be thriving. Grasses grow differently in each region, and the ones that are native to each area have adapted themselves to their related soils and climates. There are rain forests in the Pacific Northwest and real deserts, like the Sonoran, that rival any of the world's great deserts. Frigid prairies in the winter are subjected to subtropical heat in summer months. Not only the grasses but many of the plants that naturally survive under these

Many California grasslands, though picturesque, are not what they used to be. Overgrazing in times of drought and the introduction of aggressive annual grasses have greatly reduced the extent of native species.

Meadows and prairies can be found throughout the American West, though little remains pristine. Even the driest parts of the Southwest have moist areas that are hospitable to grasses.

conditions—annuals, perennials, bulbs, and corms—make good components for meadows, suiting all kinds of sites, from full sun to shade, from soil that is permanently wet to soil that gets the bare minimum of rainfall and needs drought tolerant planting.

From the sandiest shores at the lowest altitudes near ocean shorelines to the highest mountaintops, you can find native grasses and the plants that associate well with them, making natural grass ecologies. While these can share similar characteristics, each region has its own unique native and exotic (non-native) components. Making successful meadow gardens has everything to do with how these components work together. Aggressive species can dominate to the point of being a given—unkillable and unstoppable. Some grass ecologies, such as cattails (*Typha*) and common reed (*Phragmites australis*), are difficult if not impossible to eliminate because the area they grow in cannot be protected against reinfestation. Knowing what grasses are currently growing in the area where you plan to make your meadow is essential.

North America's notable grass ecologies begin in the east; they include New Jersey's Pine Barrens, the Smoky Mountain Balds, and the pine savannahs of Georgia and Florida. These pine savannahs continue south through Florida, terminating in one of America's great grass ecologies, the Everglades. The Great American Prairie begins

to break out just over the Appalachians and, after Ohio, does not stop until it hits the Rocky Mountains. In Colorado, the short grass prairies give way to mountain meadows until they pass the tree line to alpine heights. In the Southwest, the deserts too have grasses, although sheep, cattle, and development have greatly diminished their presence. On the West Coast, the coastal plains were once covered with oak savannah. California's great Central Valley was home to the largest grassland west of the Rockies. In the Pacific Northwest, the short grass prairies of eastern Oregon and Washington give way to the forests of the Cascades. The largest grassland west of the Cascades is the Willamette Valley. No longer resembling its original grassland, but still in grass, much of it is now home to most of America's turf grass seed production.

In meadows, flowering accents come and go with the seasons. This meadow in Oregon's Willamette Valley has both native and non-native grasses but is still beautiful. The shooting stars (*Dodecatheon*) will be followed by other flowers.

Not every meadow garden is a restoration, the putting back of the native ecology. True restorations may be impractical for many reasons, but native grasses almost always play a role in successful created meadows. I like to use the meadow grasses that best suit each individual site, either native or native adapted. It is more important that the components work together, whether native or not. Non-native meadows can be beautiful and ecologically sound if properly designed. In the end, regional natives and noninvasive exotics are the foundation of most meadows.

Northeast

The Northeast is mostly rocky and forested. At the coast, meadows have adapted to grow in the fine particles of dune sand, often receiving direct salty spray from the ocean. Moving inland, natural meadows in this region are found on the edges of forests and in generally shallow rocky soil; these areas tend to be moist or seasonally moist, supporting sedge meadows with ferns and wildflowers. Often what is called a meadow in this region is in fact pasture. And the open ground pastures and meadows of the Northeast tend to want to revert to forest.

Pasture meadows in this region, while sometimes containing native remnant prairie or grassland, are most often composed of cool-season non-natives (mostly from Europe) that have been planted or have naturalized. These pasture grasses (including species from the genera *Anthoxanthum*, *Dactylis*, and *Holcus*) were originally planted by settlers to "improve" the land, or to make pastures of known quality like back home in Europe. "Improving" to a farmer or rancher meant improving the land's ability to feed livestock better. Much to the dismay of ecologists, this "improving" became a staple part of farming and ranching, and it has led to the permanent altering of the native ecology. Original grass ecologies are hard to find in the Northeast. If a meadow existed with a good fertile well-drained soil and no trees to cut down, it was the first land to be plowed or grazed.

The European species that compose most pastures are found throughout the northern latitudes. Non-native pastures can be managed to make beautiful meadows, but first any woody plants or vines must be mowed, removed, or killed, or they will overwhelm meadow areas.

Lawn grasses used in the Northeast are primarily cool-season and non-native; bluegrass and fescues predominate.

Winters in the Northeast are long and cold. Summers can be hot and humid. Fall arrives early, and the growing season comes to an end with the onset of frosts.

Mid-Atlantic and Southeast

Down through the Mid-Atlantic states, conditions are fairly similar to the Northeast but with some important differences. Winters are not as long or as cold, but summers are hotter and more humid. Higher clay content soils begin to appear, and clay soil is increasingly the norm the further south you go. There is less snow on the ground for less time in winter, and as you approach the Carolinas, winter starts to deliver little snow

It's always a battle between the grasses and the woody plants. Unless subjected to fire or human intervention, this meadow will revert to forest.

The great meadows along Virginia's Blue Ridge Parkway include mountaintops known as balds, grasslands that are rich in species. Unfortunately, road building provides a conduit for non-native plants, and misguided management techniques exacerbate the problem.

to cover the ground. Meadows in the Mid-Atlantic are similar to those of the Northeast but with bigger and bigger clearings; many of the same species occur, but cool, rainy winters with occasional hard freezes tempt gardeners here to grow many things that will sooner or later be killed in a really hard freeze. As one travels into southern Georgia and on into northern Florida, native meadows are found in poor soils and rocky ledges. Many of the grass ecologies in this region are pine savannahs, one of America's most unappreciated grass ecologies.

Deep South and Gulf States

Eventually, Georgia clay gives way to the sugar sand of the Florida peninsula. Here, different grasses begin to show up in lawns—bahia, Bermuda, centipede, St. Augustine, and zoysia all appear and thrive. None are native to Florida. There is very little Florida prairie left in its original state. While proportionally there are large tracts of wetland grass areas still intact (Everglades National Park, for one), true Florida pine savannah is hard to come by, many acres of coastal dunes have been developed, and the citrus industry replaced much of Florida's native grasslands.

It rains a lot in Florida, but sandy soils do not hold water for long. Winters are mild and dry; summers are hot, wet, and humid. In the south, the lack of temperature differences between daytime and night temperatures keeps many species of grasses from thriving. In the Deep South, the true grasses (members of the family Poaceae) begin to disappear, and sedges and other members of the family Cyperaceae start to dominate the grasslands. Many southern grasses are aggressive colonizers. Existing lawns can be difficult to convert to meadows, as aggressive species can infect and overgrow an area in a relatively short period of time. Native grasslands here, as elsewhere, need constant burning, grazing, or mowing to prevent the overgrowth of invasive woody shrubs and trees. Sadly, non-native invasive plants are more the norm than the exception here.

Travel east along the Gulf, and many of the same conditions and species are to be found. Rainfall is generally plentiful, from 40 to 60, even 80 inches per year. Summers are wickedly hot and humid. Soils are mostly acid, and wet meadows are far more common than dry ones. Coastal dunes are represented all the way from the tip of Florida to the tail end of Texas. The grasses in Texas fall into two basic categories: those growing with 20 inches or less of rainfall, and those needing between 20 and 40 inches of rainfall to thrive. The west of Texas is hot and dry, the east, wet and humid. Temperatures can go from 80°F to below freezing in a matter of hours. This is a tough place to be a plant. Floods and drought are common. Yet Texas has the largest number of grass species of any of the 50 states. Pure native Texas grasslands—from sedge meadows in the piney woods through the black land prairies of central Texas to the blond expanses of west Texas—exert a special charm. Once you've seen them, they'll never leave you.

Southern Texas grassland is often in thick gumbo clay and grows in oppressive heat and humidity. Much if not most of this grassland has been completely altered. A lot of Texas grassland resembles South Africa. The dominant Texas grasses—Bermuda, king ranch bluestem, Johnson grass, coastal Bermuda, guinea grass—are all invasive, aggressive, non-natives.

Remnant Texas prairies that have never been improved are called hay meadows. Old farmers who knew that prairies could be productive without improvements often saved good, rich prairie ecology. Natural depressions in the flatland were called "buffalo wallows," as water from storms collected in these hollows. Many special meadow plants are unique to these ecologies. Lawn grasses in Texas are Bermuda, St. Augustine, and zoysia in the south, with Bermuda and tall fescue in the north. Cool-season grasses struggle to stay disease- and weed-free. Over time, most lawns degrade into Bermuda. Buffalo grass lawns are under constant threat from invasion by Bermuda seed, stolon, and rhizome.

As in much of California, Texas wildflower shows are "spring loaded." As the heat of summer increases, the flowers fade and the grasses provide the foliage and texture to carry the meadow through to autumn.

A dry meadow with blue grama (*Bouteloua gracilis*) and needle and thread grass (*Hesperostipa comata*). In this part of Colorado, the prairie begins to change to a mountain ecology where grassy openings give way to forest. Garden of the Gods Natural Monument, Colorado.

Midwest and Prairie States

Travel north of Texas, and you'll find the beginning of one of the world's most productive grasslands. Drier prairies stretch from Oklahoma to Iowa, Nebraska, into Colorado; these may be tall, short, or mid grass prairies, depending on the amount of rainfall, which varies from as little as 6 inches per year in eastern Colorado to 40 inches in Iowa. Iowa, once almost entirely tall grass prairie, has the distinction (if that is the right word) of having the most altered ecology (the least amount of original pre-European settlement ecology) of any state in the nation. Less than one-tenth of one percent is left. It's still grass—just corn and wheat, not bluestem and Indian grass. Lawn grasses tend to need lots of water, and as you travel north, Bermuda begins to thin out and cool-season grasses start to dominate. Lawns in this region are subject to greater temperature extremes the further north you go.

Remnants of the Midwest's once vast prairies are a rarity. Buffalo are truly the symbol of the prairie. Shaw Nature Reserve, Missouri.

Before it was properly understood, prairie was thought to be unproductive. In fact, prairie soil is usually deep, rich, and fertile. Snapper Prairie State Natural Area, Wisconsin.

Prairies are generally taller grass ecologies than meadows. Meadows are generally found in shady ecologies, near rivers under trees. In the prairies, trees are mostly found in the depths of the river valleys. Meadows are often seasonally flooded and usually have been improved for pasture or farmed.

Travel north into the heart of the Midwest—Ohio, Illinois, and Wisconsin and into the forest of the northern interior states. Once again, the climate and grasses change. Now the forest comes back into play, with stretches of prairie broken up by forest and development. Special meadow ecologies occur throughout the Midwest on limestone formations, along the dunes of the Great Lakes, and in forest openings along the lakes and streams of the heartland. Much can be learned about how to create meadows by studying these places, while they can still be found.

Lawns in this region are almost always a mix of cool-season grasses: blue, rye, fescue, and bent are the most common. Lawns and meadows left unmowed usually degrade into forest and shrubby, viney thickets. Again, non-native trees, shrubs, and vines have invaded grass ecologies. The growing season starts to shorten as one travels north into the Midwest. Harsh cold winters are followed by short springs and hot summers. Fall can be nice and springlike, or cold and wintry, and precipitation falls throughout the year. Count on snow to cover the ground for much of winter.

Mountains

Head west, and the prairies eventually hit the great Rocky Mountains. Here, elevation (in addition to rainfall and temperatures) begins to affect which grasses thrive. By the time the prairies touch the Rockies, the elevation has reached 5,000 feet—a mile high. An amazing transition takes place as prairie morphs into alpine meadow. Warm-season grasses begin to drop out at 5,000 feet; cool-season grasses dominate elevations above this height and to about 8,000 feet, at which point sedges take over.

An alpine meadow is, perhaps for many people, what a real meadow is all about: a carpet of grasses and flowers, from spring into summer and even into fall. At high elevations, no grasses are evergreen, and even cool-season ones turn into burnished copper colors. Rain falls throughout the year, and snow can cover the ground from fall through late spring. The growing season is therefore often short in this region, and temperature swings are legendary. Air gets drier, and winter winds often create conditions that can freeze-dry landscapes. Plants have got to be tough to be at home on the "Front Range."

Continue toward the Pacific, and the Intermountain West begins to unfold. Tall, seemingly endless mountain ranges give way to valley floors, only to heave upward again. Many pastures were improved in the past with non-native species. Soils become increasingly alkaline, and many contain odd components that may be serpentine or saline. Less rain falls in the summer and precipitation starts in fall to set up a winter rain–summer dry pattern. Newcomers to this rapidly urbanizing region are challenging the harsh natural landscape and its related climate in order to create gardens. Lawns tend to be water-thirsty cool-season grasses (fescues, ryes, blue, bent), but water availability is increasingly an issue. Throughout the West, most cool-season grass lawns are summer irrigated.

Alpine meadow, Rocky Mountain National Park, Colorado. Alpine wildflowers and their hybrids can often be found in nurseries. The true native alpine grasses are just now becoming available for meadow making.

In autumn, early rains green up cool-season grasses. Meadowy forest understory makes a nice backdrop for the warm colors of autumn foliage. Big Tesuque Trail, Santa Fe National Forest, New Mexico.

Southwest

Heat and water are the principal factors in the landscape of this region. The original grasslands of the Southwest (New Mexico, Arizona, parts of Texas, Nevada, and southern California) are some of America's greatest natural treasures. The shorter grass prairies of pinyon pine ecology, in particular, are magical in their silvery splendor. Sadly, very little of this ecology remains. Xeric (dry) ecologies are always more fragile than mesic (moist) ones, and desert meadows are some of the most altered of all grass ecologies. Pristine desert grassland, close to water sources, has disappeared fastest of all, as there was so little of it to begin with.

Irrigation, for good or evil, has changed the face of the Southwest: apply water to land, and many more kinds of plants will grow. Population in this region is ever increasing, which in turn places an increasing strain on the region's natural eco-systems. Many parts of the Southwest are literally running out of water.

Here, scant rain falls in summer, with little more falling in winter. Summer temperatures can be extremely high, and cool winters have occasional freezes. Bermuda is the primary lawn grass, with zoysia and *Buchloe dactyloides* (buffalo grass) making minor appearances. Areas at higher elevations can grow cool-season grasses (fescue, blue, rye) if irrigated.

Pacific Coast

Travel across the desert and one or two more mountain ranges, and you will finally hit the Pacific Coast. The cold waters of the Pacific Ocean create a climate with rainy winters, dry summers, and ocean breezes moderating temperatures—a Mediterranean climate, in short, and one of the most desirable, as evidenced by the huge population concentrated along the coast. Irrigation plays a major role in creating the cultivated landscape in this region; left unwatered in summer, grassland and meadows in a Mediterranean climate turn beige and brown, not a color scheme most gardeners want to see. Here, in direct contrast to how they grow back east, many native grasses are green in the rainy western winters and brown and dormant in summer, remaining so till the rains of fall and winter green them up.

Traveling inland from the ocean and northward, the landscape changes. With hotter summers and colder winters, subtropical grasses begin to drop out. Annual grasses and flowers dominate most grassland and meadow ecologies in the West. These grasslands are "spring loaded"—green and with flowers only in the winter and spring. From early summer to late fall they are dormant, crispy, dry, and flammable. Eastern and Midwestern meadows and prairies, by contrast, with their greater percentage of perennials (both

West Coast grassland makes its biggest show of color in early spring, fueled by winter rains. While fleeting, these spring shows are spectacular. For designed meadows, you can add later-blooming accents to prolong the display. Fort Hunter Liggett Reserve, California.

At higher elevations, summer can be the showiest season. Once the snow has melted and the days get longer, more and more wildflowers come into bloom. Big Meadows, Eldorado National Forest, California.

grasses and flowers) bloom from summer through fall, and then, with the approach of shorter days and cooler temperatures, show autumn colors.

Western lawns are primarily planted with tall fescue, perennial rye, and bluegrass; minor players include kikuyu, zoysia, St. Augustine, and buffalo grass. None are native to this region. From Portland south, Bermuda grass (*Cynodon dactylon*) increasingly muscles in; a warm-season grass, Bermuda is dormant in winter but grows aggressively with the addition of summer water.

Finally, reaching the Pacific Northwest, the climate is still essentially a Mediterranean one, just cooler. Moving inland by even just a few miles into the mountains of

the Pacific Northwest, temperatures drop considerably and the face of the landscape becomes intermountain. Lawns in the Pacific Northwest are primarily cool-season grasses (fescue, blue, rye, bent).

It's ironic that Oregon's once-beautiful Willamette prairies are now home to most of the turfgrass seed production in America. What little native prairie remains is mostly wet ecology.

— — —

Sadly, for many, the native meadows and prairies of the past are a distant memory. It's time we put some of our natural heritage back. Let's rethink our lawns. Let's put some nature back into our lives. Let's make a meadow garden.

CHAPTER 3

MEADOWS FOR A PURPOSE

In this garden, it would be a mistake to plant grasses that need lots of water. Site-appropriate and locally adapted plants are much more in sync with the borrowed landscape in the distance.

Properly selected, grasses are excellent on slopes. Many grasses give the effect of water cascading down a hill, and are good for erosion control as well.

PURPOSEFUL MEADOWS will solve garden problems as well as be a joy to behold and a pleasure to be in. The key to making a successful meadow garden is to partner with nature, but first you must be site specific.

Mastering the site

The first thing to do is to analyze your site thoroughly. Start by examining the topography: where are the slopes? which way does the grade fall, and is it gentle or steep? Where and what are the immovable features of the site? Buildings, walls, fences, paved driveways, patios and walks, mature trees, shrubs, and hedges—all affect a site, particularly when combined with aspect. The soil in shade cast by north-facing walls and trees will be cooler, more moist, than ground that is very open or seldom in shade. Underly-

ing bedrock may be evident close to the surface. Hollows in sunken areas may indicate areas with poorer drainage.

Does water stay in certain areas, permanently making damp, boggy conditions, or do these areas drain over time? Sites on top of hillsides will drain more readily, but may also be exposed to strong prevailing winds. Drainage of the site may be seasonally affected—for example, swales for ground drainage can be incorporated into meadows in an aesthetic way. Paths can be planned that either meander directly through proposed meadows, if the ground is well drained at all times, or float above them as catwalks or boardwalks linked by bridges over deeper gullies, swales, or streams.

Armed with knowledge of your site, consider to what purpose the meadow is to be put. Is it to be viewed from a distance primarily—for example, in larger gardens? Or is to be walked through and experienced every day? This will be the case in smaller spaces—for example, where you are turning a front yard with traditional lawn, driveway, and walk-to-entrance combination into a meadow garden that runs right up to your house. What purpose you want your meadow to serve will usually affect the theme or

Scale is important: large gardens need large plants or large sweeps of smaller grasses. Go big or stay home!

style that you adopt as well as influencing your design plans, both spatial and planting. That is, purpose has to be factored into the scientific part of good design: location + topography + climate + site conditions + existing vegetation formula. That's not to say that taking all these factors into account is to limit your horizons. A meadow can be whatever you want it to be—to a point. There can be a difference between what you want in your garden and what nature wants to be in your garden.

Working with nature sounds so simple, but many people just don't get nature. Many gardeners are sadly ignorant of their local ecology, but your knowledge of it will be critical to your meadow's success. You've got to get to know your site, starting with its history. Every garden and every area in a garden, wherever it may be, was something else before you and your house arrived on site. Ancient events shaped your land's present-day character. If you could turn the dial back on a time machine, your garden might be under primeval seas, with layer after layer of sea bottom compressing slowly into limestone. Or you might find yourself under a glacier, under a thick sheet of ice, carving solid granite into glacial moraine. Continuing down this timeline, grazing animals may have cleared the site of your garden, or it may have been farmed to produce useful crops. Some ground may have been left for nature to "garden," undisturbed by man until relatively recently. The immediate past matters, too. For example, many suburban tract homes are built on land on which the topsoil has either been removed or altered, so that the entire lot is on "engineered" soil, heavily compacted and devoid of natural components.

Soil type

Knowing your soil type is an absolute prerequisite if your meadow is going to solve problems rather than create them. Current thinking on sound ecological principles advises us not to fight the site. Don't try to change the soils—that's working against nature rather than joining in partnership with her. Instead, acknowledge the givens of your site—plan and plant accordingly.

Thankfully, the majority of grasses tolerate an amazingly wide variety of soil conditions, from sand to clay. Sandy soils have fine particles and are often lacking in nutrients and organic matter; they may need some added nutrition to get plants going. If your soil is sandy and free-draining, choose grasses that thrive in light, sandy soil. What if the soil is clay and compacted? Often soils have been compacted by heavy grading equipment, particularly when new homes are constructed or older ones remodelled extensively. Clay soils are heavier and stay wet once they get wet, and there are plenty of grasses that will thrive in them.

If you don't know what kind of soil you have, don't worry—you're not alone. Ask for some professional help. Landscape contractors and horticulturists can save you a lot of grief if you call them in early on. One hour of paid consultation goes a long way toward saving time and money and the heartbreak of dead plants. A local professional will know what kind of soil you have and how it affects plant selection and growth. Grasses will grow differently in different soil types. Sand-lovers may grow more slowly, and clay-lovers may need more water. When plants are being tortured as opposed to

(previous page top) With its diverse meadow plantings, this front yard is far better for the environment than the neighbor's lawn across the street.

(bottom) Grasses and stone are a natural match: the hardness and weight of the rocks are countered by the softness of the grasses.

Many plant species thrive in dry climates, and while some may be familiar garden plants, in meadow settings they take on a whole new character.

(previous page top) Mexican feather grass (*Nassella tenuissima*) is a good choice for dry soils. Grasses are ideal for softening the look of harsh, dry environments.

(bottom) Native grasses are a good bet for coastal sites; in fact, many beach communities restrict plantings to native species. Like many other endangered ecologies, pure coastal prairie can be hard to find.

If your neighbor has a lawn of creeping, invasive grasses next to your meadow, you may need to create a barrier or no-man's-land to protect your meadow from invasion.

being coddled, they may grow lower or shorter. This is not always a bad thing, just something worth noting.

And what about the natural state of soil—is it wet or is it dry? Dry soils can usually be irrigated, and wet soils can often be drained, but why not plant the grasses that thrive in the given soils? Why drain a wet area when there are plenty of grasses that love getting their feet wet? Resources are precious, and many areas of the country are experiencing water shortages and droughts. Wise planning should take into account that water will probably never be more plentiful or less expensive. Just because you can irrigate to your heart's content doesn't mean that you should.

Get to know the plants growing on your site

Many gardeners, ready to make a meadow, look at their yard and see an old dying lawn. Are you sure that's the case? Appearances can be very deceptive—and nature can be a mistress of disguise.

Imagine you invited me to come take a look at your lot and give you a consultation on your meadow prospects. First, we would identify the type of old lawn you have. Although it may all look like one type of grass—say, tall fescue—there are usually others mixed in with it. Invariably, I'll find an invasive grass—Bermuda grass, kikuyu, or nutgrass. Maybe I'll find morning glory. All are potentially noxious weeds that will infect any meadow you are trying to make if you don't get rid of them right at the start.

Knowledge is power—knowing every single plant in a dull-looking old lawn is essential. It's not really that hard and can even be fun! Or, again, call in a pro. You've got to know the enemy in order to defeat them—and noxious weeds are the enemies of new meadows.

Just as important is to be aware of what's growing next door. Johnson grass, smooth brome, Bermuda, golden bamboo—all kinds of enemies might be hiding in that idyllic-looking planted garden or so-called cleared field. It may look empty, or innocuously cultivated, but it might harbor weed seeds, rhizomes, stolons, or all three. Any or all of these can reinfect or come to dominate your intended meadow. How you eliminate the weeds, and keep them out, depends on what weeds they are, and the time of year you intend to make your meadow or natural lawn. Learn more about weeds in Chapter 7.

Green needle grass (*Nassella viridula*) has invaded this Colorado meadow. You may decide to leave it and work with it rather than try to eliminate it. Remember: a weed is just a plant out of place.

Natural problem solvers

I have made meadows in various locations, some of them extremely challenging—for example, the intense conditions of Death Valley. I know that meadows can be made in many different soil types, and I have made them in a range of styles. I have encountered very few problem sites that cannot be solved by a meadow.

You can make a meadow in any part of your garden, whatever size it is. They can be in a front yard, in a backyard, down a narrow side yard, or even on a roof. Meadows are not just for people with rolling acres of space, so urban and suburban garden owners needn't despair. My friend and colleague Matt Moynihan's garden shows how a rich, diverse, dramatic meadow can be created in a relatively small space (for more on this garden, see Chapter 5). Really spatially challenged gardeners can make tiny pocket meadows in containers, whatever their aspect and location might be. Choose the right grasses and other meadow components, and meadows will thrive in just about any setting, however large or small.

Slopes and hillsides are tricky to mow and expensive to maintain as an area of conventional lawn or traditional plantings. Many grasses will grow on slopes, but some are better than others on steep slopes, where water drains quickly. While it seems obvious that grasses on the top of a slope get less water than grasses at the bottom, many people forget that simple fact. It's best to use drought tolerant grasses on the top of the slope; and obviously, the bottom of a slope can be wetter, so be sure to select suitable varieties.

When planting grasses on a slope, use more drought tolerant species at the top and moisture-loving species at the bottom. You can also position plants more closely on center at the top of a slope and more widely at the bottom.

(previous page top) This backyard in Santa Monica, California, may be small, but it can still contain a beautiful meadow. The lawn consists of California dune sedge (*Carex pansa*); accent grasses include muhlys (*Muhlenbergia*) and sugar cane (*Saccharum officinarum*).

(bottom) A postage-stamp-size meadow with native sedges and wildflowers. Small meadows can be great spaces for quiet contemplation and rest.

Many sites have combinations of upslopes and downslopes, so just remember that if you are planting the same species on upslopes and downslopes, they will grow differently with different amounts of moisture. Shaded slopes can be more forgiving for some grass varieties.

Dogs, kids, and other wildlife

Dogs will always be dogs. They are territorial and love to patrol their domain. Dogs (especially large dogs) and conventional lawns are not always a good mix, and so planting a meadow can also be an easy solution to a common suburban problem. For your dog run, why not provide a pathway of mulch and cover the ground with taller grasses? You have to get the grasses established before letting animals traffic them heavily, but meadow runs are far more aesthetically pleasing than muddy patches of bad lawn. Several species of grass are salt tolerant and are fairly resistant to female dog urine. *Zoysia*, *Paspalum* and *Distichlis* are three genera of grasses that take the toxicity of dog urine.

Though they must be sited sensitively (they can look out of place in some suburban settings and with many kinds of architecture), a tall meadow is a natural, welcoming habitat for wildlife. Butterflies and other pollinators and beneficial insects live in the meadow understory, and many species of birds from goldfinches and bluebirds to meadowlarks and hummingbirds love tall grassy fields filled with flowers. Make one and they will come.

Children too love tall meadows, and so do adults who want to feel like kids. Kids love them because they can get lost in them—taller meadows with narrow paths are perfect for making forts and secret spaces. Even adults can revel in a wonderful sense of freedom that comes from roaming through taller plants and grasses. Try making a maze of paths through the meadow, or even consider making a formal maze or labyrinth in your meadow, as a special seasonal effect or a permanent garden feature. Tall meadows can also hide the sins of the site, such as old concrete pads and unsightly features too difficult or too costly to remove. And in urban gardens, really tall grasses can shield you from an ugly neighborhood.

Variations on a theme

In any site, one of a meadow's main functions is to help blur the boundaries between your land and the wider landscape around it. Meadows make the perfect transition between garden and natural landscape—ideally, it will be hard to tell where one ends and the other begins.

Whatever the underlying conditions of your site, with the myriad of grasses and grasslike plants available, meadows can be stylistically whatever you want them to be. Why not create a tropical meadow with decidedly bold tropical foliage and flowers? Grasses, palms, and cycads make excellent companions. Clearly tropical grasses such as papyrus, *Setaria palmifolia* (palm grass), and *Thysanolaena latifolia* (tiger grass) are stalwarts of tropical meadows: plant palm grass with birds of paradise and an understory of carex and "walls" of tiger grass, and the result is a setting straight out of the islands. But many

(next page top) Dogs and cats love grasses. Be sure to choose varieties that suit your breed—big dogs may need big grasses. In dog runs, get grasses well established before subjecting them to heavy traffic.

(bottom) Watching birds come and go in a meadow is a real treat. Many of our most treasured songbirds prefer meadow edges and grass ecologies.

This lawn of European meadow sedge (*Carex remota*) blends seamlessly with the surrounding shore vegetation. Grasses and conifers are another natural fit: their textures go hand in hand.

The large leaves of palm grass (*Setaria palmifolia*) create a rustling sound when moved by the breeze. Big-leaved grasses are essential in tropical gardens.

The bright yellow-green of *Sesleria autumnalis* makes it a standout groundcover grass. Evergreen and drought tolerant, it looks good year-round. The slender, demure flowers are never messy.

In the Colorado garden of Scott Ogden and Lauren Springer Ogden, taller grasses and perennials underpin the orchard. Winding, narrow paths let you pick the fruit and enjoy the meadow at the same time.

The rolling drifts of Fairy Tails fountain grass (*Pennisetum* 'Fairy Tails') in this meadow create a Zen-like effect. Sometimes large plantings of just a few species can be the way to go. Simple plantings are often the best.

(next page) This lawn of California dune sedge (*Carex pansa*) is shown in its bronzy winter coloration, while the Fairy Tails fountain grass is still green and flowering. The simple one-two of the sedge and the fountain grass is strong.

other grasses, including those native to colder northern latitudes, can be used to create outstanding tropical effects. Many of these have leaves strongly evocative of the tropics. Sometimes it's hard to say exactly what it is that makes a grass tropical-looking, but plant habit and foliage size, texture, and color all play an important part. Many of the taller tropical-effect grasses are short-lived, growing two or three seasons at most, or are annuals in colder climates. Many are moisture-loving, as the tropics usually are associated with rain.

Still other grasses have foliar attributes that help to accent meadow plantings. New spring growth or fall and winter color may be a particular tour de force of some grasses. The New Zealand sedges are good examples of such a versatile foliar accent; their gradations of colors, from oranges and iridescent greens through to amazing shades of bronze, copper, and chocolate brown, can be tropical in one setting, or part of a drought tolerant scheme in another.

GRASSES FOR FOLIAR EFFECTS

These are grasses with colors other than green.

Silvers and blues

Andropogon
Carex laxiculmis Bunny Blue (= 'Hobbs')
Elytrigia elongata
Eragrostis chloromelas
Eragrostis elliottii
Festuca
Helictotrichon sempervirens
Juncus patens 'Elk Blue'
Juncus polyanthemos
Leymus
Muhlenbergia emersleyi
Muhlenbergia lindheimeri
Panicum amarum
Paspalum quadrifarium
Sorghastrum nutans 'Sioux Blue'

Yellows, golds, and whites

Acorus gramineus 'Ogon'
Acorus gramineus 'Pusillus Aureus'
Alopecurus pratensis 'Aureus'
Arrhenatherum elatius var. *bulbosum* 'Variegatum'
Calamagrostis ×*acutiflora* 'Avalanche'
Calamagrostis ×*acutiflora* 'Overdam'
Carex dolichostachya 'Kaga Nishiki'
Carex oshimensis 'Evergold'
Carex siderosticha
Cortaderia selloana 'Gold Band'
Glyceria maxima 'Variegata'
Hakonechloa macra 'Aurea'
Luzula sylvatica 'Aurea'
Milium effusum 'Aureum'
Miscanthus
Phalaris arundinacea 'Feesey'
Phalaris arundinacea 'Luteopicta'
Phalaris arundinacea 'Picta'
Phalaris arundinacea 'Woods Dwarf'
Schoenoplectus tabernaemontani 'Albescens'

These are naturals for tropical effects.

Carex (wide-leaved varieties)

Cymbopogon

Cyperus

Eleocharis

Hakonechloa macra

Isolepis cernua

Juncus

Miscanthus (wide-leaved varieties)

Muhlenbergia dumosa

Paspalum quadrifarium

Paul's China Mystery Grass
(Neyraudia sp.)

Rhynchospora latifolia

Saccharum officinarum

Setaria palmifolia

Thysanolaena latifolia

Desert-themed meadows work just as well. Nothing softens the harsh geometric forms of cactus quite like grasses do. The cloudlike blossoms and fine textures of desert grasses are indispensable in western-themed gardens.

You can also create edible meadows. Plant them with asparagus, artichokes, berries, rhubarbs, and onions threaded through the grasses and along the paths. Graze your way through the meadow while reaching for cherry tomatoes or searching for strawberries. What's not to like? Meadows make a great understory for orchards and vineyards. A "walk on" meadow or natural lawn is a great way to deal with the problem area beneath orchard trees and vines. Try silver-foliaged grasses under the silvery leaves of olives, or use a green-leaved sedge beneath apple trees. Or vice versa: you can blend or contrast with the overhead foliage; the choice is yours.

For a quiet, more contemplative background, consider making a type of Zen meadow. Try combining traditional Asian plantings with grasses. The hard formal elements of Japanese and Chinese gardens contrast nicely with the softness of grasses. Combine bamboos with pines and grass for an incredibly subtle mix of colors and textures. Seasonal changes of color provided by the grasses can be a powerful and reflective component of the meadow.

How about a moonlight meadow as a theme, with grasses and flowering accents in yellows, golds, and whites, chosen to capture the moonlight? A golden garden with grasses in shades of yellow-green and chartreuse with flower accents of lemon and white will literally glow in the light of the moon. Silver foliage is equally effective. Border the meadow with gilt-leaved shrubs and glossy-leaved trees, and the effects are guaranteed surreal.

Finally, whatever the style or theme, your meadow must look purposeful. Most lawns are a couple of inches high, so it takes careful planning to make sure your meadow looks like a meadow, not just a lawn that needs mowing. It needs to announce, "I'm a meadow." Most meadows will look their best at from 1 to 4 feet in height. Don't be afraid of tall grasses: the taller the meadow, the more apt it is to catch the light and wind—one of the most beautiful purposes of all the many to which meadows may be put.

Grasses with flowers that dance above their foliage are particularly effective at catching light.

CHAPTER 4

ACCENT ON DESIGN

Making a meadow look completely natural is not as easy as it might seem. This sublime California meadow manages to look serene and inviting while incorporating steps, trees, a house, large boulders, and a swale.

The following grasses give "verticality" to meadow plantings.

Andropogon

Bouteloua curtipendula

Calamagrostis ×acutiflora

Elytrigia elongata

Juncus

Molinia

Muhlenbergia

Pennisetum spathiolatum

Saccharum ravennae

Schizachyrium scoparium

Schoenoplectus

Typha

Vetiveria zizanioides

MY APPROACH TO MEADOW DESIGN is based on two main strands: Know what you have ("Don't fight the site"), and know where you're going. Analyzing the site—incorporating the best existing landscape features into the type of meadow I am creating and then selecting plants that will thrive in those site conditions is the key.

Successful meadow design is based on sound horticultural decisions. But it's much more than choosing the right plants and putting them in the right place in your meadow. Just as a musician has to learn scales, so too the garden designer must learn the plants. When do they do their thing? What is their thing exactly? Is it the color of the new growth? Why are you choosing that plant for this meadow?

A meadow can be quiet and green, or filled with riotous displays of flowers and color. Perhaps you want to blend with the dark green foliage of nearby trees and shrubs? The mid height *Carex divulsa* would fit that bill. Or perhaps you want to contrast their dark verdancy with bright yellow-green? Try *Sesleria autumnalis*, then. Grasses and grasslike plants offer a phenomenal range of greens, but meadows can also be subtly threaded with silvers and grays, or boldly scattered with bright reds, yellows, and oranges. Color is never static in a meadow: sunlight and shade create drama out of the simplest palette; changing seasons provide sparkling highlights, with minimal input after planting.

The shape, habit, height, and foliage of each grass combine to give them different textural qualities. They also have a varying visual weight, which to me is like a brushstroke. Combining grasses with different brushstrokes means I can use plants in the same way as an artist applying color from his palette to build up a meadow picture. For example, grasses with vertical growth, or slender spiky flowers, are one sort of brushstroke in the meadow. Billowy flowering grasses are another, adding a gauzy, misty watercolor quality to the meadow.

Groundcover grasses

Start by choosing your groundcover, or base, grasses. These are the backbone of the meadow, the framework on which all else will hang. Whenever possible, use grasses native to your region. Keeping the main groundcover grasses to mostly two or three varieties, it's hard to go wrong. You can always add components if you feel the meadow needs more accents. Or choose multiple species of one genus, like *Carex* or *Festuca*. The percentage of one variety in a mixed base often varies in concentration throughout my meadow plantings.

Base grasses are mostly cool-season growers that stay evergreen and are valued for their ability to cover the ground. Their strength is dependable foliage texture and color. In colder climates, many turn bronze or are blasted dormant by the cold, but they do not die to the ground like warm-season grasses. The best base grasses are fairly tidy and relatively long-lived. They tend not to have showy flowers, nor do they have messy flowers. Cool-season groundcover grasses "green up" quickly in the spring; they are already in full leaf, some even flowering, when warm-season grasses are just poking out of ground.

Knowing what
individual grasses
do is key to putting
them together. Once
you understand
the plants, the
combinations are
endless.

Blue grama (*Bouteloua gracilis*) and buffalo grass (*Buchloe dactyloides*) form the base grasses in this meadow; accents and background grasses grow up through them.

(previous page top) This meadow exploits the subtle textural contrast between Atlas fescue (*Festuca mairei*) and slender veldt grass (*Pennisetum spathiolatum*). Grasses that are similar-looking make good companions. Combining too many grasses, with different kinds of flowers and foliage types, can look messy.

(bottom) The flowers in this scene seem to float above the meadow, while the grasses anchor them to the site. As in a good painting, different brushstrokes contribute different effects.

BEST GROUNDCOVER GRASSES

The grasses listed here are my favorite base grasses. Most perform astonishingly well in most gardens.

Bouteloua gracilis
Brachypodium sylvaticum
Bromus benekenii
Carex
Deschampsia cespitosa
Festuca mairei
Leymus triticoides
Muhlenbergia
Pennisetum spathiolatum
Poa arachnifera
Schizachyrium scoparium
Sesleria

BEST BACKGROUND GRASSES

These are all tall grasses for backdrops.
Arundo
Cortaderia selloana
Miscanthus
Muhlenbergia
Panicum virgatum
Paul's China Mystery Grass
(*Neyraudia* sp.)
Pennisetum
Saccharum ravennae
Setaria palmifolia
Spartina bakeri
Sporobolus wrightii
Thysanolaena latifolia
Tripsacum dactyloides
Vetiveria zizanioides

Grasses that have similar foliage and texture make good base grasses. Subtle differences in grasses add simplicity and complexity simultaneously. Too many different textures can create a hodgepodge and look messy. Too many different kinds of flowers, too, can be problematic. Try to combine grasses whose flowers are similar, like *Festuca mairei* (Atlas fescue) and *Pennisetum spathiolatum* (slender veldt grass).

It's OK to vary colors and textures of the base grasses as long as the overall effect reads "simple." Knowing how each species of grass grows is key to the meadow's appearance. Different grasses may grow at different rates, so spacing can be tricky as well. Slower growing grasses may need to be planted more closely on center and "edited" at a later date, so as not to be crowded.

Background grasses

I use background grasses both to define the meadow as an enclosed space and to blend or transition a meadow into surrounding plantings. They often serve to hide unsightly views or the sins of infrastructure. Also, because they are taller, many are effective at capturing light and movement in the garden. Background grasses need plenty of room, so space them accordingly.

With its plumelike flowers, Korean reed grass (*Calamagrostis brachytricha*) makes an assertive background grass, useful for dramatic autumn displays.

(previous page top) European meadow sedge (*Carex remota*). This groundcover grass is simple but effective. It can handle sun as well as shade as long as moisture is sufficient.

(bottom) Fairy Tails fountain grass (*Pennisetum* 'Fairy Tails').

Autumn moor grass (*Sesleria autumnalis*) provides a dab of "chartreusity." Its bright yellow-green foliage makes it an effective filler among the other grasses.

Filler grasses

Filler grasses are used in between base grasses, covering the ground until the clumping grasses overshadow them. Lower filler grasses are also good wherever meadows come close to walkways. Planting taller grasses too close to walkways is a common mistake of gardeners inexperienced with grasses. Grasses flopping too far over paving are unsightly, and shearing them can destroy the natural look of the grasses. Low filler grasses can hold pathway edges and also are useful for surrounding pop-up sprinkler heads (taller grasses would block the arc of their spray).

Filler grasses can be short-lived grasses like *Anthoxanthum* or long-lived genera like *Carex* or *Sesleria*. Shorter clumping species of filler grasses are more expensive to use than creeping filler grasses because they must be planted more closely on center. When these grasses can be planted from seed, money can be saved, but many of the best filler grasses have to be planted from plugs or starts, and therefore cost more per square foot than creeping grasses.

Pathways

Meadows are sensory places to be in and experience, not just grassy areas to look at from a distance. Even a small meadow calls out for you to enter it, even if the invitation is seldom taken up. I always plan a path through each meadow. Circulation is important in any garden, and meadows are no exception. Done properly, pathways will greatly enhance the way you experience the meadow. Narrow pathways with twists and turns will create drama and a sense of mystery; they force garden visitors to fall single file into the meadow and to admire specific views and features. Wide, broad pathways that accommodate two or more people walking abreast have a different effect. A pathway that cuts through between two sloping banks gives the viewer a bug's-eye perspective. Paths will aid in the maintenance of the meadow (in larger gardens, consider pathways wide enough for maintenance vehicles).

Don't be surprised if you make a path and garden creatures use them too! In snake country, you may want to widen the path so you'll both have a chance to see each other. In areas with serious lyme tick problems, you may want to keep paths wide to avoid contact with ticks. To keep taller meadow grasses from flopping over and obscuring the path, try supporting them with slender stakes with string or fishing line; wattles or willow fences, or bamboo will serve the same purpose, attractively.

Pathways can be made of many surfaces. In addition to simply mown grassy pathways, meadow paths can also be bark, stone, mulch, gravel, hardscape, or decomposed granite (DG). Logs or stones might bridge muddy spots. Permanently wet meadows can be enjoyed from pathways suspended above them. Catwalks are a great way to get into bogs and swampy sites. They can be as simple as a flat-sided log or highly engineered custom-built wooden plankways with rails and steel or concrete posts.

Mulches and gravels can be both functional and aesthetic, keeping feet dry and shoes clean, but grassy pathways are also effective at keeping the meadow more natural. Grassy pathways blend in with the surrounding meadow. Turf grass can be used, but creeping

GOOD FILLER GRASSES
Acorus
Agrostis
Alopecurus (foxtail grass)
Anthoxanthum odoratum
Bouteloua gracilis
Briza media
Buchloe dactyloides
Carex
Eragrostis
Festuca rubra
Koeleria macrantha
Poa
Sesleria

This path of California dune sedge (*Carex pansa*) is flanked by taller grasses and perennials. Only occasional mowing is required.

turf grasses may invade the meadow and prove problematic. Mowed turf also needs traditional lawn care to look its best, and this can prove to be both expensive and environmentally unsound. Meadow lawn pathways can be a solution to this problem.

Fragrant grasses were some of the original strewing herbs of medieval times; their cut foliage was strewn on the floors of houses and public buildings to "sweeten" the room. Many of these grasses also have herbal properties and are used for medicines and as flavorings. Such grasses can be placed on or near paths where they will be walked on or brushed by. Many people are unaware that grasses can be fragrant, so it's fun to watch visitors to the meadow try to figure out what smells so good as they walk the meadow path. Locate these grasses where you can touch them.

Dark green Berkeley sedge (*Carex divulsa*) is the workhorse of many of the meadows I have made. Its lustrous, arching leaves really set off flowering plants.

Grassy walkways can be gardens in their own right. Weave *Acorus gramineus* into a sedge pathway, and as you stroll along it, a fragrance is released from an unknown source—the grass beneath your feet. The pungent *Anthoxanthum odoratum* (sweet vernal grass) releases the perfume of fresh cut grass. Brush past *Cymbopogon citratus* (lemon grass): the air is overlaid with just a hint of lemon. Grassy pathways bring you in contact with grasses up close and personal.

Best grasses to use for pathways are low growing and tolerant of both foot traffic and mowing. Ideally they need be mowed infrequently, or almost not at all. Many ground-cover grasses like to be cut several times a year to thicken them and rejuvenate their foliage. In all but the hottest south and southwest areas, the cool-season grasses and sedges tend to make the best paths.

Grassy paths can also have flowering accents. These can either be off to the side or crushable underfoot. As a nation, we've grown to fear stepping on flowers. But in my opinion, we need to change our thinking on this—please, please step on the flowers in your grassy pathways! Once you begin to experience what it is like walking on nature, you'll realize why we all need to walk more gently on the planet in general. Low-growing bulbs (*Habranthus*, *Zephyranthes*), or low perennials like *Phyla nodiflora* (creeping vervain) and violas can be networked into grasses.

And the grasses for these pathways? Well, first what color green? Or maybe some shade of blue? When it comes to the best grasses and sedges for pathways, the trick is to choose running grasses that are not too invasive, or clumping grasses that are not so lumpy as to turn an ankle. The best clumping grasses for pathways are mat-forming

clumpers, so that people can stroll them more easily. For lists of my favorites, see Chapter 1's section on natural lawns.

Meadow accents

Once your grasses have been decided, and pathways considered, the next step is to decide which accents to use. If the base (groundcover) grasses are the framework of the meadow, it is the accents—grass, grasslike, and non-grass (flowers, shrubs, even art)—that set the tone for the meadow. The best meadow accents come and go as the seasons progress; properly strategized, the meadow can be a nonstop, ever-changing tapestry. Remember, you can always add things later as the meadow matures.

Well-placed art in the meadow can be as integral to the site as the plants. Consider the backdrop each piece—sculpture or other objets d'art, or useful features such as seats and benches—may require, where it is to be viewed from one or two spots. If the art/feature is to be viewed in the round, from many different angles, and is sufficiently tall, it may not require any backdrop to stand out above the meadow. You can select plants to contrast or blend with the colors of the art or its base. Much complicated art is at its best in the simplicity of meadow fabric.

Accents can be coordinated to burst heavy at certain seasons, or spread out over time so the accents are singular moments throughout the year. Meadow accents can also be color themed. I use them to inject exactly the colors I want, and plant them where I want a particular highlight, in a particular season. Color can be used with specific intention to create exactly the mood you want, when you want. For example, meadows can be constructed to have cool-colored accents in the spring and hot colors in the fall. Tropical and Mediterranean climates can have flower color throughout the year, even in winter. Cold climates may need to depend on trees, shrubs, and stone to carry interest on into the winter.

Where light falls at certain times of the day may affect my choice of accent plants for a particular situation. Maximizing the luminosity of grasses is for me one of the joys of designing meadows—the backlighting at dawn of *Austrostipa ramosissima* or the fiery tones that the setting sun adds to *Eragrostis trichodes* add a great sense of drama and theater to a garden. The cloudlike blossoms of certain grasses catch the light beautifully, giving a meadow an indefinable, almost surreal quality. Use this group of grasses to soften the meadow. In particular, taller fuzzies are excellent along meadow margins and edges, helping to blur transitional areas between formal and informal.

Many grasses have particularly good flowerheads, and well-designed meadow gardens offer grasses that bloom throughout the season. When combining flowering grasses as accents, try not to include too many types of flowers: too many competing forms can look messy and lack cohesion. Sticking to a succession of different spiky flowers, for instance, offers complexity with continuity. For more details of bloom season, see the descriptions in Chapter 6.

GRASSES FOR BILLOWY OR CLOUDLIKE FLOWERS

These grasses give gauzy, fuzzy effects.

Aristida purpurea
Blepharoneuron tricholepis
Briza media
Calamagrostis brachytricha
Deschampsia
Eragrostis
Melica
Melinis
Miscanthus
Muhlenbergia
Nassella
Panicum virgatum
Sporobolus

Catlin sedge (*Carex texensis*). This native sedge works in most American gardens coast to coast. Best in part shade, it makes a fine natural lawn.

Little bluestem (*Schizachyrium scoparium*), in its reddish fall color, makes an eye-catching accent plant as well as a fine base grass and is adaptable to meadows across North America. It comes in various foliage colors, from blue to green. Many named varieties exist, and local genotypes may be available in your region.

The grasslike foliage of bulbs like this ornamental onion (*Allium maximowiczii*) makes them indispensable meadow accents. Remember that most alliums have a pungent odor when crushed so keep them away from paths.

Unlike many other plants, grasses tend not to compete with sculpture in the garden. Their foliage can blend or contrast with the art.

The chartreuse foliage and purple flowers of Sweet Kate spiderwort (*Tradescantia* 'Sweet Kate') provide a strong color accent for most of the summer. Meadow accents of silver or gold really show up under gray skies or on moonlit nights.

(next page top) Autumn sunlight brings out the warm glow of streambank wheatgrass (*Elymus lanceolatus*), blue grama (*Bouteloua gracilis*), and buffalo grass (*Buchloe dactyloides*). Autumn is a magic time in the meadow as grasses go through their subtle changes.

(bottom) Although foxtail barley (*Hordeum jubatum*) can aggressively reseed in some situations, no other grass quite matches its shine. The flowers beg to be touched.

Could there be a more versatile grass than blue grama (*Bouteloua gracilis*)? Tough as nails, it can make a natural lawn or a meadow, and is native to most of the lower forty-eight states.

(next page top) The seasonal changes that grasses undergo can mean that some grasses will be bright green while others are already in their brown or golden autumn coloration.

(bottom) The verdant colors of the meadow in spring make that season my favorite time of year. This is my old Pomona, California, garden. With its early blooms, *Rosa* 'Sally Holmes' made a great background for the grasses.

Seasonal accents

Grasses come in every shade of green imaginable. Bright chartreuse to deep black-greens. Medium greens to blues and silvers. But grass foliage changes as the season progresses, so try to anticipate how the seasonal changes will affect your compositions. The flush of the new season's growth can be the most amazing thing any plant does, and many grasses are no exception. Early season grass foliage is often brighter and shinier, with new growth spectacularly iridescent. As the leaves mature, the shades will darken and not be so glossy. Some grasses pick up shades of pink and red in their foliage as they emerge in the spring. Many variegations of cream, white, or yellow are pronounced as they emerge and fade as the season progresses. The great-looking spring foliage of many cool-season grasses declines quickly as the plant puts its energy into flowering and fades soon after. A common mistake is to put these in prominent foreground positions, where they look poorly in summer and fall. They are much better employed further into the meadow, where other grasses will hide their unattractive summer leaves.

As summer turns to fall, grasses bring ephemeral autumn color to the lower plane of the garden, taking on just about every shade of orange, yellow, or red imaginable. Some grasses have rich fall colors that quickly fade to the dried grass colors of winter; others, like *Schizachyrium scoparium* (little bluestem), hold their fall color long into the winter, even when dry. Some grasses are dependably one fall color: yellow, orange, or red. Others have seedling variation in the full spectrum of autumn hues. *Panicum virgatum* (switch grass) is one such grass; the straight species may be mostly yellow, while named varieties offer reds and purples. Many of these reddish clones will not produce true seed strains, and their progeny may emerge in various colors, changing the meadow over time.

(left) The pink autumn coloration of Florida love grass (*Eragrostis elliottii*) is suffused with purple and even tints of orange. These foliar effects are magical. Fall color can be added in subtle dabs or big sweeps.

(right) In contrast, prairie dropseed (*Sporobolus heterolepis*) autumn color is yellow-green.

Warm-season grasses with fall color can be marvelous accents in the meadow. In mild Mediterranean or subtropical climates, many cool-season grasses won't go all the way dormant and dry, but they will take on fall and winter highlights. *Vetiveria zizanioides* blushes red, and its leaf tips curl like New Year's confetti. *Eragrostis elliottii*, a Florida love grass, turns from metallic blue to a surreal color like that of a gas flame with plum purple and orange suffused throughout. Sedge lawns will blush copper if frosts are hard. These shifting foliar effects are part of the magic of the meadow. Add more of one color, less of another, by adjusting your choice of grasses. Remember to position grasses that offer seasonal color shows where they will be backlit by early or late light.

Winter grass foliage varies from region to region. Most grasses in cold northern climates are dormant and brown in the winter. Even cool-season grasses are blasted by freezing temperatures. Sedges are brown or copper-colored, and warm-season grasses die completely to the ground. What's left, if not covered by snow, are subtle accents of white to brown and even black. Oddly, sometimes the "warmest" colors in the win-

The skeletons of warm-season grasses can light up the winter garden. Many birds will gather grass seeds throughout the autumn and winter and collect nesting materials in early spring.

ter garden are the dried grasses catching the low light of leaden January skies. Grasses that stand up to winter snow can add great interest to otherwise sleeping gardens. For instance, the first hard rains or wet snows smash the taller molinias to the ground, but many *Miscanthus* varieties are still standing after a hard winter of snow and rain.

Bulbs, daisies, and other sweeteners

The best non-grassy meadow accents—what I call meadow sweeteners—are plants that combine well with grasses and add something special to the meadow. Maybe it's a flower, maybe a seedhead. Maybe it's the color of the stems or the fragrance of the foliage. Truly versatile meadow accents are mowable and rebloom when cut. And you can add them to grassy paths through the meadow. They have many attributes similar to the grasses. Perennials with thin wiry stems, for example, are indispensable in meadow situations, as they flex with the breeze in a way similar to grasses. *Gaura lindheimeri*, whose slender stems blush reddish purple in fall and winter, is a perfect example: its white

(left) New York ironweed (*Vernonia noveboracensis*) as a meadow "sweetener." Ironweed is a butterfly magnet and tough as the day is long. New varieties of these great tall background bloomers are showing up all the time.

(right) Daylilies (*Hemerocallis*) are perfect in a meadow setting. The foliage of many daylilies can become unattractive, and meadows hide their sins. I like dwarf varieties among short grasses and longer-scaped varieties among taller grasses. Deciduous and spider-type daylilies are particularly suited to meadows.

or pink flowers float like the butterflies they attract among the grasses. Low-growing annuals and perennials with interesting foliage and flowers (*Ajuga, Ranunculus*) are also very effective when woven into the meadow. Many of the best meadow accessories have low basal foliage that hides among the grasses, paired with flowers that shoot up above or are carried at the same height as the grasses—heucheras, for example. A meadow is the perfect place for tall flowering daylilies (*Hemerocallis*) and other plants whose foliage combines well with grasses. In fact, an entire meadow can be made of accent plants with grasslike foliage—*Agapanthus, Nolinia, Yucca, Hesperaloe, Restio, Ophiopogon, Liriope, Dasylirion, Lomandra, Ephedra.* Whether sprinkled throughout or planted in groups, any plant with grasslike leaves, whether narrow or broad, can find a home in the meadow.

If this book were to list all my favorite sweeteners for each region of the United States, readers would need a large wheelbarrow to cart it around. To simplify matters, here, in broad strokes, are my very top picks in various plant families; many of the gen-

Bugleweed (*Ajuga*) is completely at home in a meadow. There are many selected forms with differing foliage types and flowers. They're mowable, too.

Foxtail agave (*Agave attenuata*) in a meadow dune garden. Succulents are natural partners for grasses; their bold foliage contrasts nicely with the fine textures of the grasses. In fact, most of our treasured succulents are native to grass ecologies.

era mentioned have species or naturally occurring varieties that are better adapted than others to your region. Be aware that varieties can vary greatly by color, height, season, and longevity. To learn more, see the bibliography, or work with the resources in the back of this book.

Suffice it to say, a meadow without bulbs is hardly a meadow. It's not surprising that most of our beloved bulbs are from grass ecologies. *Crocus* from the Turkish steppes, *Crocosmia* from the South African veldt, *Camassia* from the North American prairies—all can find a home in the meadow. A carefully designed meadow can have bulbs blooming in almost every season. This is particularly true in the Mediterranean meadow. Wayne Roderick, a giant in the field of bulbs, had a meadow composed almost entirely of bulb foliage. Many Mediterranean bulbs have grassy foliage that completely disappears into the meadow. Look for true species or species crosses, which naturalize, for more natu-

ralistic effects. Some overly hybridized bulbs like amaryllis and lilies can be too garish or over-the-top for meadow settings.

Bulbs (including plants with tubers or corms, not just true bulbs) make meadows look more mature more quickly; they are excellent fillers between clumps of tall background grasses, especially those that grow actively when the grasses are cut back. After blooming, the bulbs retreat, having provided both flower and foliage, giving interest to the meadow while grasses are waiting to push new growth. Although a surprising number of popular bulbs are available as container plants and can be acquired from mail order/online nurseries throughout the year, most bulbs are available only in the fall and are best ordered in summer, when nursery inventories are up and the best and the largest sizes are in stock. For more on timing and the other practicalities of meadow planting, see Chapter 7.

Cape reed (*Chondropetalum tectorum*) belongs to a group of grasslike plants known as restios. They're the sexy newcomers for Mediterranean meadows and range from compact growers to tall background and specimen plants.

(previous page top) Wayne Roderick's amazing meadow, composed almost entirely of bulbs. In a Mediterranean climate, there are bulbs in leaf and flower year-round. Carefully orchestrated bulb color can dance through the seasons.

(previous page bottom) Rain lilies (*Zephyranthes*) are native to North and South America and can work in natural lawns from Florida to California. They come in many colors and many are drought tolerant.

(this page left) Ithuriel's spear (*Triteleia laxa*), a western North American lily relative. Western American bulbs are often the crown jewels of European gardens. It's amazing that so few western U.S. gardens include these bulbs, for many are native to dry meadows.

(this page right) Nodding onion (*Allium cernuum*) is an easy, hard-working bulb for meadow gardens. Their drooping flowerheads have a special charm. Many color forms are available.

BULBS FOR TEMPERATE NATURAL LAWNS AND LOW-GROWING MEADOWS

The following are low-growing bulbs that work well in short grasses and sedges.

Chionodoxa (glory of the snow). Late winter, early spring flowers. Blue, purple, white.

Colchicum. Fall flowering. Pink, white.

Crocus. Spring and fall flowers. Many species, varieties, and colors.

Freesia. Many varieties, range of colors. Fragrant.

Galanthus (snowdrop). White flowers in late winter.

Hyacinthoides (bluebells). Spring flowers. Blue, white, pink.

Ipheion (starflower). Early to late spring flowers. Blue, white.

Muscari (grape hyacinth). Spring flowers. Blue, purple, white.

Narcissus (daffodil). Dwarf forms. Excellent for spring color. Fragrant.

Oxalis (wood sorrel). Many different flower and foliage colors.

Scilla. Dwarf forms. Early spring flowers. Blue, purple.

Scilla peruviana, a Mediterranean bulb. Tough and dependable, it is one of my favorite bulbs for California gardens. It's effective both as a single specimen and in large groups.

BULBS FOR HOT, DRY NATURAL LAWNS AND LOW-GROWING MEADOWS

These bulbs are great in hot climates.

Allium (ornamental onion). Lower growing forms. Flowers spring through fall in many colors.

Babiana (baboon flower). Spring flowers. Blue, purple, white.

Calochortus (mariposa lily). Many varieties. White, orange, cream.

Lachenalia (wild hyacinth). Many varieties. Spring and summer flowers. White, yellow.

Ledebouria. Many varieties, most with striped or spotted leaves. Spring flowers in green, white, yellow.

Rhodophiala (schoolhouse lily). Red flowers in fall.

Sparaxis (harlequin flower). Many varieties and colors. Summer flowers, hot colors.

Tritonia. Many varieties, summer flowers, in warm colors, mostly.

BULBS FOR MID HEIGHT MEADOWS

Allium (ornamental onion). Many colors, various bloom times.

Camassia. For damper areas. Late spring flowers. Blue, pink, white.

Fritillaria. Spring. Yellow, orange, green, purple.

Narcissus (daffodil). Spring. Many varieties, mostly white or yellow, some fragrant.

Ornithogalum. Late spring and summer flowers. White, yellow.

Tulipa (tulip). Spring. Many species, varieties, and colors.

Zantedeschia (calla lily). Summer. Many varieties, many colors.

BULBS FOR TALLER MEDITERRANEAN MEADOWS

Albuca. Many varieties, white summer flowers.

Amaryllis. Many varieties, spring and summer flowers. Many colors.

Asphodeline. Many varieties, summer flowers. White, yellow.

Bulbinella. Yellow flowers in winter and spring.

Chasmanthe. Winter flowers. Orange, yellow.

Crocosmia (montbretia). Many varieties, summer flowers. Orange, red.

Cypella. Many varieties, summer flowers. Yellow, blue.

Eremurus (foxtail lily). Stately flower spikes in summer. Orange, yellow, white.

Gladiolus. Many varieties, some fragrant. Summer flowers in spectrum of colors.

Moraea. Summer flowers. Blue, white, purple.

Urginea maritima. White summer flowers.

BULBS FOR TROPICAL MEADOWS

These bulbous corms or tuberous perennials make exotic-looking tropical flower and foliage accents in a meadow of that style. Some are hardy in cooler climates, while others must be dug up and overwintered in a frost-free place for replanting the following season. Many also make excellent container plants.

Begonia. Many varieties, summer flowers in spectrum of colors.

Canna. Tall, excellent colored foliage and summer flowers in range of colors.

Colocasia. Many foliage colors, some with spectacular variegation and markings.

Crinum. Tall lily with summer flowers. White, pink.

Haemanthus. Summer flowers. Red, orange.

Hedychium (ginger). Fragrant flowers in summer. Cream, yellow.

Hippeastrum. Many varieties and colors, summer flowers.

Veltheimia. Pink summer flowers.

Xanthosoma. Excellent summer foliage plant.

Achillea 'Moonshine' is just one of dozens of fabulous yarrows that can add dazzle to a meadow. They're also essential for attracting wildlife—butterflies and moths can't resist them. They offer a wide range of flower colors and foliage that varies from silver to green.

Bulbs are sweet, but members of the daisy family (Asteraceae) are truly workhorses of the meadow, working well in most and tolerating a wide range of conditions. Most grow best in sunny situations, but some will grow in shade. Daisies range from miniatures such as *Bellis perennis*, which can tolerate being mowed in natural lawns, to giants like *Helianthus angustifolius*, which can reach up to 16 feet high. Most daisies attract butterflies and other pollinators to your garden and meadow, and these in turn attract birds, bringing the meadow alive.

(left) Meadow blazing star (*Liatris ligulistylis*) is another hard-working native accent for meadows.

(right) *Silphium trifoliatum*. Silphiums range from compact forms to taller varieties, mostly in various shades of yellow. Most are easy to grow.

BEST DAISIES FOR MEADOWS

Look for native and non-native daisies that thrive in your region. The choices are mind-boggling. There are daisies for wet and dry meadows.

Achillea (yarrow). Many varieties in a range of color, flowers summer through fall.

Aster. Many varieties, flowering spring through fall.

Bidens. Grows naturally in many American grasslands.

Chrysanthemum. Upright plants, many varieties with flowers in a spectrum of colors.

Echinacea (coneflower). Bold prairie perennial, flowers in summer.

Echinops (globe thistle). Strong heads of thistle flowers.

Erigeron (fleabane). Range of mid to lower height daisies, spring through fall.

Eupatorium (hemp agrimony), *E. purpureum* (Joe Pye weed). Taller growing.

Grindelia (gum plant, rosinweed, tarweed). Summer flowers.

Helenium (sneezeweed). Many varieties.

Helianthus (sunflower). Taller growing.

Inula. Robust, mostly taller daisies, summer flowers.

Liatris (blazing star, gayfeather). A true prairie native, flowers in summer.

Ratibida (Mexican hat, prairie coneflower). Strong, woody stems carry spring and summer flowers with distinctive centers.

Rudbeckia (coneflower). Varieties in range of heights and colors.

Solidago (goldenrod). Robust.

DAISIES FOR MEDITERRANEAN MEADOWS

These daisies are perennial in mild Mediterranean climates and tolerate heat and drought.

Argyranthemum. Spring, summer, and fall flowers.

Artemisia (sagebrush, wormwood, mugwort). Silver foliage, flowers in spring and summer.

Cotula. Lower growing with silvery foliage and flowers in spring and summer.

Encelia. Spring and summer flowers.

Erigeron (particularly *E. glaucus*). Spring and summer flowers.

Euryops. Feathery foliage, flowers in winter and spring.

Felicia (blue daisy). Spring and summer flowers.

Gazania. Summer flowers.

Montanoa. White flowers. Tall background.

Osteospermum. Many varieties in many colors, year-round.

Santolina. Silver or green foliage with summer flowers.

Tagetes (marigold). Many varieties with winter and spring flowers.

Tanacetum. Feathery foliage of silver or pale green.

Upright prairie coneflower (*Ratibida columnifera*) is one of those flowers that children are magnetically drawn to. They bloom for a long period and thrive in hot, dry climates.

Queen Anne's lace (*Daucus carota*) is a meadow stalwart. With butterflies flitting about its airy flowerheads, how could any meadow be complete without it? Its naturalizing tendency isn't necessarily bad.

Many unusual perennials that are difficult to place in typical perennial borders are at their best in meadows. The Apiaceae, or carrot family, harbors some prime examples, including that common grassland component, Queen Anne's lace (*Daucus carota*). Perhaps no other flower says "meadow" more loudly. But there are other magnificent umbellifers that are unmatched in meadow settings. While some are heavy reseeders, others make fine meadow appointments, serving individually as focal points or in groups as tall backdrop planting. The strange seedheads and colored bracts of eryngiums are particularly wonderful architectural meadow accents; these underused perennials are found in cold, tropical, Mediterranean, and desert climates. Fennels are spectacular, with their ferny, aromatic foliage and chartreuse flowers. Umbellifers frequently come with the site, and building meadow around them is often a better solution than trying to eradicate them. Most grow in damp places.

UMBELLIFERS FOR MEADOWS

Aegopodium (bishop's weed). Good groundcover.

Angelica. Sculptural giant, good as specimen or background.

Anthriscus (chervil). Mid height, 2 to 3 feet.

Astrantia (masterwort). Mid height, 2 to 3 feet.

Daucus carota (Queen Anne's lace). Mid height, 2 to 3 feet.

Eryngium. Mid height, 2 to 3 feet.

Ferula communis (giant fennel). Tall, good as specimen or background.

Foeniculum (fennel). Tall, good as specimen or background.

Hydrocotyle (pennywort). Good groundcover.

Myrrhis odorata (sweet Cicely, garden myrrh). Tall, good as specimen or background.

Pimpinella. Mid height, 2 to 3 feet.

Eryngium planum. With their thistle-like flowers, eryngiums, or sea hollies, are a natural combo with meadow grasses. They display metallic shades of blue, purple, and white, and many are attractive even when dry. Most are drought tolerant and attractive to insects.

Castilleja (paintbrush)

Chelone (turtlehead). White, pink, blue.

Diplacus aurantiacus (orange bush monkeyflower). Orange, yellow.

Mimulus (monkeyflower). Yellow, orange, red.

Penstemon barbatus (beardlip penstemon). Pink, coral.

Penstemon 'Blue Midnight'. Blue.

Penstemon cobaea (showy purple beardtongue). Purple.

Penstemon digitalis (smooth penstemon). Blue, white.

Penstemon ×*gloxinioides*. Many varieties and colors.

Penstemon grandiflorus (large beardtongue). Blue, white.

Penstemon parryi. Reddish pink.

Penstemon pinifolius. Red, orange, yellow.

Penstemon pseudospectabilis. Pink to purple.

Penstemon rostriflorus (Bridge's penstemon). Red.

Penstemon strictus (Rocky Mountain penstemon). Blue, purple.

Penstemon superbus. Rose to red.

Penstemon tubiflorus. White.

Penstemon virens. Blue.

Veronica (speedwell). Many varieties. Blue, purple, pink, white.

Veronicastrum virginicum (Culver's root). Pink, purple, white.

Rocky Mountain penstemon (*Penstemon strictus*). More and more named penstemon hybrids and selections are being offered by nurseries. Most have a long bloom period.

Panayoti Kelaidis of the Denver Botanic Gardens dubbed penstemons "children of the steppes," and certainly no high country dry or desert meadow should be without a representative of the largest plant genus endemic to North America. Some (*Penstemon digitalis, P. grandiflorus*) can brighten even eastern meadows. Penstemons are at their best associating with meadow grasses, and all are hummingbird magnets. They offer both attractive foliage and luscious flowers in colors that have to be seen to be believed— vibrant, eye-catching shades from ragingly iridescent to sublimely soft. And while some are short-lived, lasting only two to three years, many will naturalize and spread about. Penstemons and their cousins, some other important meadow sweeteners among them, vary in size from miniatures up to flowering accents that reach 3 to 4 feet. Culver's root, monkeyflowers, and many others tolerate moist conditions; most excel in hot, dry meadows. All benefit from good drainage.

Bridge's penstemon (*Penstemon rostriflorus*). Penstemons deliver valuable color to dry western meadows. Their colors can be electric, and most species are irresistible to hummingbirds. As a bonus, many thrive on neglect.

Showy purple beardtongue (*Penstemon cobaea*). The sheen and luminosity of penstemon flowers can be breathtaking. The flower stalks often lean with the weight of visiting bumblebees.

(left) Hummingbird sage (*Salvia spathacea*) is at home in dry western settings. The tall rocketships of reddish flowers draw hummingbirds from near and far. This sage looks good with muhly (*Muhlenbergia*) and needle grass (*Nassella*).

(right) Clary sage (*Salvia sclarea*) makes tall candelabras of pink flowers. Many salvias are deer resistant, rabbit resistant, and have fragrant foliage.

Sages (*Salvia*) and related perennials in the mint family (Lamiaceae) are another stellar group of flowering meadow sweeteners. Though most prefer sun and drier, well-drained sites, there is a salvia for all meadows in all soil conditions: in nature, salvias are found from first exposure seacoast through deserts and up to alpine mountaintops, and their versatility is reflected in both their flowers, which come in just about every color imaginable, and their many sizes, ranging from 6 to 10 inches to 4 to 6 feet high and wide. Tall salvias are especially useful as backdrops and transition accents on meadow edges. They too are irresistible to bees, butterflies, and hummingbirds. Many are annuals in colder climates, but they grow so easily that even as annuals they are effective in the meadow. Most are both deer and rabbit resistant.

(next page) Texas hummingbird mint (*Agastache cana*) is a bullet-proof accent for western meadows. Many new forms and hybrids are now being offered. They're deer resistant, rabbit resistant, and attractive to butterflies.

SAGES AND COUSINS FOR MEADOWS

Agastache 'Ava' (Ava hummingbird mint). Tall, rose-pink. Good for backdrop, meadow edges.

Agastache cana (Texas hummingbird mint). Pink.

Ajuga (bugleweed). Many foliage types for low meadows. Blue, purple.

Lamium (dead nettle). For low meadows. White, pink.

Monarda (bee balm). For moist meadows. Red, white, purple.

Physostegia (obedient plant). For moist meadows. White, pink.

Prunella (selfheal). For low, moist meadows. Purple.

Salvia apiana (California white sage). For hot, dry meadows. White.

Salvia azurea (pitcher sage). For hot, dry meadows. Blue.

Salvia clevelandii (Jim sage). For backdrop, meadow edges. Blue.

Salvia coccinea (scarlet sage). For hot, dry meadows. Red.

Salvia greggii (autumn sage). For hot, dry meadows. Red, cream, pink.

Salvia guaranitica (Argentine sage). Drought tolerant. For backdrop, meadow edges. Blue.

Salvia leucantha (Mexican bush sage). For backdrop, meadow edges, dry gardens. Purple.

Salvia lyrata (cancer weed). For low meadows. Blue.

Salvia nemorosa. For low meadows. Blue.

Salvia repens. For low meadows. Blue.

Salvia reptans (west Texas sage). For hot, dry meadows. Cobalt blue.

Salvia sclarea (clary sage). Drought tolerant. Lilac to lavender blue.

Salvia spathacea (hummingbird sage). Magenta to rosy red.

Salvia uliginosa (bog sage). Native to damp grasslands, good as edge or backdrop in moist meadows. Blue.

FERNS FOR MEADOWS

Adiantum (maidenhair fern). For small spaces.

Athyrium (ladyfern). Foliage mixes silvers and greens, for small spaces.

Blechnum (hard fern). For small spaces.

Chilanthes (lip fern). Silvers and greens, for small spaces.

Cibotium (Hawaiian tree fern). Tall, good as background.

Cyathea (Australian tree fern). Good tall background.

Dennstaedtia (cup fern, hay fern). Turns yellow in fall.

Dicksonia (New Zealand tree fern). Good tall background.

Dryopteris (wood fern). Good en masse.

Marsilea (water clover). Silvers and greens, grows in water.

Matteuccia struthiopteris (ostrich fern). Good en masse.

Onoclea sensibilis (sensitive fern). Good en masse.

Osmunda (flowering fern). Takes full sun with sufficient moisture, orange to red fall color.

Pellaea (cliffbrake). Silvers and greens, for small spaces.

Polypodium (polypody). Good en masse.

Polystichum (holly fern, sword fern). Good en masse.

Pteridium (bracken fern). Goes drought dormant.

Pteris (slender brake fern). Silvers and greens.

Woodwardia (chain fern). Tall, good as background.

Japanese painted fern (*Athyrium niponicum* var. *pictum*). The combination of grasses, sedges, and ferns is often overlooked—strange, because in nature you often find them growing together.

Providing effects from tropical dramatic to woodland calm, ferns are a natural accent for shady meadows or meadow margins. Many form extensive colonies that fit, hand in glove, with the textures of grasses and sedges; many are deciduous, bringing fall color to the lower plane of the meadow and new spring growth color as well. As the new leaves unfurl, fiddleheads provide unique architectural effects. Yet ferns and grasses have yet to become iconic garden combinations—it's hard to understand why. Ferns vary from petite miniatures like maidenhair ferns, growing just inches high, to giant tree ferns, some of which can reach 20 to 30 feet. Some are solitary and clumping, others spread to form large colonies. Short clumpers can be blended into moist shady areas in or near sedge lawns; colony-forming ferns can be used in masses or drifts in taller meadow grasses. Many are strong groundcovers, especially in shady or moist settings; others, like the lip fern, tolerate searing desert heat and dry air, as long as moisture and drainage at root level is sufficient. Especially the ferns native to North America belong not just in nature, but in our meadow gardens as well. When you're thinking about adding them to the meadow, look for ferns native to your particular climate and region.

Sword ferns
(*Polystichum*) with
Mexican feather
grass (*Nassella
tenuissima*). This
meadow planting
of ferns and grasses
is more drought
tolerant than you
might think.

Irises and grasses, too, were meant to be together. The slender blades of irises intertwine with grasses with seamless perfection. There are irises, from miniatures to giants, that will work in sand or clay, on dry slopes or wet bogs, and in virtually any climate zone. The iris family (Iridaceae) is quite large, and many iris relatives are at home in the meadow. Perhaps first and foremost is the genus *Sisyrinchium* (blue-eyed grass), whose star-shaped flowers work in many types of meadows. Species irises are especially good meadow flowers; while most prefer full sun, some will grow in light to moderate shade. Although common bearded hybrids can be used to good effect if mixed with other, softening flowers, it is the species iris, the ones native or adapted to your region, that make the best meadow grass companions. Miniatures are perfect accents for natural lawns. Taller irises make great accents with taller background grasses. A good range may be hard to find in general nurseries; the irises you'll want are best obtained from specialty nurseries.

IRISES AND COUSINS FOR MEADOWS

Belamcanda (blackberry lily). 1 to 2 feet. Orange, yellow, red, pink.

Dierama (wandflower). 3 feet and up. White, pink, purple.

Iris confusa (bamboo iris). Shade tolerant. Bluish white.

Iris cristata (dwarf crested iris). Shade tolerant, 4 to 12 inches. Blue, purple, white.

Iris danfordiae (Danford iris). 4 to 12 inches. Blue, purple, white.

Iris douglasiana (Douglas iris). Many varieties, shade tolerant, 1 to 2 feet. Blue, purple, white.

Iris ensata (Japanese iris). 3 feet and up. Many varieties, multicolored.

Iris foetidissima (stinking iris). Most shade tolerant of them all, 1 to 2 feet. Brownish green.

Iris innominata (beardless Pacific Coast iris). 1 to 2 feet. Blue, purple.

Iris japonica (Japanese crested iris). Shade tolerant. Blue, white.

Iris laevigata. 3 feet and up. Many varieties.

Iris latifolia. Parent to many Dutch iris hybrids, 1 to 2 feet. Blue, white.

Iris missouriensis (Missouri iris). 1 to 2 feet. Blue, purple.

Iris reticulata. 4 to 12 inches. Blue, purple, white, bicolors.

Iris setosa. 1 to 2 feet. Blue, purple.

Iris sibirica (Siberian iris). 3 feet and up. Multicolored.

Iris spuria (spuria iris). 3 feet and up. Yellow, white, blue, bicolors.

Iris tectorum (roof iris). Shade tolerant, 1 to 2 feet. Bluish white.

Ixia (corn lily). 4 to 12 inches. Orange, yellow, red, peach.

Nemastylis geminiflora (prairie celestial). 4 to 12 inches. Blue, white, purple.

Neomarica. Shade tolerant, 3 feet and up. Purple and white.

Orthrosanthus. 4 to 12 inches. Blue.

Sisyrinchium (blue-eyed grass). 4 to 12 inches. Blue, white, purple, yellow.

Tigridia (tiger flower). 1 to 2 feet. Red, orange.

Watsonia humilis. 1 to 2 feet. Pink, orange, magenta.

Douglas iris (*Iris douglasiana*). The western North American irises have been increasingly hybridized, and many new cultivars are now available. Some are orchid-like in their form, venation, and color. They truly enjoy meadow settings.

Blue-eyed grass (*Sisyrinchium*). With their grasslike foliage, the sisyrinchiums are cheerful little accents. Their flowers come in blues, purples, yellows, and whites. Their foliage varies from green to silver. Many are drought tolerant.

POPPIES FOR MEADOWS

Argemone (prickly poppy). Good heat and drought tolerance. White.

Eomecon (snow poppy). Shade tolerant. White.

Eschscholzia californica (California poppy). Many varieties. White, pink, cream, orange, red.

Eschscholzia californica subsp. *mexicana* (Mexican poppy). Good heat tolerance. Yellow, orange.

Macleaya cordata (plume poppy). White. Good for tall backdrop.

Meconopsis (blue poppy). Many varieties, shade tolerant. Blue, purple, white, yellow.

Papaver nudicaule (Icelandic poppy). Yellow, orange, peach, pink, red.

Papaver orientale (oriental poppy). Needs some winter chill to grow well. Red, white, pink, black, bicolors.

Papaver rhoeas (Shirley poppy). Red, white, maroon, red, orange.

Papaver somniferum (opium poppy). Red, white, pink.

Romneya coulteri (Matilija poppy). White.

Sanguinaria (bloodroot). Shade tolerant. White, pink.

California poppy (*Eschscholzia californica*) is a truly beloved flower. Recently, many new color forms, as well as other species of *Eschscholzia*, have become available. Their cheerfulness makes them irresistible.

Poppies are the most well loved meadow accessory, a quintessential meadow accent. The magic of poppies is the way they catch light: a mass of poppy flowers mingling with the seedheads of grasses, swaying on their thin stems in a breeze, is a captivating sight. Most are short-lived perennials or annuals, ranging in size from miniatures to towering; some tall members of the poppy family (*Romneya coulteri, Macleaya cordata*) make good backdrops to waves of meadow grasses. Poppies are most at home in dry, sunny meadows, but some work in shade. Their irresistible flowers come in many colors, from electric oranges and reds to pinks, purples, and yellows. Some produce white blooms, and others have dark, nearly black flowers. Most are spring or summer bloomers. Many are easy to establish from seed and are deer resistant.

Finally, no meadow should be without buttercups. Most members of the Ranunculaceae are real grassland natives and are perfectly suited to meadows. Some are good in shade; others can handle full sun. Most *Ranunculus* species crave moist settings, but some will tolerate seasonal dryness. Some (*Ranunculus repens*, for example) are wicked spreaders, but most are well behaved. The simple charm of buttercups is undeniable, and their range of color and form help knit them into almost any kind of meadow. Many are familiar garden plants, like larkspurs, hellebores, columbines, and anemones; it is just that many gardeners are used only to seeing these plants in traditional perennial borders, not in meadows. Buttercups have a wide range of blooming periods; hellebores even produce flowers in winter, in a range of colors from white to black and lots in between: greens, pinks, creamy yellows, and almost reds.

Japanese anemone (*Anemone ×hybrida*) is indispensable as a fall flowering accent for a shady meadow. Just when most other flowers have quit, Japanese anemones send their wiry-stemmed flowers into the air.

Some of the most versatile buttercups are the woody vines or perennials of *Clematis*; these are useful in a variety of meadow settings, scrambling and rambling through meadow grasses, and many have attractive seedheads as well. Flower color and form range from clusters of small flowers to large flowering types with blooms 6 to 7 inches across. As with so many meadow sweeteners, the straight species will look more natural in most meadow settings.

Rocky Mountain columbine (*Aquilegia caerulea*). Columbines are versatile meadow components and come in a wide range of colors and forms. While the hybrids have their value, the unimproved native species are equally charming.

BUTTERCUPS FOR MEADOWS

Aconitum (monkshood). Shade-loving. Yellow, pink, white, purple, blue.

Actaea (baneberry). Shade-loving. White.

Anemone blanda. Spring-flowering low-growing sun-lover. Red, pink, white, purple, blue.

Anemone coronaria. Spring-flowering sun-lover. Red, pink, white, purple, blue.

Anemone hupehensis var. *japonica*, *A.* ×*hybrida* (Japanese anemone). Shade-loving, fall-blooming. White, pink.

Aquilegia (columbine). Shade-loving. Pink, white, orange, yellow, scarlet.

Cimicifuga (snakeroot). Shade-loving. White, pink.

Clematis tangutica (golden clematis). Yellow.

Clematis terniflora (sweet autumn clematis). White.

Clematis texensis (scarlet clematis). Scarlet.

Clematis virginiana (virgin's bower). White.

Consolida ajacis (larkspur). Blue, purple, white.

Delphinium cardinale (scarlet larkspur). Orange, red.

Delphinium elatum (tall larkspur). Blue, purple, white.

Helleborus (hellebore). Winter-blooming, shade-loving. White, green, pink, yellow, black. Good foliar effects, too.

Hepatica (liverleaf). Shade-loving. White.

Pulsatilla (pasqueflower). Sun-lovers. White, blue, pink, purple, blue.

Ranunculus aconitifolius (bachelor's buttons). Good for naturalizing. Yellow, white.

Ranunculus cortusifolius. Good for naturalizing. Drought tolerant. Yellow.

Ranunculus ficaria (celandine). Good for naturalizing. Yellow, white; some forms with interesting dark silver foliage.

Ranunculus gramineus. Good for naturalizing. Silver leaves, yellow flowers.

Ranunculus repens (creeping buttercup). Good for naturalizing. Yellow. Golden-foliaged forms, too.

Thalictrum (meadow rue). Shade-loving, pair tall forms with tall grasses. Yellow, white, pink, purple.

CHAPTER 5

A PORTFOLIO OF MEADOW GARDENS

A meadow garden of mowed sedge in Arcadia, California. Accents can be grasslike plants as well as flowering perennials. The light green sweet flag (*Acorus*) here gives off a fragrant scent when bruised or stepped on.

The lawn in this front-yard meadow consists of Catlin sedge (*Carex texensis*) and California dune sedge (*Carex pansa*). It's only mowed a few times a year and is loaded with spring bulbs. The photo shows the lawn in autumn.

NEVER BEFORE has there been such an amazing array of grasses and grasslike plants from which to choose. Long may it be so! But how to combine them is another matter. With that in mind, here are some examples of successful designed meadows. Some are small, some are large. Some are simple and quiet; others are full of color and complexity. But they are all fine examples that illustrate many of the key points I make in this book.

It's important to study the context of each of these meadows to see how it fits into the site. Notice how some have "doors" and "windows"; some have backdrops of buildings, others of the trees and skies of the wider landscape around. Each meadow is uniquely suited to its location, climate, and setting. Some may not be from the region that you live in, but the same underlying principles apply when it comes to the design and "construction" of a beautiful meadow. All these gardens are purposeful—they are all meadows by design.

This opening garden shows that sedge lawns can replace conventional turf grass and still be beautiful and functional. The traditional planting of lawn and perennial border can be achieved with natural sedge lawns without sacrificing beauty. Here, low-growing *Carex texensis* is mixed with *Carex pansa* to create the lawn. The lawn is mowed three or four times a year, which allows for bulbs to come and go, giving the lawn a flowering component as well.

Christine London designed slope planting, Los Angeles, California

Grasses work well on slopes and, properly chosen, thrive underneath a canopy of trees. The graceful sheets of grasses and sedges in this meadow don't compete with the drama and sculpture of native live oaks. The simplicity of the meadow is a perfect canvas for the ever-changing shadows being cast upon it. By restricting groundcover grasses to a selection of quiet green foliage and subtle flowers, landscape architect Christine London of Beverly Hills, California, has achieved an overall effect of peaceful coolness. The groundcover grasses are primarily *Carex divulsa*, *Carex texensis*, and *Sesleria autumnalis*. Occasional flecks of *Juncus polyanthemos* provide meadow accents. The simplicity of this meadow suits the modernism of the house and terrace.

This slope in a Los Angeles canyon makes use primarily of sedges (*Carex*) and autumn moor grass (*Sesleria autumnalis*), with accents of Australian gray rush (*Juncus polyanthemos*). The simplicity of the planting doesn't need the addition of flowers.

Autumn color in Dave Fross's garden. Reds and greens always look good together. Add a touch of silver (courtesy of blue oatgrass, *Helictotrichon sempervirens*) and *voilà*!

Dave Fross, Native Sons Nursery, Arroyo Grande, California

Dave Fross is the owner of Native Sons Nursery in Arroyo Grande, California, not too far from the coast. It is one of the West Coast's finest nurseries, supplying a wide range of great plants for gardens in Mediterranean climates. I find it refreshing that, while Dave could have filled his garden with hundreds of fabulous flowering perennials and shrubs, he opted instead for a garden of grassy meadows, quiet and full of texture.

Misty coastal fogs lift and settle on this garden and nursery, making the air magical. Sedges play a big role in the garden, offering subtle changes in color and texture, from the dark or orangey greens of *Carex divulsa* and *Carex testacea* (respectively) through the coppers and bronzes of *Carex flagellifera*. Accents are provided by the warm glow of *Anemanthele lessoniana* and the stray grays of *Muhlenbergia rigens*. Brilliant flecks of California poppies (*Eschscholzia californica*) and restrained clouds of blooming heucheras add dabs of color, with splashes of silver and blue provided by fescues, *Helictotrichon*, and *Leymus*. These all work exceptionally well with the bronzes and dark greens of the plant palette. It's a garden with a heavy native bent, but with good Mediterranean accents as well. The grassy garden rooms connected with threads of sedges are each unique and appropriate for the amount of shade cast by the spreading tree canopy overhead.

Phormiums and the bark of a madrone (*Arbutus menziesii*) provide dark accents along a path. The orange- and copper-colored grasses blend exquisitely with these darker colors. It's chocolatey goodness!

Canyon Prince giant wild rye (*Leymus condensatus* 'Canyon Prince') plays a major role in the garden. The silvery blue blades weave along the path. In misty or foggy weather, the sky and meadow become one.

Low flowering bulbs and perennials evoke a mountain meadow in this hot Napa Valley courtyard. The garden is more heat and drought tolerant than it might seem.

Hess Winery garden, Napa, California

I created this garden in collaboration with landscape architect Peter Walker of Berkeley, California. The challenge was to create an "alpine meadow" for owner Donald Hess, who is from Switzerland, in a hot, dry Napa Valley courtyard. Walker, a noted modernist, conceived of a meadow bisected by angled pathways of decomposed granite—a grid superimposed on the meadow style planting.

The base meadow is composed of *Carex remota* and *Carex texensis*. The accents are numerous, with a heavy reliance on Mediterranean bulbs and perennials, which in this climate offer the possibility of bloom almost every month of the year. Ixias, babianas, scillas, ipheions, narcissus, cypellas are but just a few of the bulbs that come and go as the seasons progress. Flowering grass accents are kept to a minimum, with just a few to add

some sparkle: *Briza media* (quaking grass) and *Deschampsia cespitosa* add a haze of fuzziness over the foliage of the base sedges. *Schizachyrium scoparium* 'The Blues' provides bold brushstrokes as its foliage turns from metallic blue to red-orange in fall and winter.

Flowers of geranium and clematis tumble through the low grassiness, and red-veined dock (*Rumex sanguineus*) naturalizes throughout the meadow, blending with dapples of electric blue eryngium. Butterflies and bees add an additional layer of animation to the scene. I specifically selected low-growing perennials (*Scabiosa*, *Gaura*) that throw their flowers into the air—I think such plants associate particularly well with grasses and often include them in my meadows.

The meadow is laid out in strips, separated by decomposed granite pathways. It's a garden for strolling and contemplation.

Most clematis are native to grasslands and prairies and are really at home in a meadow. The showy flowers are followed by attractive seedheads. Species clematis, in particular, can add a special charm to a meadow.

Lady Bird Johnson Wildflower Center, Austin, Texas

Just because you live in the punishing climate of central Texas, with its rocky or clay soils, doesn't mean you can't make a meadow. At the Lady Bird Johnson Wildflower Center, interpretations of rich hill country meadows are testament to the possibilities that await hot climate gardeners. Many of the best grasses and sedges for the hot south are finally readily available in the southern nursery trade, wonderful plants like *Carex retroflexa*, *Carex perdentata*, *Muhlenbergia reverchonii*, and *Poa arachnifera*. These plants mix well with lupines (*Lupinus*) and paintbrush (*Castilleja*), both icons of hill country landscapes. Native and adapted bulbs like rain lilies (*Zephyranthes*) and schoolhouse lilies (*Rhodophiala*) are now finding their way into hot climate meadows.

Hot southern meadows must have a strong foundation of meadow grasses, as most color from flowering accents is fleeting under the relentless heat and humidity of the region's climate.

The sheets of bluebonnets (*Lupinus texensis*) that sparkle in the Texas hill country are obvious meadow sweeteners. Because their flowers are fleeting, they need a foundation of grasses.

A lawn of Berkeley sedge (*Carex divulsa*). This sedge is equally at home in full sun or shade. Its tolerance of a wide variety of soils and climates makes it a go-to groundcover for meadow gardens across the country.

Private residence, Malibu, California

Not half a mile from the famous surf of Malibu is the two-acre meadow that really launched our nursery. One of L.A.'s largest meadow gardens, it is home to a working horse ranch set among some of the largest native sycamores (*Platanus racemosa*) along that stretch of coast. Tall billowing grasses surround a large lily pond fed by a tumbling waterfall; the grasses caress the water and sway in the afternoon breeze. Most of the meadow is a matrix of low groundcover sedges (*Carex pansa*, *Carex divulsa*). Carpets of *Sesleria autumnalis* blend with the yellow-green sycamore leaves, suffusing the area in chartreuse light effects.

The size of the property allows for many types of grasses to be used without the meadow becoming busy or jumbled. In one section, *Carex texensis* makes a carpet with snow in summer (*Cerastium tomentosum*) and *Oenothera berlandieri*. This flowering lawn is mowed two or three times a year. In another area, the endangered Texas bluegrass, *Poa arachnifera*, blends with evening primrose in a combination that is both drought tolerant and beautiful. In deep shade and under the canopy of Chinese elms (*Ulmus parvifolia*), *Carex divulsa* thrives with camellias as a backdrop—simple and elegant. *Carex divulsa* can handle the aggressive roots of these beautiful trees. The mixed *Miscanthus* varieties surrounding the pond help create garden rooms of shorter groundcover grasses that sweep to the water, allowing visitors to stroll right up to the edge and gaze at the rushes and waterlilies growing in the shallows. In this garden, texture rules. Flowers and color—well, they are just the cherries on the sundae.

I designed the dune garden meadow, along Malibu's broad beach, to be quiet. Coastal Commission rules mandate only native grasses and sedges, but this doesn't mean we have to sacrifice beauty. Several native species blend in a subtle weave of colors and textures: *Carex pansa* creates a walkable, usable natural lawn that is pleasant to walk on; the two wild ryes, *Leymus mollis* and *Leymus triticoides*, are close cousins with similar slender

Sycamore foliage bathes this sedge lawn in bright green light, which is reflected in the autumn moor grass (*Sesleria autumnalis*) growing among the sedges.

Many coastal communities insist that only native species be used in dune plantings. Native grasses also provide a habitat for insects and other wildlife.

flowers that have powdery and silvery blue leaves; deer grass (*Muhlenbergia rigens*) adds grayish brushstrokes and movement to the plantings; it's tall (3 to 4 feet) but its top couple of feet are see-through flower stems. Succulents, so easy to grow in this climate, provide bold and colorful accents. The added diversity mixes in complex textures yet maintains the simplicity of the planting.

Matus-Sheehan garden, Pasadena, California

With a backdrop of mature conifers on a hilltop, a meadow of drought tolerant grasses and succulents spills over steep slopes and pools around a beautiful 1930s California Spanish-style home. As you wind along the bouquet canyon flagstone paths, you pass from sunny hot terraces to shady cool grottoes. The meadow is complex, layered with bulbs, perennials, and succulents; it is bordered by fragrant roses, camellias, and citrus in true old Pasadena tradition.

The grasses and sedges, although numerous, read simple. Many varieties are similar in flower form and foliage, so they combine easily. *Carex remota*, *Carex divulsa*, and *Bromus benekenii* are the primary groundcover grasses. Since all three grow equally well in sun or shade, they move through the garden with ease. The main flowering grass accents are *Pennisetum spathiolatum*, *Pennisetum macrourum*, and *Pennisetum* 'Fairy Tails'. *Muhlenbergia lindheimeri* and *Nassella tenuissima* excel on the hotter and dryer soil of the steeper slopes. Behind the house, at the very top of the property, a "waterfall" of *Setaria palmifolia* (palm grass) spills down the hill with a decidedly tropical flair; thriving in dry shade, this species delivers both beauty and durability for not a lot of water.

This garden is perfect for strolling with drink in hand. You'd never know that it's in the heart of the city.

Much more visually satisfying than a mowed lawn, this meadow is also more filled with wildlife.

McLeod garden, Long Beach, California

The McLeod garden, set atop a bluff in Long Beach, California, is a series of garden rooms whose grasses and grasslike plants provide textural swirls, some soft, some bold, that suffuse the entire garden. Many of the spaces are formal, and the grasses, although relaxed, are never messy. The small rarely used front lawn is a natural lawn of *Carex pansa*. The larger, often used back lawn is bordered by a sweep of meadow grasses that helps to connect the conventional lawn to the site, giving it more cohesion. These grasses help blend the garden into the borrowed landscape of the adjacent golf course.

Eastern gamagrass (*Tripsacum dactyloides*) is one tough character, and is evergreen in mild climates. Here, it's doing a great job at erosion control on a shady slope.

Berkeley sedge (*Carex divulsa*) cascades down a bank. Grassy slopes can be fun for kids. With their weeping leaves, many grasses evoke falling water.

Unusually large for an L.A. garden, this one seems even bigger as you move from one garden room to the next. The formal rose garden has an understory of mixed varieties of blue fescue to create a dappled blue underpinning to the hybrid teas. Another garden room, with an aviary full of colorful chirping birds, is decorated with tropical grasses and foliage plants. The soothing sound of water from the koi pond, planted with rushes and waterlilies, adds to the sensuality of the scene. Previously unusable slope was made usable by cutting trails and adding secret spaces for children and adults to enjoy; these shady trails, descending to the golf course below, are a true delight of the garden. Grasses flow over the hill and blend into the golf course plantings below.

In the shade, *Tripsacum floridanum*, *Tripsacum dactyloides*, and *Carex divulsa* are the drought tolerant evergreen understory to the trees overhead. Sunnier meadow grasses include the mid height *Festuca mairei* and *Pennisetum* 'Fairy Tails'. Multi-colored New Zealand flax (*Phormium*) adds color along with the colorful rocketships of kniphofia.

Private residence, Santa Cruz, California

This meadow garden sits on a coastal bluff, overlooking Monterey Bay, in what was orig-inally native coastal grassland. Years of overgrazing and mismanagement left the original prairie substantially degraded, but still intact. The surrounding garden was meant to pay homage to its original character, yet at the same time create a fire-safe meadow rich with sophisticated Mediterranean accents, filled with color and diversity.

The size of the garden (more than two acres) allows for a series of garden rooms that amply accommodate many horticultural treasures—succulents, roses, bamboos, conifers—with grasses as the glue that holds it all together. A spring-fed creek ambles between ponds and creates opportunities for networking bog and water plants into an overall scheme that is basically both drought tolerant and low maintenance. Grassy

Gauras, lavenders, salvias, and verbenas lead the way in this drought tolerant meadow. Have fun with color—make changes as you see fit.

Sculpture can set the tone of a meadow, imposing its own mood. Siting sculpture well is an art in itself.

(next page top) The grasses here blend the plants together almost invisibly.

(bottom) Berkeley sedge (*Carex divulsa*) in flower with blue oatgrass (*Helictotrichon sempervirens*). Dark green can really make silver and blue pop. Berkeley sedge is a dependable dark green in either sun or shade.

pathways of *Carex pansa*, *Carex praegracilis*, and *Carex perdentata* thread their way through masses of taller perennials and meadow grasses, like the mid height *Carex divulsa*. Drifts of silver- and blue-leaved grasses like *Helictotrichon sempervirens* and *Leymus triticoides* 'Gray Dawn' complement seams of blue- and silver-foliaged plants. The garden features the largest collection of restios on the California coast. Durable, long-flowering accents (gauras, salvias, lavenders, verbenas) blend together to add both color and movement to the garden; they are covered with butterflies and bees, giving the meadow a constant animation. Fragrant foliages and flowers mix with the ocean air and afternoon breezes to create an intoxicating mix.

Fog, which is typical in coastal settings, adds a special dimension to the meadow: nothing blends with foggy skies more subtly than grass. Sometimes in this garden, it's hard to tell where the earth ends and the sky begins.

The slope in front of the house, graded like a rice paddy, is clothed in just two grasses: Fairy Tails fountain grass (*Pennisetum* 'Fairy Tails') and golden Texas sedge (*Carex perdentata*). It helps to have the beautiful Santa Barbara mountains in the background. The simplicity of the foreground honors the distant view.

Frances Shannon designed garden, Montecito, California

Helping designer Frances Shannon create a themed meadow was a unique opportunity for me. The house, a beautiful tropical colonial, was styled for the owners' love of the tropics. The goal of the meadow was to evoke rice paddies. A south-facing slope was graded, in the true character of rice terraces, and planted with only two taxa, *Pennisetum* 'Fairy Tails' and *Carex perdentata*. The swaying flowers of the fountain grass catch the light but don't compete with the stunning views to the Santa Barbara Mountains in the distance.

Most fountain grass flowers arch, but *Pennisetum* 'Fairy Tails' really adds verticality to the scene. Evergreen in mild climates, it is also reasonably drought tolerant.

Parks and public gardens don't have to be all lawn. Pathways through masses of grasses can be a relief from the surrounding concrete of the city. A bit of urban wildness is good for the soul.

Jeffrey Open Space, Irvine, California

This Orange County park, among the most successful large-scale meadow plantings on the West Coast, proves that meadows have their place in public spaces. Acres of groundcover grasses are massed in huge sweeps, the scale of which demands a big brush. *Pennisetum spathiolatum* and *Carex divulsa* are the biggest players. The dark green of the carex is complemented by the golden green of the pennisetum. Threads of silver and

gray are provided by *Leymus condensatus* 'Canyon Prince' and *Juncus polyanthemos*. Drifts of *Pennisetum orientale* 'Tall Tails' animate the meadow with their nodding, fuzzy-caterpillar-like flowers. There's still plenty of conventional turf to use, but pathways through the meadows offer so much more visually than just plain turf ever could. Meadows are maintained by a one-time mowing over the late winter months. Color from bulbs and succulents are being added as time and city budgets permit.

A mass planting of slender veldt grass (*Pennisetum spathiolatum*), a great choice for California gardens. Its golden flowers are showy from spring to autumn. It looks best in sweeps and masses.

Alliums and clipped boxwood punctuate this midwestern sedge meadow. What's wonderful about this garden is that the color moments come and go like magic. Matt's careful orchestration keeps flecks of color dancing through the meadow.

Moynihan-Smith garden, Clayton, Missouri

My good friend landscape architect Matt Moynihan and his partner Brian Smith have a lovely 1920s brick home near St. Louis, and together we had a lot of fun making one of the first truly sophisticated meadow gardens in the Midwest.

The meadow surrounds three sides of the house, with the best part in an enclosure of rare boxwoods that are planted in the front yard. These drifts of boxwood are unique in their own right: they hide the street but only partially screen the house, so they create a semi-private grassy room. This low meadow is marvelously seasonal—a succession of bulbs and perennials in sheets and waves of color as spring and summer progress. Early spring's flush of daffodils gives way to camassias, irises, and alliums, and to summer's true lilies and daylilies.

The base grasses of this subtle meadow—not more than 40 feet wide by 60 to 70 feet deep—are a mix of sedges: *Carex remota*, *Carex perdentata*, and *Carex divulsa*. Also present are lawn remnants of *Poa pratensis* and *Festuca elatior*. These occasional lawn "fragments" work well with the base sedges. Drifts of *Chasmanthium latifolium* add a flowering grass component that blends seamlessly with the true lilies that perfume the meadow in summer. The backbone of sedges is mostly evergreen when the cold of winter arrives. A simple flagstone walk allows access for strolling through this meadow garden and cutting flowers to bring indoors.

The same color theory you would apply to interiors works in a meadow as well. You can even choose your meadow accents to go with the colors of the room from which you view the garden.

Autumn is my favorite time in my northern California garden. The rich greens of the grasses make the yellows and oranges really shine.

My present garden, Brisbane, California

Moving from Pomona to northern California, I got to make a meadow in the rarefied climate of the San Francisco Bay area. With water on three sides, the San Francisco Peninsula is a special climate—in fact, a series of many microclimates—moderated by the Pacific Ocean, which allows us to grow plants that would either melt or turn crispy in the hotter, drier southern California sun. This cooler climate allows for more plants that require some chill or vernalization to thrive. Taking advantage of these cooler conditions, I made a meadow on our smaller Bay Area lot. The natural lawn around the gnarled pepper tree is *Carex texensis*, with accents of bulbs and buttercups.

The base grasses include *Oryzopsis miliacea*, *Dactylis glomerata*, *Carex divulsa*, *Bromus benekenii*, and *Deschampsia cespitosa*. Mostly evergreen foliage and airy flowers dance throughout the garden. *Amsonia*, dogwoods, and Japanese maples are at home on the north, wind-protected side of the house. Raspberries and blueberries are scattered throughout the garden, and one can literally munch one's way through the meadow on the way to cut flowers and foliage to decorate the house.

Catlin sedge (*Carex texensis*) surrounds steps made from recycled concrete. This is the perfect setting for a sedge lawn—a conventional lawn would make no sense here. Sedge lawns are great in any postage-stamp-size yard.

Much of my knowledge has come from experimenting. The art and science of making meadows is fairly new, so there's no road map. It's ok to kill a few plants—experimentation can lead to new combinations and discoveries.

My old garden, Pomona, California

I will always have a soft spot for my old garden in Pomona. It's where I started my nursery, and this was where I made my first garden of grasses—in a barrio in eastern L.A. I needed to make a refuge from the heat and smog of southern California, and this garden was like an experimental laboratory for me.

First I planted bamboo to screen my blighted views and then, with the help of my artist friend Simple, I made a garden of grass, my own Mediterranean meadow fantasy. The property, of almost a half-acre, seemed larger because of the winding pathways I had running through it, linking different garden rooms on their circuitous route. As I learned more about grasses—and as new grasses came into my hands—the garden changed; still later, as trees and bamboos grew and shade increased, so did the grasses I had planted change.

The base grasses are *Carex divulsa*, *Carex pansa*, *Carex perdentata*, and *Bromus benekenii*. Accents of warm-season grasses (*Pennisetum orientale* 'Tall Tails', *Panicum virgatum*), along with other deciduous trees and shrubs, add dramatic seasonality that defy the mild climate of southern California. Taller grasses like Paul's China Mystery Grass (*Neyraudia* sp.) and *Saccharum ravennae* make bold statements, adding a touch of the exotic to the scene. Antique roses provide a great flowering backdrop that is replenished by tall fall-blooming daisies (*Aster, Helianthus, Montanoa*). Maintenance was mostly in February, when the entire garden (except its bamboos and shrubs) was cut to within 3 to 4 inches of the ground. We called it "The Big Chop." The grasses and perennials would green up again in as little as two weeks.

I'd like to think the garden was a reflection of the house, a bungalow with a hint of the Asian influence that was a signature of the Arts and Craft movement. Like the earlier Craftsman style in California, my garden was a giddy and guilty realization of gardening in a Mediterranean climate: a fabulous combination of conifers and citrus, palms and succulents, knit together by grasses.

(left) Paul's China Mystery Grass. This giant grass, a species of *Neyraudia*, was collected in China by plantsman Paul Comstock. We still haven't figured out its epithet, but we know we love it! It really excels for tropical effects.

(right) *Rosa* 'Sally Holmes', a hybrid musk rose, makes a great backdrop to the many grasses. Roses and grasses are easy companions. Roses can add flowers, fragrance, fruits, and autumn color to a meadow.

Neil Diboll's meadow of little bluestem (*Schizachyrium scoparium*), Indian grass (*Sorghastrum nutans*, near the house), and prairie dropseed (*Sporobolus heterolepis*). In Neil's meadow, flowers and grasses weave in and out in fluid harmony. In autumn, the black seedheads of the wildflowers are the attention-getters.

Neil Diboll garden, Wisconsin

You'd expect the guy who founded one of the most influential U.S. native plant nurseries—Prairie Nursery in Westfield, Wisconsin—to have one of the finest native plant gardens in America, but most people can't believe that Neil Diboll's done this all himself. Though it has taken years, the 20-acre property, covered with degraded woods and remnant prairies, has been transformed over time, by controlled burns and chainsaws, into restored forest with flowering prairies, natural lawns, and woodland sedge meadows.

Trash trees and overplanted pines were thinned or removed (cut debris created a woodpile that was ritually burned for Halloween celebrations); so too were the remnant prairies burned (always with the necessary safety measures and permits), to eliminate unwanted woody plants and weeds. With this removal and burning, many of the natives were able to return to the site and flourish; and by seeding prairie grasses and wildflowers, Neil has brought the meadows and prairies back to life. The final phase has been to create natural lawns and natural lawn pathways with his own seed mix, appropriately titled "No-Mow." Just to prove he's not a dilettante, Neil has surrounded the house and barn with hostas, sedges, and gingers—an exotic necklace on a natural beauty.

The grasses are the true stars of the garden. Prairie grasses are mostly *Schizachyrium scoparium* (little bluestem), *Bouteloua curtipendula* (side oats grama), *Sorghastrum nutans*

(Indian grass), and some *Sporobolus heterolepis* (prairie dropseed); *Andropogon gerardii* (big bluestem) reappeared after the burning and the tree thinning.

Natural lawns of No-Mow seed mix are a large component of the garden. Without them, hours of mowing, watering, and maintenance would be required to maintain this much lawn and path. All were planted from seed and in just one season became fairly well established. Their fine green tousled foliage works just fine in full sun and moderate shade. Though some water is added to the hostas during dry spells, the native garden is completely sustainable. Neil's latest efforts are focused on adding woodland flowers and sedges to the woodland understory.

The key to Neil's success was analyzing his site, understanding what he had, and knowing his plants. Asters, echinaceas, and goldenrods bring in birds, bees, and butterflies, but it doesn't stop there. Monardas, blazing stars, and sunflowers bob and weave through the grasses, providing an unending succession of flowers and seedheads. It really is all about the plants.

A simple path of mowed grass invites you into the meadow. Here, the path meanders through a field of little bluestem (*Schizachyrium scoparium*).

Neil's natural lawn of No-Mow fescue. These grasses are at their best in cool, northern latitudes. In times of drought they may turn brown without supplemental water; still, they're a good substitute for turf grasses, especially in some shade.

Scott Ogden and Lauren Springer Ogden garden, Fort Collins, Colorado

The Ogden–Springer meadow garden is perhaps the most sublime meadow planting in all of North America and undoubtedly the most sophisticated. It's not just the sheer number of species of plants in the garden, but how well they are put together. Scott Ogden and Lauren Springer Ogden, exceptional plantspersons and designers both, are proponents of plant-driven design. Their own garden is a testament to the old adage that garden design is both art and science. You can only put this many plants in one place—and not have it become a mess—if you know your plants, as Scott and Lauren do. Plantings that appear so deceptively simple and so perfect are in fact quite complex. The meadow changes almost daily as elements shift in both subtle and dramatic ways. Only well-behaved plants are allowed in. Aggressive plants are avoided, and editing is swift and merciless.

The sitting area in Scott and Lauren's Colorado garden, with fescue, rush, and foxtail barley (*Hordeum jubatum*). This is the most sophisticated meadow planting in America. The stone benches and firepit are an excellent way to enjoy the plantings, day or night.

To put this many plants together and have it be so perfect is possible only if you know your plants. This garden celebrates Scott and Lauren's philosophy of "plant-driven design."

The basic construction of Scott and Lauren's "steppe" meadow is simple. The low grassy "prairie" is backed by trees and shrubs and encircled by gravel and flagstone paths. Taller grasses blend the meadow's edge into the shrubby and treed backdrop. The meadow is free of pathways but enjoyed from all angles from the paths that surround it; the pathway layout is deliberately orchestrated to create a multitude of framed vistas and secret spaces, making the garden seem larger than it really is. It is the grass panel itself that is the real star of the garden. What makes it work is the careful blending of species and varieties that are similar in color, texture, and habit. Showy flowering grasses are kept to minimum; the emphasis is on good-looking foliage and well-mannered behavior. This makes the showy flowering grasses really pop, when they do appear. When light hits the melica or the hordeum, it's as if a stage light has been pointed only at them. A preponderance of grasses with slender flowering stems keeps the flowering accents see-through, never dense or opaque.

Adding to its horticultural cachet is the open meadow's emphasis on species and species crosses of traditional hybridized bulbs and perennials. Species daylilies, irises, asters, and alliums come and go in the meadow virtually year-round, poking up through snow and enduring summer's heat. The understated charm added by straight species from such genera as *Echinacea* gives the meadow its familiar yet intriguingly unique appeal. Many of these are natives collected by Scott and Lauren themselves on countless forays into endangered ecologies. By preserving these treasures in gardens as well as in nature, all we gardeners can play an important role in the conservation of our great native plant heritage.

The strong form of the pot floats in a foam of swaying grasses, making a fine focal point.

Flowering smooth brome (*Bromus inermis*) in the Peace garden, an invasive pasture grass that the owners have chosen to live with rather than try to eradicate. Though aggressive, this thug can be "sweetened" with better-behaved grasses and perennials.

Tom and Diane Peace designed garden, Denver, Colorado

In this suburban garden, designers Tom and Diane Peace prove that you don't always have to start over completely to make a meadow. If you're clever, you might be able to work with what you have.

They started with a "waste area" of the garden that was thick with the invasive pasture grass *Bromus inermis*. It is tough to eradicate: to do so requires multiple grow-kill cycles and constant vigilance to prevent its recurrence. Knowing this, Tom and Diane opted to keep the base grass of brome, which is not an entirely unattractive plant, and augment it with ornamental grasses and accent flowers. Tough and easy flowers like coneflowers and Queen Anne's lace work with the brome, where fussier and more delicate flowers would be swallowed; classic meadow accents like gaura, knautia, and yarrow

make it a real yet more purposeful meadow garden. Native grasses like switch grass and little bluestem bring diversity and interest to the groundcover layer of brome. As left-overs from a remnant lawn, clumps of tall fescue now provide the slender brushstrokes of a flowerhead never seen when the lawn was being mowed once a week. Currently, this meadow is being mowed just once or twice a year.

The foreground of sturdy *Achillea* 'Moonshine' and *Iris pallida* 'Variegata' helps the brome look less like a weed.

In this site, a meadow just makes sense: it's beautiful, functional, and good for the planet.

(next page) Harmonious colors and textures in a dry climate: little bluestem (*Schizachyrium scoparium*), Indian grass (*Sorghastrum nutans*), dwarf goldenrod (*Solidago simplex*), and oneseed juniper (*Juniperus monosperma*). These plants are harmonious with nature as well, providing a great habitat for wildlife.

Judith Phillips designed garden, New Mexico

This meadow garden designed by Judith Phillips is a superb example of the power of using native grasses and wildflowers to make meadows. A soft cloak of native southwestern grasses, studded with colorful accents, is at one with the surrounding landscape and mountain views. *Buchloe dactyloides* (buffalo grass), *Bouteloua gracilis* (blue grama), and *Andropogon* (bluestem) create a fine base layer with ever-changing seasonal effects. Overall, water use is minimal, but some areas closer to the house are honored with additional moisture to create an oasis moment. Grasses that need more moisture in hot, dry climates (*Calamagrostis*, *Miscanthus*) are used sparingly, grouped together, and given some shade to thrive. In full sun, accent grasses (*Muhlenbergia*, *Sporobolus*) add tall flowers that catch the light and tolerate the climate's hot, drying winds. Fall color is found in the sky and on the ground, as the base grasses morph from summer silvers and greens to golden yellows, and then to rusts, oranges, and parchments in fall and winter.

Pathways throughout the meadow range in their materials from gravel to flagstone and brick. Dependable native flowering accents (*Liatris*, *Solidago*, *Rudbeckia*) provide colorful purples and yellows from summer into fall, attracting bees, butterflies, and birds to the garden. Native trees and shrubs, the backdrop for this meadow planting, add an unforgettable fragrance of pine and sage, as well as providing cover and shelter for birds.

Esparto grass (*Lygeum spartum*) beneath olive trees. The silver foliage above and below blends well with the gray trunks of the trees. The seedheads of the grass are like little flecks of cotton.

Blenheim Farms, Dana Point, California

It's only fitting that a house made of straw bales should be surrounded by a meadow. R. J. Brandes' straw bale construction is not really noticeable from the outside. The three-foot walls undulate only slightly, and the waving grasses that anchor the house to the site seem to capture the spirit of the building and how it appears in the wider landscape. Situated not too far from the historic mission at San Juan Capistrano, along the San Juan Creek, this wonderful estate was fashioned after the Argentine fazendas of R.J.'s youth.

The base grasses are some of the best for hot, dry, southern California gardens, with sweeps of *Carex divulsa*, *Bromus benekenii*, and *Festuca mairei*. Classic gray-olives are paired with the silver of *Lygeum spartum* with its flecks of cottony flowers. The "walls" of the meadow are backdrops of *Vetiveria zizanioides*, *Sporobolus wrightii*, and *Spartina bakeri*; these three tall grasses are standouts for making curtains of grass foliage.

Growing 4 to 6 feet high, Florida cord grass (*Spartina bakeri*) makes a great backdrop. It's also drought tolerant and evergreen in mild climates.

A meadow of Mediterranean false brome (*Brachypodium retusum*), Atlas fescue (*Festuca mairei*), and slender veldt grass (*Pennisetum spathiolatum*) forms the basis of a green roof in a fire-prone part of California. This green roof meadow needs comparatively little supplemental water to stay nonflammable.

Meadow roof garden, Sunol, California

This meadow garden flows from the surrounding hills onto the roof of this extraordinary house, built into a mountaintop. Landscape designer Cynthia Tanyan and I worked together, creating a roof meadow garden that blends seamlessly from native soil to 6 to 8 inches of manufactured soil media. After site visits and consultations, I prepared a palette of grasses that would be heat and drought tolerant, low, and nonflammable (the residence is in a fire-prone area). The main mix—of *Brachypodium retusum* (Mediterranean false brome), *Festuca mairei*, and *Pennisetum spathiolatum*—is a quiet blanket that melts into the surrounding landscape. Accents are few—mostly succulents, such as sedums, aloes, and sempervivums.

Slender veldt grass (*Pennisetum spathiolatum*) with Atlas fescue (*Festuca mairei*) and a carpet of *Sedum rupestre* 'Angelina' all form part of the rooftop meadow.

Broad expanses of Berkeley sedge (*Carex divulsa*) and Atlas fescue (*Festuca mairei*)—both sturdy groundcovers—reflect the character of the property's backdrop of oak savannah.

Sandy Hill garden, Santa Ynez Valley, California

Sandy Hill's Rancho La Zaca is a nugget of gold set in the crown of California's Santa Ynez Valley. The property, situated in beautiful native grassland and coastal chaparral, is bisected by the original Butterfield stagecoach line of the Gold Rush days, and Sandy's garden is a toast to a California of legend and romance—a time of ranches, horses, and guns. Substantial in acreage, the ranch includes a residence, a caretaker building, a working vineyard, a horse-ranch, and a full-sized arena with a big barn for rodeos and parties. The grasses, which flow throughout, follow the roads and surround the buildings like a soft fire-retardant quilt, offering protection in a fire-prone ecology. Agaves, aloes, and kniphofias accent the grasses, along with classic California plants like oaks, roses, and sycamores. Antique flower accents like roses and nasturtiums appear as they would have in early California gardens. And of course, the meadows are strewn with California poppies. Poppies of all colors—oranges, yellows, creams, pinks, even the tall native Matilija poppies—are sprinkled throughout the meadows. Dollops and dabs of red and orange crocosmias are used sparingly but to great effect among the breezy grasses.

Native oak savannah grasslands, originally beat-up and overgrazed, were overseeded with native species and are now being restored. The purposeful grasses are mostly cool-season, drought tolerant varieties that are both beautiful and simple to maintain, requiring little water and upkeep. Big players among them are the similarly flowered *Festuca mairei* and *Pennisetum spathiolatum*. Natural lawn pathways of *Carex pansa* criss-cross the

meadows and provide trails for people and horses. Two small formal lawns of *Carex pansa* are set in a yew-hedge-enclosed courtyard under the shade of a grove of olives. Accent grasses include tall flowering species like *Pennisetum macrourum*, *Muhlenbergia rigens*, and *Pennisetum* 'Fairy Tails'; most get some irrigation. These tall grasses help the irrigated garden segue into the nonirrigated native meadows. The silver- and gray-foliaged *Eragrostis chloromelas* and *Juncus polyanthemos* are particularly effective at hiding the seam. This meadow garden at once celebrates California's past and offers a glimpse of California's future—a turning-away from water-guzzling lawns to a future in harmony with nature.

Agaves and aloes, here in flower, flank a wooden stair and boardwalk through the grasses.

CHAPTER 6

GRASSES FOR MEADOWS

Autumn moor grass (*Sesleria autumnalis*), one of the best groundcover grasses.

A GOOD WAY to get started selecting the plants for your meadow is to break them down into groups. For ease of use, I've suggested the grasses listed in this A-to-Z chapter be considered in one or more of the following five basic categories: Groundcovers G, Fillers F, Backgrounds B, Accents A, and Natural Lawns NL.

Every meadow starts with a foundation of groundcover grasses. These species, indicated by the letter G, generally should be 45 to 65 percent of the meadow.

Fillers, indicated in the entries by the letter F, are the plants that literally fill in between the groundcover grasses and the accents. Fillers help to hold the meadow together. Fillers can be grasses or flowering plants. Bulbs make great fillers. Fillers can come and go in the meadow and be changed out to keep the meadow fresh. Low fillers are especially effective among taller grasses, so the grasses feel less crowded. Fillers can range from 15 to 30 percent of the meadow.

Background plants, indicated by the letter B, can be grasses or other plants. These plants serve as a backdrop to the meadow. They are usually tall plants that frame the bulk of the meadow and help anchor it to the space. In large settings, background grasses and plants can be used in huge masses and sweeps. Tall background grasses are good for mazes and grass "tunnels." In smaller gardens, background plants and grasses are used sparingly so that they do not overwhelm the setting. Background plants can be 5 to 20 percent of the meadow.

Accents, indicated by the letter A, are plants (grasses or sweeteners) that draw attention to themselves either by their texture, their flowers, or seasonality. With good positioning and thought to timing, many accents can be employed. If you really know your plants, the meadow can be full of accents. Remember that you can always add more as time goes on, as you learn more about your individual site. Accents can occupy 3 to 40 percent of the meadow.

The final category, natural lawns, indicated by NL, are for lawns or pathways. They are low, creeping, or mat-forming by nature; they usually require little or no mowing to stay low and walkable. Natural lawns can be grasses and sedges and can be used singularly or mixed.

The percentages recommended here, while flexible, are proven formulas that have served me well in my meadow designs. Obviously, in gardening, rules are meant to be broken. Experimenting can be fun and satisfying, as many combinations have yet to be tried. Remember, each meadow is unique to its site.

Achnatherum (spike grass)

These mostly cool-season grasses, good for flowering accents, are at their best in dry western meadows. Their flowers range from fluffy or cloudlike to slender needle-like spikes. Most bloom in the spring, following winter rains, and then go summer dormant. The western achnatherums, desert species found in dry rocky habitats, are great at softening harsh desert landscapes. For this reason spike grasses are best planted by seed to establish in the native soil media. They are easily overwatered in garden settings and thrive where neglected. Zones 5 to 9.

Achnatherum coronatum (giant needle grass). Particularly good on rocky slopes. Height, 3 to 6 feet [A]

Achnatherum hymenoides (Indian rice grass). Way underused. Fine-textured foliage and cloudlike golden flowers catch the light beautifully [G] [F] [A]

Achnatherum speciosum (desert needle grass). Fine-textured blond foliage with slender cottony plumes. Height, 2 to 3 feet [F] [A]

Achnatherum calamagrostis (silver spike grass) [G] [F] [A]

Native to the mountains of south and central Europe. Showy fluffy plumes top arching 2- to 3-foot plants. Fine-textured foliage tends to go dormant in the summer, but flowers are persistent and showy on the plant into the winter. Plants sulk in hot humid summers. Best in full sun and well-drained soil; performs poorly in moist fertile soils. Plant from pots or seed. Silver spike grass is an effective light-catcher, sprinkled throughout the meadow or in drifts.

Acorus (sweet flag)

In almost every meadow or natural lawn that I make, I will try to find a place for some sweet flags. These grasslike plants have irislike leaves that are soft and fragrant. The source of oil of calamas, these plants need moisture and shade to thrive, especially in hot southern or western climates. Most have handsome evergreen foliage that is most pronounced when brushed against or stepped upon. Forms with colored foliage are plentiful; the humble green forms are too often overlooked.

Acorus calamus [F] [B]

Native of Eurasia. This sweet flag reaches 4 to 5 feet with rich green foliage. It is winter dormant and needs a winter chill to thrive. Will not grow in water. Plant from pots 2 to 3 feet on center. Zones 3 to 9.

Acorus calamus 'Variegatus'. Leaves are linearly striped with creamy white. Height, 3 to 4 feet. Plant from pots 2 to 3 feet on center [B] [A]

Acorus gramineus (Japanese sweet flag) [G] [F] [A]

From China and Japan. Bright green grassy foliage, 8 to 10 inches. Many selections are fun to mix or sprinkle throughout the meadow. All will grow in shallow water. Good on pathway edges. Plant from pots 6 to 12 inches on center. Zones 6 to 10.

Acorus gramineus 'Licorice'. Licorice-scented, otherwise similar to the species. Plant from pots 8 to 12 inches on center [G] [F] [A]

Acorus gramineus 'Ogon' (golden variegated sweet flag). Rich golden yellow variegated foliage has great value as a bright buffer, capable of brightening shady meadows. Plant from pots 8 to 12 inches on center [G] [F] [A]

Acorus gramineus 'Pusillus' (dwarf grassy sweet flag). Bright green foliage to a height of 3 to 5 inches. Good between stepping stones and in sedge lawn pathways: it tolerates light foot traffic. Plant from pots 4 to 6 inches on center [G] [F] [A]

Acorus gramineus 'Pusillus Aureus' (golden yellow dwarf grassy sweet flag). Golden foliage, to 3 to 5 inches. Plant from pots 4 to 6 inches on center [G] [F] [A]

Achnatherum calamagrostis.

Acorus gramineus 'Variegatus'. Creamy white variegation, growing 6 to 12 inches. Does best in light shade. A good choice for massing along pond edges, streamsides, and shady paths. Plant from pots 8 to 12 inches on center G F A

Agrostis hallii (thin grass) G F NL

Widespread in western states, this low-growing cool-season creeping grass makes a fine natural lawn, forming a soft mat of blue-green foliage 6 to 10 inches high. Seed or plant from plugs 6 to 12 inches on center. Zones 7 to 10.

Agrostis pallens (California bent grass) G F NL

A drought tolerant low-growing filler for western meadows. Foliage is blue-green and creeping. Both coastal and inland forms of this native bent grass are being studied for natural lawn applications. Usually planted from seed, as seed grows quickly and evenly, or from plugs 6 to 12 inches on center.

Ammophila arenaria (European beachgrass) G F A

Native to Europe, North Africa. This sand-loving base grass has naturalized on the shores of beaches from Los Angeles to Canada and along the East Coast, forming dense monostands and displacing *Leymus mollis* and other native dune grasses. Basically evergreen, this gray-green, flat-bladed grass grows 2 to 3 feet high and spreads from underground runners. Vilified by native plant purists, this species nevertheless has value as groundcover and for dune stabilization. Drought tolerant by the coast, it is best in full sun to light shade, and has adapted to grow well in heavy soils. Usually sold as bareroot divisions by nurseries. Plant from divisions 12 to 18 inches on center.

Ammophila breviligulata (American beachgrass) G F A

This native American version of *Ammophila arenaria* covers dunes from the Great Lakes to the Carolinas. Gray-green foliage grows 3 to 4 feet high and spreads from underground rhizomes, forming extensive colonies. Like *Ammophila arenaria*, it is usually sold in bareroot divisions available from fall to spring. Choose locally adapted clones, as they are usually better suited to particular climates, and plant from divisions 1 to 2 feet on center. This classic dune plant is iconic in coastal settings. Zones 5 to 9.

Acorus gramineus 'Ogon'.

Ammophila arenaria.

Ampelodesmos mauritanica (Mauritania rope grass) B A

Native to the Mediterranean. This clumping evergreen background grass can form huge clumps, 6 to 8 feet high and wide, topped by showy golden flowers that are long lasting on the plant and stunning in arrangements. The sharp leaves have been used to tie grape vines (hence the common name) and are similar to pampas grass, only a lustrous dark green in color. Tolerates sand or clay and handles seacoast conditions and wind. Best in full sun or light shade. Plant from plugs or pots 4 to 6 feet on center. Slow growing but worth the wait. Zones 9 and 10.

Anthoxanthum odoratum (sweet vernal grass) G F A NL

This pungent clumping grass is found across the northern half of North America and is common in pastures, fields, and roadside ecologies. It has delicately pointed flowers that emerge green and dry to a golden brown. Green foliage grows 6 to 8 inches; flowers are carried 12 inches atop the plant. This is one of my favorite grasses to mix with sedge meadows to add both fragrance and flowering accent. Tolerates a wide variety of soils; prefers sunny, moist soils. It needs light shade in hot interior to humid southern climates. Plant from plugs or pots 12 to 18 inches on center. Sprinkle throughout the meadow or plant in drifts along pathway edges.

Aristida purpurea (purple three-awn) G F A

Native to the U.S. Southwest. This fine-textured desert grass has showy flowers that bloom red-purple in early spring. Flowers and foliage turn gold as heat of summer arrives. A great choice for hot, dry sites. Avoid too much summer water, as plants prefer to be dry. Tolerates a wide variety of soils, best in sun or light shade. Plant from plugs, pots, or seed 18 to 24 inches on center. Purple three-awn will naturalize freely but is easily controlled. Sprinkle throughout the meadow or plant in drifts. Zones 6 to 9.

Arrhenatherum elatius var. *bulbosum* 'Variegatum' (striped tuber oatgrass) F A

This sweet little variegated plant is a classic cool-season grass that looks splendid in early spring. Soft white-striped foliage makes a nice mound of leaves 6 to 12 inches high with showy little white flowers that dry to tan. Best in filtered light shade with regular water. Tolerates a wide variety of soils. Plant from

Aristida purpurea.

Arrhenatherum elatius var. *bulbosum* 'Variegatum'.

Austrostipa ramosissima.

pots 8 to 12 inches on center. Best used as an accent or filler, as it disintegrates in summer heat.

Arundo donax (giant reed) B A

Native to southern Europe and Africa. This woody Mediterranean background grass can easily grow 14 to 18 feet in one season, producing upright arching slowly spreading clumps of gray-green leaves on stout woody stems. Evergreen in mild climates, freezes to the ground in cold climates. Thick rhizomes can be extremely difficult to dig and remove in older well-watered stands. This plant, introduced by mission fathers, was the "bamboo" of the American Southwest, used in constructing all manner of shelters, fences, and animal pens. Cut canes were strapped to burros, where they could withstand several days' ride up the trail before being planted by sticking them in the ground and watering them.

Planted by well-meaning soil conservators and reviled by native plant zealots as an invader (it has naturalized in highly disturbed riparian corridors), this species has a possible future in biofuels and biofiltration. Like switch grass, it grows in sand or clay and tolerates first-exposure seacoast. Its variegated forms are many, and much less troublesome than the straight species. Zone 6.

Arundo donax 'Gold Chain'. A compact clumper, to 6 feet, that stays brilliant yellow throughout the year. Its well-mannered tendencies will boost this plant's popularity. Zones 7 to 10 B A

Arundo donax 'Slender Gold'. This new form is tall, to 14 feet, but with leaves and canes more slender and more finely textured. Holds its variegation throughout the year. Zone 7 B A

Arundo donax var. *versicolor* (variegated giant reed). New foliage is strongly variegated but fades to green by summer. You can get color later and keep plants lower by cutting canes to the ground in July. Zones 6 to 10 B A

Arundo formosana (Taiwan grass) B A

Perhaps nomenclature is confused, but at least two different plants are sold in U.S. markets as *Arundo formosana*. Our plant is similar to *Arundo donax* but a wicked spreader with sharp pointed leaves that can be impossible to eradicate once established. Named clones appear to be a different, finer-textured plant that makes a good garden citizen as a background grass and seems to pose no environmental threats. Plant from plugs or pots 5 to 8 feet on center. The straight species, while dangerous to plant, is absolutely Jurassic in its effect. Zone 6.

Arundo formosana 'Oriental Gold'. Beautiful variegated 4- to 8-foot golden foliage that stays gold year-round graces this selection, discovered by Greg Speichert. Makes an amazing tall golden backdrop B A

Austrostipa ramosissima (pillar of smoke) B A

This unusual background grass from Australia grows 6 to 8 feet in an upright clump that literally looks like smoke rising from a fire. Thin woody canes have glossy evergreen leaves that shimmer among the silky cloudlike blossoms. It is best in full sun to part shade and moist, well-drained soil. Will tolerate drought and heavy clay. Plant from plugs or pots 4 to 6 feet on center. Stunning when backlit. Zones 8 to 10.

Baumea rubiginosa 'Variegata' (striped twig-rush) F A

New Zealand. This clumping slow-spreading rush has slender gold-striped flattened leaves and grows 12 to 18 inches high. Prefers moisture in soil and grows in water. Best in full sun to part shade. Plant from plugs or pots 12 to 18 inches on center. Makes a great brushstroke in moist meadows. Zones 7 to 10.

Blepharoneuron tricholepis (mountain mist, pine dropseed) G F A

Western United States. This clumping warm-season grass makes a fine groundcover for high desert and mountain meadows in the interior West. Gray-green foliage grows 12 to 18 inches with showy, airy plumes another 12 to 18 inches above the leaves. Tolerates a wide variety of soils and grows best in full sun to light shade. Plant from plugs or pots 1 to 2 feet on center. Zones 4 to 9.

Bothriochloa barbinodis (silver beardgrass) F A

Native to the western United States. This semi-evergreen cool-season grass has showy, cottony flowers that catch the light as they dance in the breeze. Slender clumping medium green foliage is carried on slender arching stems, 2 to 4 feet high. Best in full sun to light shade; it will grow in a wide variety of soils, including coastal conditions, and is also drought tolerant. Seed or plant from plugs or pots 12 to 18 inches on center. Good flowering accent in dry meadows. Zones 7 to 9.

Bothriochloa barbinodis

Bouteloua curtipendula.

Bouteloua curtipendula (side oats grama) G F A

Among America's best native flowering grasses for meadows, side oats grama grows well in almost every state in the union, from Minnesota to Arizona. It is one of the toughest, showiest, most versatile flowering grasses you can plant. The gray-green clumping, warm-season foliage grows 18 to 24 inches high and is topped by slender pennant-like flowers that emerge purple and dry to tan as they mature. In fall, both foliage and flower spikes turn rich colors of bright purple, orange, and bronze. Tolerates a wide variety of soils; best in full sun or light shade. Heat and drought tolerant when established. Easy from seed, or plant from plugs or pots 12 to 18 inches on center. Effective scattered throughout the meadow or planted in groups; the flowers in particular are delicate brushstrokes. Zones 4 to 9.

Bouteloua gracilis (blue grama, mosquito grass) G F A NL

This low-growing species is native to a vast majority of the United States, growing in some of the country's hottest, driest parts. It is a warm-season grass but is only briefly dormant in mild climates. The blue-green foliage grows 4 to 6 inches high and is topped by showy flowers that look like eyelashes, or pennants. The flower can also resemble little clouds of insects (hence mosquito grass). Although it is a clumping grass, if planted closely on center, 4 to 6 inches, or better yet seeded, it can make a fine natural lawn. It grows best in full sun and suffers in too much shade. Mowing keeps lawns easier to walk on but also cuts the attractive flowers. Often plants will rebloom after cutting. Uncut meadows of blue grama are stunning backlit in setting sun or early light. Blue grama is often mixed with *Buchloe dactyloides* (buffalo grass), as they have almost identical foliage color and texture. The creeping habit of buffalo grass feels good underfoot and fills in between clumps of blue grama. Blue grama, too widely spaced, can be difficult to walk on. So for lawns it is better to seed than plug this grass.

Blue grama grows in sand or clay. When planting seed, 4 pounds per 1,000 square feet is a good rate. It's best to plant in late spring or early summer, as soil and air temperatures begin to warm. You can seed in early fall but remember the first frost will shut down growth. Zones 3 to 9.

Bouteloua gracilis 'Hachita'. Vigorous seed strain preferred by many western gardeners G F A NL

Bouteloua gracilis.

Brachypodium sylvaticum (false brome) `G` `F` `A`

Found throughout the northern latitudes, this clumping to slowly creeping warm-season base grass is naturalized across the northern tier of the United States, a frequent component of pastures. Declared noxious in the Pacific Northwest, it nonetheless makes a fine meadow, bringing bright green glossy foliage and slender, attractive flowers; it is probably always going to be a part of pastures and meadows there. This grass has many distinct valuable forms (we have grown a sterile form at Greenlee Nursery for years), but some clones will naturalize. Plant from plugs 12 to 18 inches on center. For sun to medium shade; best with regular water; prefers climates with cool nights. Great in woodland settings combined with ferns. Zones 3 to 9.

Briza media (quaking grass) `F` `A`

Native to Europe. This cool-season grass makes tidy mounds of bluish green foliage growing 6 to 12 inches high and wide. Foliage is topped by sweet little golden flowers that resemble rattlesnake tails. Flowers grow 12 to 18 inches above the foliage; they appear in early spring and are showy on the plant into summer. Tolerates a wide variety of soils and grows best in full sun to part shade; somewhat drought tolerant in climates with adequate summer rain, but looks best with regular water. Plant from plugs or pots 12 to 18 inches on center. This species makes a good flowering accent in low groundcover with sedges (*Carex*) and moor grasses (*Sesleria*). Zones 4 to 9.

Briza media 'Russells' (striped quaking grass). Attractive white-striped leaves. Plant from plugs or pots 12 to 18 inches on center `F` `A`

Bromus benekenii (Denver brome) `G` `F` `A`

Panayoti Kelaidis of the Denver Botanic Gardens brought this fine groundcover grass to my attention. Plants are bright yellow-green in full sun and darker green in shady situations. The beautiful leaves are soft to the touch; downy foliage is particularly stunning with morning dew or etched in frost. Flowers are slender and noticeable but not showy. Evergreen in mild climates. I have seen this brome looking good in cultivation in both Malibu and Denver. Grows in sun or shade; good in dry shade with tree root competition. Plant from plugs 12 to 18 inches on center. Naturalizes. Zones 4 to 9.

Briza media.

Bromus benekenii.

Buchloe dactyloides (male).

Calamagrostis ×*acutiflora* 'Avalanche'.

***Buchloe dactyloides* (buffalo grass) G F NL**

This sod-forming warm-season native, one of the main components of the North American short grass prairies, grows from Texas to Montana. It is best sited on dry clay soils in full sun. The plant is dioecious, with male and female plants. Sod companies have released mostly female clones, which have insignificant flowers held down inside the foliage. For many years we have grown male clones, which have showy little flowers over the gray-green leaves. Female clones are pollen-free, but male clones have a sparkle that makes them more meadow-like.

If you grow buffalo grass from seed (Cody and Tatanka are two popular seed strains), you get boys and girls. Sod, on the other hand, is almost always female (female forms include 609, Prairie, and Stampede). Plants are slow to establish from seed (even if sown in spring, the optimum time) and need careful attention to establish. Buffalo grass is much faster to establish from plugs planted 6 to 12 inches on center; plugs fill in faster if mowed every 30 days after planting. Plants spread from stolons, and mowing and fertilizing helps the meadow fill in.

One of our best native lawn grasses, buffalo grass does have its drawbacks. Its worst fault is that it is easily overtaken by Bermuda grass, which it strongly resembles. Once Bermuda gets in, it's almost impossible to get it out before it overtakes the buffalo grass. Buffalo grass is also easily overrun with cool-season weeds, especially in coastal meadows. It is also sensitive to most broadleaf weed killers, so many people find it hard to manage. One way to avoid many of these problems is to keep buffalo grass extremely dry, once it's established. Keeping it dry will favor the buffalo grass and discourage invaders. At our nursery in Malibu, we have 20-year-old lawns that we water only two or three times a month in the summer, and they look great. Most buffalo grass failures come from overuse of water and fertilizer. Zones 4 to 9.

Buchloe dactyloides 'Surfer Boy'. A showy flowering male clone from David Douget G F A NL

***Calamagrostis* (reed grass)**

This large genus offers some of the best foliage and flowers for meadows. Some are North American natives; others are European and Asian species. Some are cool-season and evergreen; others go dormant in cold winter climates. Species from northerly latitudes do poorly in hot humid climates and need a winter chill to thrive. Most of the reed grasses prefer full sun and fertile moist soil. The western species (*Calamagrostis foliosa*, *Calamagrostis nutkaensis*) are good for Pacific Coast gardens near the water. Those described here are some of the more valuable ones for a flowering meadow. They are mostly evergreen and suffer in hot, dry interior climates. Zones 5 to 9.

Calamagrostis ×acutiflora (feather reed grass) G F A

Perhaps the best known of the reed grasses, feather reed has fluffy pinkish vertical plumes that emerge in May and soon turn slender and golden brown. The flowers are showy and persistent into the winter. A poor bloomer in hot climates lacking sufficient winter chill. Effective in drifts or sprinkled throughout the meadow. Flowers in most garden settings top out at 3½ to 4 feet. Plant from pots 2 to 3 feet on center. Feather reed grass is the quintessential brushstroke of flowering grasses. A warm-season grower.

Calamagrostis ×acutiflora 'Avalanche'. A white variegated selection G F A
Calamagrostis ×acutiflora 'Overdam'. Pink and cream in early spring then fades to white until the fall G F A

Calamagrostis brachytricha (Korean reed grass) G F B A

This woodsy warm-season grass has arching foliage and flowers 3 to 4 feet high and wide. Spring foliage is iridescent green; fall color is orangey yellow. Flowers emerge fluffy greenish pink in the fall. Tolerates full sun with adequate moisture. Plants prefer light shade and are one of the better flowering grasses for shady situations. Good backdrop, scattered throughout or in drifts. Plant from plugs or pots 2 to 3 feet on center. Great in combination with groundcover sedges. Zones 4 to 9.

Calamagrostis epigeios (meadow reed grass) G F A

This warm-season grass is a strong spreader that makes a good accent in old pasture meadows challenged by other aggressive species. The foliage and flowers of this species are more naturalistic than the tight clumps of *Calamagrostis ×acutiflora*. Plant from plugs or pots 12 to 18 inches on center. Good on the water's edge in big sweeps.

Calamagrostis brachytricha.

Calamagrostis foliosa (Mendocino reed grass) G F A

Low arching gray-green foliage and flowers to 18 inches. Light shade is best; regular water. Plant from plugs or pots 12 to 18 inches on center. A good choice for accenting low meadows by the coast. Good with fescues. Somewhat short-lived. Zones 8 and 9.

Calamagrostis nutkaensis (Pacific reed grass) G F A

Medium green foliage 3 to 4 feet high. Full sun to part shade; regular water. Plant from pots 3 to 4 feet on center. Zones 7 to 9.

Carex albolutescens (Florida meadow sedge) G F NL

Native to Florida. This clumping sedge makes a 4- to 8-inch lawn of glossy bright yellow-green foliage in sun or shade. Aggressively reseeds, a tendency that may prove problematic where it's not wanted. It seems to be less aggressive in dry spots. Makes an especially fine lawn in hot humid climates, and its bent for naturalizing can be a plus in highly trafficked areas like dog runs. Tolerates most soil types. Plant from plugs 6 to 8 inches on center. Zones 7 to 9.

Carex appalachica (Appalachian sedge) G F NL

Occasional to rare from Maine to Ohio down to North Carolina and Tennessee. This sweet 4- to 6-inch fine-textured clumping sedge makes a fine natural lawn in dry shade. It can handle full sun with adequate moisture but is best in some shade. Good in small meadows. Plant from plugs or pots 6 to 8 inches on center. Zones 4 to 8.

Carex 'Beatlemania' G F NL

Possibly a selection of but more probably a hybrid involving *Carex caryophyllea*, this plant is a slowly creeping slightly variegated sport of *Carex* 'The Beatles'. Regardless of its true parentage, it makes a good 4- to 6-inch natural lawn in light shade. It will tolerate full sun with adequate moisture but is happier with some sun in the hottest part of the day. The yellow variegation is subtle, acting more as a highlight. Best in well-drained soils. Plant from plugs or pots 6 to 8 inches on center. Zones 4 to 9.

Carex buchananii.

Carex buchananii (leatherleaf sedge) F A

A short-lived New Zealand sedge with upright chocolate- to copper-brown foliage 1 to 2 feet. Good drainage is needed for winter survival in colder zones. Plant from plugs or pots 18 to 24 inches on center. Zones 7 to 9.

Carex buchananii 'Viridis'. Silvery green foliage, otherwise identical to the type. Plant from plugs or pots 18 to 24 inches on center F A

Carex comans (New Zealand hair sedge) F A

One of the many native New Zealand sedges with variable clonal traits that remain mixed up in the U.S. nursery trade. Short-lived plants are usually pale silvery green. Fine-textured clumping foliage grows to 1 foot with hairy leaves that want to spill over rocks or walls like water. It grows best in moist yet well-drained acidic soils, but it is drought tolerant and will grow in almost any soil as long as drainage and moisture is sufficient.

Not for hot humid summers. Best in light shade. Plants naturalize in gravelly situations. Plant from plugs or pots 18 to 24 inches on center. Zones 7 to 9.

Carex comans 'Bronze'. Rich, fine-textured bronze foliage with pink tints, 8 to 12 inches tall. Plant from plugs or pots 12 to 18 inches on center [F] [A]

Carex comans 'Frosted Curls'. Pale green leaves with distinctive curly twisted leaf tips. Plant from plugs or pots 12 to 18 inches on center [F] [A]

Carex dipsacea (copper green sedge) [F] [A]

An interesting New Zealand sedge with bronzy green foliage. Often short-lived, growing to a height of 18 inches. Zones 7 to 9.

Carex divulsa (Berkeley sedge) [G] [F]

Native to Europe. This dark green clumping sedge is one of the best groundcover grasses for meadows. It can be kept lower than its usual 12 to 18 inches with occasional cutting. Tolerant of sun or shade, clay or sand, this sedge is the workhorse of most every meadow I make. It is evergreen in all but the coldest climates. It tolerates tree root competition and will even grow in first-exposure seacoast, in dune sand. Also takes moist to boggy conditions. It has insignificant flowers followed by brown seedheads; many gardeners cut these before ripening to keep plants tidy. Plant from plugs or pots 12 to 18 inches on center. Some will naturalize. This is by far one of the most versatile and manageable of all the groundcover sedges. Zones 5 to 9.

Carex dolichostachya (miyama kan suge) [G] [F] [A]

From Japan and Taiwan, this is yet another Japanese carex with good evergreen foliage and fine texture, growing 10 to 18 inches high and wide. Longer lived than many Japanese sedges, and, as with many of them, only a variegated form is offered by U.S. nurseries. Best in light shade with good moisture and drainage. Plant from plugs or pots 8 to 12 inches on center. Zones 5 to 9.

Carex dolichostachya 'Kaga Nishiki' (Gold Fountains). Gold variegation is subtle: the plant reads more gold than variegated. Reversions that sport back to green make good groundcovers as well. Plant from plugs or pots 8 to 12 inches on center.

Carex divulsa.

Carex dolichostachya 'Kaga Nishiki'.

Carex eburnia.

Carex flagellifera.

Carex eburnia (ivory sedge, bristleleaf sedge) G F NL

This widespread sedge grows from Newfoundland to British Columbia and south from Texas to Virginia. Like *Carex pensylvanica* and *Carex praegracilis*, it probably has many clones and forms. It makes a fine lawnlike panel in dry shade. Plants may brown a bit in high summer but green up again with cool temperatures in the fall. Plant from plugs or pots 6 to 8 inches on center. Zones 2 to 8.

Carex filifolia (thread leaf sedge) G F NL

Found from the Great Plains to the foothills of the Rocky Mountains, usually on mineral soils. Slowly creeping, 4 to 6 inches high. Full sun to light shade. Makes a very drought tolerant natural lawn. Turns a burnished copper color in winter. Plant from plugs 6 to 8 inches on center. Zones 4 to 9.

Carex flacca (gray sedge, carnation grass) G F NL

Native to Europe, North Africa. Though not for large areas, this slowly creeping sedge, when well sited, will make a fine silver-blue lawn, 4 to 6 inches high. Grows in lightly shaded conditions. The many forms in the trade can vary from short blue clones to tallish greener ones; plants are usually lower and bluer with sunnier and drier conditions. In western and southern climates, it's best in shade. Plant from plugs 6 to 12 inches on center. Zones 4 to 9.

Carex flagellifera (weeping brown sedge, mophead sedge) F A

Another short-lived New Zealand sedge consistently mixed up in the U.S. nursery trade. Many plants are sold unknowingly under incorrect names, and seedling strains may produce varied individuals, further confusing matters. Regardless, this clumping plant is stunning when well sited, growing to 18 inches with long lax leaves, in varying shades of brown, that elongate when in full seeding stage. Best in full sun or light shade with moisture and good drainage. Plant from plugs or pots 2 to 3 feet on center. Zones 7 to 9.

Carex flagellifera 'Bronze Delight'. Bronze-toned leaves F A
Carex flagellifera 'Coca Cola'. Cola-colored leaves F A
Carex flagellifera 'Toffee Twist'. Light caramel-colored leaves F A

Carex grayi (Gray's sedge, mace sedge) G F A

A beautiful bright green tropical-looking sedge, with showy bright green seedheads. Clumping warm-season foliage reaches 2 to 3 feet and is at its best in rich woodland situations (shade and moisture) with plenty of humus in the soil. Good sprinkled throughout shady meadows. Plant from plugs or pots 2 to 3 feet on center. Seedheads are like little spiked clubs (hence mace sedge). Children love them. Zones 3 to 9.

Carex laxiculmis (glaucous woodland sedge) G F A

A great native American groundcover sedge with evergreen foliage growing in neat clumps, 6 to 8 inches high and wide. Tolerates the heat and drought of the eastern United States. Grows well with tree root competition. Best in shade with regular water but widely adaptable. Plant from pots 8 to 12 inches on center. Zones 4 to 9.

Carex laxiculmis Bunny Blue (= 'Hobbs') is a particularly nice blue-green form. Will grow in the heat of Zone 9 G F A

Carex morrowii (kan suge) G F A

This popular groundcover sedge is longer lived in northern latitudes and makes a fine clump of glossy dark green, mostly evergreen foliage that grows to 8 to 12 inches high. It is often confused with *Carex oshimensis*, another of the Japanese sedges. The straight species is rarely offered; only the variegated forms are commonly encountered in nurseries. Best in light shade with regular water and good drainage. Save any reversions to green forms, as these are useful, too. Plant from plugs or pots 12 to 18 inches on center. Zones 5 to 9.

Carex morrowii 'Gold Band'. Leaves have creamy yellow margins G F A

Carex morrowii 'Ice Dance'. Creamy white margins G F A

Carex morrowii var. *temnolepis* (hosoba kan suge). A fine-textured form with white variegation that approaches silver. Best in light shade. Surprising heat tolerance with adequate moisture once established G F A

Carex morrowii 'Variegata'. Thin silver-white margins are more of a highlight than a noticeable variegation. An older variety but still worthy G F A

Carex morrowii 'Gold Band'.

Carex muskingumensis.

Carex muskingumensis (palm sedge) G F A

This slowly creeping warm-season sedge is yet another great groundcover for sun or light shade. Prefers moisture in hot climates; otherwise, it is surprisingly durable, growing in a variety of soils and conditions. Bright green foliage has a tropical feel and comes in miniature and variegated forms. Fall and winter copper-colored foliage is superb. Plant from plugs 12 to 18 inches on center. Zones 4 to 9.

Carex muskingumensis 'Ice Fountains'. Bright white variegations G F A

Carex oshimensis 'Evergold'.

Carex pansa.

Carex muskingumensis 'Little Midge'. Sweet dwarf form to 8 inches G F A

Carex muskingumensis 'Oehme'. Good gold margins G F A

Carex oshimensis (Oshima kan suge) G F A

This durable, popular, and widely sold groundcover sedge is very adaptable. It produces thick tussocks of fine evergreen foliage, to 16 inches tall. Zones 7 to 9.

Carex oshimensis 'Evergold'. This is the variegated form, often incorrectly listed as 'Old Gold', 'Everbrite', 'Variegata' and 'Aureo-variegata'. Good performer but suffers on sunny sites in extreme heat. Usually short-lived but worth replanting if it disappears.

Carex pansa (California dune sedge) G F NL

California to Alaska. This creeping native sedge makes a fine natural lawn. The clone we've grown at Greenlee Nursery for more than 20 years is perhaps the most widely planted and tested meadow sedge. Native to coastal sand dunes, it handles both hot interior climates and heavy clay soils. Some botanists group this with *Carex praegracilis*, but whatever species they decide on, this sedge has proven itself over time. *Carex pansa* can be kept to 1½ to 2 inches with three to four mowings per year. It is both versatile and dependable. Best in sun or light shade. Plant from plugs 6 to 12 inches on center. Zones 6 to 9.

Carex pendula (drooping sedge) G F B A

A versatile flowering accent for sun or shade, this mostly evergreen sedge has dark green lustrous foliage 3 to 4 feet high and wide, with long 2- to 3-foot arching flower stems from which 4-inch catkin-like chocolate flowers hang. A great tall background flowering grass, especially for shady moist woodland gardens. It will grow in the sun with plenty of moisture. Tolerates a wide variety of soils and climates as long as moisture is sufficient. Plant from plugs or pots 3 to 5 feet on center. Great en masse with ferns. Zones 7 to 9.

Carex pensylvanica (Pennsylvania sedge) G F NL

Widespread in eastern and northeastern North America. Native to woodlands. A highly variable species, often found in dry sandy soils. It can grow in full sun with adequate moisture, but it always looks better in some shade. A slow creeper, it can handle foot traffic and abuse. Clones may vary greatly, so it's best to search out local clones or sources close to home. More selections are bound to appear as plants become more widely used. Plant from plugs 6 to 12 inches on center. Zones 4 to 9.

Carex pensylvanica var. *pacificum.* A West Coast form, native from Oregon to British Columbia, growing in sandy coastal soils G F

Carex perdentata (golden Texas sedge) G F NL

Native to the southeastern United States. Bright yellow-green foliage on this sedge can appear almost chartreuse in full sun; it is darker green in shadier situations. Grows in sun or shade, making a 4- to 8-inch lawn of soft clumping leaves; but, again, color will vary depending on its exposure. Grows well under oaks. Plant from plugs 6 to 12 inches on center. Zones 4 to 9.

Carex phyllocephala (Chinese palm sedge, tenjiku suge) G F

Unique clumping warm-season grass, with architectural foliage, to 2 feet, resembling a 4th of July sparkler. Rarely offered as a species, so save reversions. Zones 7 to 9.

Carex phyllocephala 'Sparkler' (fuiri tenjiku). This appropriately named white-variegated selection is the form usually encountered. Prefers partial shade and will grow in full sun if it has plenty of moisture G F A

Carex plantaginea (plantainleaf sedge, broad-leafed sedge) G F

Native to the northeastern United States, this is a beautiful long-lived low-growing groundcover sedge. A warm-season sedge, its rich bright green leaves grow in a neat clump, 6 to 12 inches high and wide. Leaves resemble the foliage of plantains. Best in shade with rich humus and adequate moisture; too much sun causes the leaves to turn yellow. Plant from plugs or pots 6 to 12 inches on center. Great with ferns planted in sweeps and drifts. Zones 4 to 9.

Carex platyphylla (silver sedge) G F A

Similar to *Carex plantaginea* and may be put to the same uses, but more evergreen, with rich silvery blue leaves. Grows to 6 inches. Another great native sedge that should be used as

Carex phyllocephala.

Carex plantaginea.

Carex praegracilis.

groundcover in shady meadows. Plant from plugs or pots 8 to 12 inches on center. Zones 4 to 9.

Carex praegracilis (western meadow sedge) G F NL

This wide-ranging sedge can be found throughout western North America, from Baja to Alaska. Many forms exist, varying in height, texture, and habits. It is closely related to *Carex pansa*, which botanists and horticulturalists have confused, and its status remains unsettled. It's best to understand where your supplier has obtained their particular clone, as many may be taller or more moisture-loving than others. The type is a slowly creeping, mostly evergreen sedge that makes a great natural lawn. It tolerates first-exposure seacoast and a wide variety of soils, including sand and clay. Best in full sun to light shade. Plant from plugs or pots 6 to 12 inches on center. Zones (5)6 to 9.

Carex remota (European meadow sedge) G F

A good clumping groundcover sedge, evergreen in mild climates, turning bronze in parts of the country where winters are cold. Grows in sun or shade; prefers regular water. Fine-textured medium green foliage grows 8 to 16 inches but can be kept shorter with occasional cutting. Stays smaller in shadier or drier situations. Plant from plugs or pots 12 to 18 inches on center. Neat and tidy, it is an excellent choice for massing. Zones 5 to 9.

Carex retroflexa (old field sedge) G F NL

Native to the southeastern United States and one of the best natural lawns for the hot Southeast and Texas, this 4- to 6-inch clumper is best with some shade in the hottest part of the day. Mostly evergreen. Plant from plugs or pots 6 to 8 inches on center. Zones 5 to 9.

Carex siderosticha (creeping broadleaf sedge) G F A

This warm-season sedge from Japan and Korea is similar to *Carex plantaginea* and *Carex platyphylla* in culture and leaf. Several variegated and gold-leaved forms exist, but the straight species is worthy, though rarely offered. Plants form low colonies and are great as tropical or woodland accents in sweeps or drifts. Plant from plugs or pots 6 to 12 inches on center. Zones 6 to 9.

Carex siderosticha 'Banana Boat'. Leaves have yellow-green centers with dark green margins G F A

Carex siderosticha 'Lemon Zest'. Solid yellow-green leaves G F A

Carex siderosticha 'Variegata'. Green leaves with white stripes, notably at their margins G F A

Carex testacea (orange New Zealand sedge) F A

Perhaps the most orange of all sedges but, like most New Zealand sedges, usually short-lived. This has fine-textured clumping foliage and grows to a height of 2 feet. Best in sun, as orange coloring fades to green if given too much shade. Otherwise, same culture as most New Zealand sedges: moisture with good drainage. Plant from pots or plugs 2 to 3 feet on center. Zones 7 to 9.

Carex testacea.

Carex texensis (Catlin sedge) G F NL

This clumping sedge makes a fine natural lawn, especially in shady situations. Yellow-green in full, hot sun, plantings always look better in the shade. Long, lax flower stems resemble foliage, and flower and seedheads are noticeable. Its mat-like habit makes it easy to walk on. Grows 4 to 6 inches high. Grows in sand or clay and is drought tolerant when established. Good with tree root competition. I first encountered this fine-textured sedge growing in the bonsai pots of California plantsman Jack Catlin. Plant from plugs or pots 6 inches on center for a full lawn effect. Mow once or twice per season. Zones 5 to 9.

Chasmanthium latifolium (northern sea oat) G F A

North America. This showy shade-loving flowering grass is native to streams and riverbanks throughout the eastern United States. Bright green bamboo-like foliage, 3 to 4 feet high, often flops over under the weight of its delightful nodding seedheads. A warm-season grass with good fall color and winter form. Flowers, like oats pressed flat, emerge greenish pink and dry to gold; they are persistent and good-looking well into winter. Grows in almost any soil. Drought tolerant when established. Plant from seed or pots 12 to 24 inches on center. Self-sows readily in moist soils but is manageable in most garden settings. Zones 4 to 9.

Cortaderia selloana (pampas grass) B A

Other than arundos, no other grass seems to be vilified the way pampas grass is along the coast of California. While some

Chasmanthium latifolium.

Cortaderia selloana 'Gold Band'.

Cyperus alternifolius.

species do naturalize in moist or disturbed soils, the vast majority of horticultural selections are not invasive and are unfairly maligned by native plant purists, who are unaware that most pampas sold by specialty grass nurseries are virtually sterile. Clumping, drought tolerant pampas grass can grow 6 to 10 feet high and wide. Showy plumes rise 4 to 6 feet above the gray-green, sharp-edged foliage. Pampas tolerates almost all soil conditions, as well as both coastal and hot, dry winds. As an evergreen background grass, *Cortaderia selloana* adds drama few other grasses can match. There are many varieties in the trade—some of the best are listed here. Plant from pots 4 to 6 feet on center. Zones 8 to 10.

Cortaderia selloana 'Gold Band'. Compact, golden-edged foliage 3 to 6 feet high and wide, with showy flowers that grow straight up, 4 to 6 feet above the foliage. A superb backdrop or specimen B A

Cortaderia selloana 'Pumila'. A "dwarf" form with foliage 3 to 6 feet and showy flowers 3 to 4 feet above. More compact in drier sites and noninvasive B A

Cortaderia selloana 'Silver Stripe'. White variegated foliage 4 to 5 feet high. Flowers are not as showy as others B A

Cymbopogon citratus (lemon grass) B A

Native to India, Asia. Evergreen, tropical-looking foliage grows 3 to 4 feet high and wide, in dense clumps. Yellowy bluish green foliage is strongly lemon-scented and will perfume the air on warm days, even when not brushed against. Tolerates any soil and thrives in hot humid climates. Best in full sun but will take light shade. Tolerates desert conditions as long as moisture is adequate. Plant from pots 3 to 5 feet on center. Good near dog runs as natural dog deodorizers. Leaves and stems are used in Asian cuisine. Showy flowers are produced only in subtropical settings. Zones 9 and 10.

Cymbopogon nardus (lemon oil grass) B A

Native to Eurasia. Similar to *Cymbopogon citratus* but with narrower leaves and more free flowering. Fragrant foliage, the source of citronella oil, repels insects. Zones 9 and 10.

Cyperus albostriatus (broadleaved umbrella plant) G F A

Native to South Africa, this beautiful clumping dwarf papyrus grows to 18 inches with rich evergreen foliage. Excellent groundcover in mild climates, it does best in shade with moist soil. Not really suitable for growing in water. Plant from pots 12 to 18 inches on center.

Cyperus albostriatus 'Nanus'. More compact plant, 8 to 12 inches, with green foliage Ⓖ Ⓕ Ⓐ

Cyperus albostriatus 'Variegatus'. Diffuse gold-white variegation. Plants do not survive temperatures 28°F and below. Zones 9 and 10 Ⓖ Ⓕ Ⓐ

Cyperus alternifolius Ⓑ Ⓐ

Native to East Africa. Another papyrus useful as an evergreen background, this easy-to-grow species naturalizes readily and can be invasive in moist soils. Usually makes a clump 5 to 6 feet high and wide. Dark green leafless stems are topped by whorls of umbrella-like flower bracts. A more refined, noninvasive species, *Cyperus textilis*, is darker green, more columnar, hardier, and better behaved. Plant from pots 3 to 5 feet on center. Good on the water's edge and boggy sites. Zones 8 to 10.

Cyperus involucratus (umbrella plant, umbrella sedge) Ⓑ Ⓐ

This is the common umbrella plant, the one usually offered by water plant nurseries as *Cyperus alternifolius*. Fast growing and spreads somewhat invasively from seed. Evergreen glossy foliage grows 4 to 5 feet high and wide, in sun or shade and just about any soil.

Cyperus involucratus 'Gracilis'. A fine miniature form, growing only to 2 feet, with no reseeding tendencies Ⓖ Ⓕ Ⓐ

Cyperus longus (hardy dwarf papyrus) Ⓖ Ⓕ Ⓐ

European native reaching 3 to 4 feet with slowly spreading warm-season papyrus-like foliage. Good for planting in cooler climates and will grow in water or moist soil. Also thrives in sun or shade and tolerates a wide variety of soils as long as moisture is sufficient. Good orange-brown fall color. Plant from pots 12 to 18 inches on center. Zones 7 to 9.

Cyperus papyrus (papyrus) Ⓑ Ⓐ

With its classic slender green stems and large round starburst-like terminal flowerheads, papyrus is a dramatic evergreen backdrop in tropical settings, growing 10 to 15 feet high in large upright slowly spreading clumps in sun or light shade. This

Cyperus papyrus.

Deschampsia cespitosa 'David's Choice'.

species prefers moisture and can be grown in water. Foliage is damaged at 32°F and killed in the low 20s. Plant from plugs or pots. Zones 9 and 10.

Cyperus papyrus 'Tutankhamun'. A compact form, growing 3 to 4 feet tall

Cyperus prolifer (miniature papyrus)

From South Africa. This is the common dwarf form also listed as *Cyperus haspan* or *Cyperus isocladus*. It makes a neat column of tropical-looking foliage growing 2 to 3 feet with umbellate heads 3 to 4 inches across. Grows in water or moist soil in sun or shade as long as moisture is adequate; it is also noninvasive. Plant from pots or plugs 12 to 18 inches on center. Zones 9 and 10.

Deschampsia cespitosa (fairy wand grass)

This cool-season clumping grass makes a strong flowering groundcover for much of the northern tier of the United States. Although it will grow in mild climates, it will not thrive where it does not get significant winter chill, nor can it grow in desert or hot humid southern climates. Where it does grow, it is spectacular in bloom and magical in the meadow. Many selected varieties of European clones exist (the German forms in particular are too numerous to mention), but North American native forms have their charms as well. Fairy wand prefers regular water and full sun to light shade. Plant from plugs 18 to 24 inches on center. Zones 4 to 9.

Deschampsia cespitosa 'David's Choice'. An especially fine choice for western gardens

Deschampsia cespitosa 'Goldgehänge'. Grows 2 to 3 feet with pendulous flowers

Deschampsia cespitosa 'Goldtau'. A valuable compact form at 1 to 2 feet

Deschampsia cespitosa 'Schottland'. A tall form whose flowers emerge as clouds of silky green foam and dry to gold. Stunning when backlit

Distichlis spicata (salt grass)

This creeping warm-season grass is one tough character. Although new growth is prickly, this bright yellow-green grass makes a lawn that will grow in any soil, sand or clay, and tolerates saline and alkaline conditions. Unmown, it grows 2 to 18 inches. Tolerates extremes of soil moisture from dry to boggy (it is an aggressive creeper in moist situations). Useful in bioswales and pathways, staying low with very few mowings. Tolerates first-exposure seacoast and also dog urine. Plant from plugs, as seed is difficult to obtain and establish. Zones 4 to 9.

Eleocharis acicularis (needle spike rush) G F

This creeping warm-season rush makes a low colony in boggy soils. Good groundcover in wet soils and a great filler in moist meadows, growing 6 to 12 inches high with fine-textured soft threadlike stems with terminal bulbous flowerheads. Grows in any soil as long as moisture is present. Good in moist bioswales. Takes sun or light shade. Plant from pots 8 to 12 inches on center. Zones 4 to 10.

Elymus canadensis (Canada wild rye) G F A
Elymus virginicus (Virginia wild rye) G F A

Native to northern and eastern United States. These two similar native American grasses are found along streams and rivers throughout the eastern half of North America and are truly at home in meadow settings. Both self-sow and naturalize in their settings. Green to sometimes gray-green foliage on Canada wild rye can reach 3 to 5 feet, with nodding green bristly foxtails that turn tan and are attractive into winter. Virginia wild rye, its southern counterpart, has a similar look and fills the same ecological role. Both grow in a wide variety of soils and habitats and are often used as nurse crops for meadow and prairie seed mixes, as they are quick to grow and provide cover for slower growing prairie and meadow plants. Both take sun with adequate moisture, but both are fairly drought tolerant. Plant from seed or pots 2 to 3 feet on center. Beautiful in drifts and groups on the meadow's edge. Zones 3 to 9.

Elymus hystrix (bottlebrush grass) F A

This slender cool-season grass, one of the best for shady meadows, grows 2 to 4 feet in a fairly vertical clump. Flowers open greenish with flecks of white, becoming tan when mature. June flowers are attractive into the fall. Tolerates a wide variety of soils and full sun with adequate moisture. Plant from seed or plugs 12 to 18 inches on center. At its best sprinkled throughout the shady meadow and on woodland edges. Zones 3 to 9.

Elymus virginicus.

G Groundcovers F Fillers B Backgrounds A Accents NL Natural Lawns

Equisetum hyemale.

Elytrigia elongata (tall wheatgrass) G F A

Native to the Mediterranean. Fairly new to ornamental horticulture, this cool-season grass was originally bred for forage and erosion control but is now finding its way into meadow gardens for its beauty as well as its versatility. Growing in upright clumps, tall wheatgrass creates a striking column of slender vertical flower spikes up to 5 feet. Both its bluish green foliage and flowers turn straw yellow in fall, and its sturdy stems stay upright all winter, adding drama to the winter meadow. Tolerates a wide variety of soils including saline and alkaline soils. Heat and drought tolerant as well. Plants naturalize and can be problematic where unwanted. Plant from seed, or plugs or pots 1 to 2 feet on center. Zones 3 to 9.

Elytrigia elongata 'Jose Select' is a particularly tall strong-growing variety introduced by David Salmon of High Country Gardens. Plugs or pots only. B

Equisetum (horsetail)

Found throughout the northern hemisphere, in nature and in gardens. *Equisetum* includes many species and subspecies, in various sizes, but these grasslike plants are primarily of two forms: upright and hollow-stemmed, and many-branched and horsetail-like. All are aggressive spreaders, creeping from underground stems and growing in any soil—since the time of the dinosaurs—as long as moisture is sufficient. Though native in many situations, they can be problematic and difficult if not impossible to eradicate, requiring repeated applications of herbicides. Most gardeners with equisetums in their lots inherit them, and many who plant them wish they hadn't and resign themselves to living with them. Still, horsetails are loved by many and can have a place in the meadow if sited with caution. Plant from pots 12 to 18 inches on center. They work well as container subjects, in pots without drain holes. Zones 4 to 10.

Equisetum hyemale (scouring rush). Upright cylindrical segmented stems, to 3 feet. Evergreen in mild climates G F A

Equisetum scirpoides (dwarf scouring rush). A warm-season horsetail with bronze fall color. Makes a good low groundcover, to 4 inches G F A

Equisetum telmateia (giant horsetail). Many-branched stems, grows 4 to 6 feet. Evergreen in mild climates. This one looks like a horse's tail G F A

Eragrostis (love grass)

Members of this genus are known and loved for their cloud-like blossoms and handsome foliage. Most are heat and drought tolerant and easy to grow. Most naturalize and move about in the meadow if conditions are favorable. Some are behaved in colder climates and naughty in warmer climates. Most take a wide variety of soils and conditions. Love grasses in flower are unmatched for their ability to catch light—even the slightest breeze makes them shimmer. Zones 7 to 9.

Eragrostis chloromelas (Boer love grass) G F A

Warm-season grass with beautiful glaucous blue fine-textured foliage, 18 to 24 inches high. Cloudlike blossoms are carried 2 feet above the foliage in arching blowsy panicles—stunning on a full-moon night. Tolerates heat, drought, and a wide variety of soils. Best in full sun to light shade. Plant from pots 2 to 3 feet on center. Good in drifts. Boer love grass naturalizes freely in warm climates and is often incorrectly sold as *Eragrostis elliottii*.

Eragrostis curvula (weeping love grass) G F A

This fine-textured warm-season grass forms dense green clumps 2 to 3 feet in height. Their weeping flowers on slender 2-foot arching stems—black on emergence in mid summer, drying to a tan color—are see-through and light catching. Fall color is reddish bronze becoming brown. Weeping love grass is a notorious self-seeder. Be ready to edit seedlings. Good on hot, dry slopes, this is a good plant for erosion control. Grows in full sun to part shade. Plant from seed or pots 2 to 3 feet on center. Zones 6 to 9.

Eragrostis spectabilis (purple love grass) G F A
Eragrostis trichodes (sand love grass) G F A

Native to the eastern United States. These two native grasses create clouds of pink-red to reddish purple flowers in mid summer that glow in early light or setting sun. *Eragrostis spectabilis* makes a neat 18- to 24-inch mound of bright foliage that is completely covered by the flowers. *Eragrostis trichodes* is nearly identical but taller, to 4 feet, with flowers so profuse, it often drapes over its closest neighbor in the meadow. Both prefer full sun and sandy soil and are often found in nature in moist swales. Both are heat and drought tolerant once established. Plant from seed or plugs 2 to 3 feet on center. These love grasses

Eragrostis curvula.

are breathtaking in sweeps and masses. Both naturalize where happy. Zones 5 to 9.

Eragrostis superba (saw-tooth love grass, rattlesnake love grass) G F A

Native to South Africa. This showy warm-season love grass tolerates high and low desert conditions with ease. Flowers, like flattened rattlesnake rattles, sparkle over the foliage on sturdy stems. Gray-green foliage 1 to 2 feet high, with 2-foot green flower spikes emerging in early summer, becoming tan when mature. Tolerates a wide variety of soils and is heat and drought tolerant. Occasional seedlings are easy to control. Plant from plugs or pots 2 to 3 feet on center. Rattlesnake love grass is a hit with kids.

Festuca amethystina (tufted fescue) G F A
Festuca glauca (blue fescue) G F A

These two closely related species are among the most popular ornamental grasses on the American gardening scene. Their botanical heritage is murky, and nurseries often mix up varieties and names. Regardless, the species and many of their cultivars make beautiful low flowering and foliar accents in meadows. Fine-textured, densely clumping foliage grows 6 to 12 inches

Festuca amethystina.

Festuca californica.

and can range from dark green to metallic blue with every conceivable shade in between. Most cultivars have showy slender flowers that appear in late spring and remain attractive through summer. *Festuca amethystina* has particularly nice flowers that have purplish pink stalks in early summer. Plants are best in full sun to light shade. Fescues need excellent drainage in hot summer climates and are short-lived and prone to soil diseases in moist humid climates. Fescues are at their best in cool night, dry summer climates. Plant from plugs or pots 6 to 8 inches on center. Zones 4 to 9.

Festuca californica (California fescue) G F A

This native West Coast fescue grows in fine-textured mounds with blue-green to bluish foliage 18 to 24 inches high and wide. Dainty, airy flowers are held 1½ to 2 feet above the foliage. California fescue tolerates a wide variety of soils as long as drainage is good. Plants do best on north-facing slopes with some shade; they are not happy in hot southern climates and can be short-lived unless kept somewhat summer dry. Plant from pots 2 to 3 feet on center. Good accent for dry shady West Coast meadows. Zones 7 to 9.

Festuca idahoensis (Idaho fescue) G F A NL

Native to the western United States. This fine-textured clumping cool-season grass is useful as a low natural lawn, a drought tolerant meadow or pathway, and a filler. Growing in nature from the coast to the mountaintops, this grass usually has gray-green foliage 6 to 12 inches tall with typical fescue flowers in late spring. Tolerates a wide variety of soils and is best in full sun to light shade. More heat tolerant than *Festuca rubra* and other fine fescues, it prefers to be summer dormant and turns blond in summer meadows. Resents summer water and low mowings. Best from seed, or plant from pots or plugs 6 to 12 inches on center. Zones 3 to 9.

Festuca mairei (Atlas fescue) G F A

This clumping grass, native to the Mediterranean, is one of the best groundcovers for large areas. Growing 2½ feet tall by 3 feet wide, its tidy foliage blends well with a variety of looks and styles. Flowers are noticeable but never messy or overbearing. Atlas fescue takes sun or light shade and a wide variety of soils. Drought and heat tolerant, it grows well in almost any climate except hot tropical and low deserts. Plant from pots or plugs 2 to 3 feet on center. Atlas fescue's unique khaki green color is particularly attractive in western meadows. Durable and long-lived, it makes a great foil for showy flowering accent grasses. Newly arrived seedling strains may have taller flowers and coarser foliage. Zones 5 to 9.

Festuca rubra (creeping red fescue) G F NL

This fine-textured cool-season grass has been hybridized and grown as a lawn grass for many years. It is the prime component of many No-Mow mixes and makes a fine natural lawn. Creeping red fescue is at its best in northern tier states in loam, dry sand, or rocky soils, in sun or part shade; it tends to "patch out" in hot climates. Once it forms a dense thatch, it is prone to typical turf type diseases. It is sometimes added as an overseed component to sedge meadows. Easy from seed or plugs 6 to 12 inches on center. Zones 4 to 9.

Glyceria maxima 'Variegata' (variegated manna grass) F A

Eurasia. This spreading, warm-season grass grows up to 2 feet high. White linear variegation is tinted pink in the spring. Best in full sun to part shade and tolerates a wide variety of soils, as long as it is constantly moist. Plant from pots or plugs 12 to 18 inches on center. Needs a winter chill to thrive. Zones 5 to 9.

Hakonechloa macra (Hakone grass) F A

Native to Japan. Long-lived clumping warm-season grass with rich green bamboo-like foliage. At its best in cool moist soil with light shade and pronounced winter chill. It does poorly in hot, subtropical desert and dry southwestern climates with alkaline soils and hard water. When it's well sited, it's a glorious foliar accent. Though the many variegated and golden forms are useful as accents, the simple green species is one of the best woodland meadow grasses you can plant. Stunning coppery orangey red fall and winter color. Plant from plugs or pots 18 to 24 inches on center. Good in drifts and groups sprinkled throughout the meadow. Zones 4 to 9.

Helictotrichon sempervirens (blue oatgrass) F A

Europe. This densely clumping cool-season grass is a popular ornamental grass for perennial borders but can also find great use in many meadow situations. Metallic blue foliage grows to 2 feet high and, where winter chill is sufficient, is topped by showy flowers, 12 to 18 inches above the leaves. Not usually

Festuca mairei.

Hakonechloa macra (autumn color).

long-lived, it must have good drainage to thrive. Best in full sun to light shade, in climates with cool summer nights. Drought tolerant when established. Plant from pots 18 to 24 inches on center. Effective as accents in drifts and groups. Zones 5 to 9.

Hierochloe occidentalis (vanilla grass) G F A

Native to western United States. Clumping, fragrant, and mostly evergreen grass. Needs shade, moisture, and acidity to flourish. Plant from plugs or pots 12 to 18 inches on center. Zones 7 to 9.

Hierochloe odorata (sweet grass, seneca grass) G F A

Circumboreal. This widespread warm-season grass is often cut and braided to make incense. It prefers moist soils and light shade. Grows 1 to 2 feet, forming creeping colonies of fragrant oily green foliage. Flowers are delicate and sweetly scented. Use on pathway margins. Plant from pots 8 to 12 inches on center. Zones 3 to 9.

Hordeum jubatum (foxtail barley) F A

North American native. This showy flowering grass is found throughout the United States except in the hot humid Southeast, but because it is bad for cattle, it is considered a noxious weed and rarely planted. Flowers are ethereal. Reseeds readily. Clumping gray-green foliage, grows 2 to 2½ feet.

Imperata cylindrica 'Rubra' (Japanese blood grass, red baron grass) F A

Native to Japan. The amazing blood-red foliage of this warm-season grass propelled it into commerce with amazing speed. The original plant is a compact clone that slowly forms a spreading colony of crimson-tipped leaves, which turn flaming red in the fall. Growing only 12 to 16 inches tall, it normally does not flower and is not invasive. Sadly, this plant has a tendency to revert to the aggressive genetics in its background (the straight species is listed as a noxious weed, with sale or distribution restricted). This bent is most pronounced in mild climates with insufficient winter chill, and especially from plants propagated by tissue culture. The U.S. nursery trade has managed to ruin this plant by spreading tissue-cultured plants throughout the country. Many states have banned any *Imperata* taxon from being shipped, so check your sources before ordering.

Japanese blood grass grows best in fertile, moist, well-drained soil in full sun. Plant from pots 8 to 12 inches on center. Despite its potential problems, no other grass is quite so magical when backlit by late or early light. Amazing as a foliar accent. Grows poorly if it does not receive a pronounced winter chill. Zones 5 to 9.

Isolepis cernua (fiber optics grass, mop-sedge) F A

This densely clumping spike rush has bright green stems that end in small flowerheads, resembling the thin threads of fiber optics. Grows in water or in moist soil, in sun or shade, as long as moisture is sufficient. Grows in a wide variety of soils. Plants make a dense hummock that will die out in the center with age. Plant from pots 12 to 18 inches on center. Fiber optics grass makes a great accent in bog gardens, and its mop-headed foliage fascinates children. Zones 7 to 9.

Juncus (rush)

Juncus is cosmopolitan genus of grasslike plants with species native to every state in the continental U.S. Their natural habitat is moist or wet soils. They range from miniatures to taller species, growing to 5 or 6 feet. Most rushes have cylindrical stems and mainly vertical foliage. Their leaves come in various shades, from bright green to dark green, silver to gray. Some clump; some are strongly rhizomatous and can form dense colonies. Most are evergreen in mild climates, and many stay green even in cold winter climates. Regionally native species can be important components of wetland ecologies. For your meadow garden, use locally native clones whenever possible; strongly spreading varieties are for large meadows only. Most rushes tolerate a wide variety of soils, and although they thrive in moist settings, many can tolerate seasonal dryness. Regional natives are too numerous to list and are usually grown by regional grass nurseries. Some of the more notable ornamental species are described here. Spiral-stemmed forms in particular are great accents and loved by children. Most are planted from plugs or pots, some from seed. Zones 2 to 10.

Juncus effusus (common rush, soft rush) G F A

Clumping and upright, arching, green, to 4 feet. Zones 3 to 10.

Juncus effusus 'Carman's Japanese'. A selection by California nurseryman Ed Carman brought from Japan and traditionally planted to bring good fortune. Green, fine-textured stems combine with showy brown seedheads G F A

Juncus effusus 'Gold Strike'. Upright straight stems with subtle linear gold variegation G F A

Juncus effusus 'Unicorn' (corkscrew rush). Dark green spiraling stems F A

Juncus inflexus (hard rush) G F A

Hard rush grows to a height of 2 to 4 feet. Its gray foliage is quite stiff and tolerates drier conditions. Plant in sun or light shade. Zone 4.

Juncus inflexus 'Afro'. A strongly spiral-stemmed form, one of the best curly rushes for mild and hot climates. Plant from pots 2 to 3 feet on center F A

Juncus mexicanus (Mexican rush) G F

Native to the western United States. Aggressively creeping, salt tolerant rush with bronzy green foliage growing 2 to 3 feet. Good for bioswales and constructed wetlands. Zones 7 to 10.

Juncus pallidus (slender South African rush) F B A

Vertical green stems growing 4 to 5 feet in height. One of the best tall evergreen rushes for hot climates. Plant from plugs or pots 2 to 4 feet on center. Zones 9 and 10.

Juncus patens (California gray rush, wire grass) G F A

Evergreen in mild climates, and capable of withstanding drought for short periods. Zones 7 to 10.

Juncus patens 'Elk Blue'. A blue-green-stemmed form from Randy Baldwin in California. Plant from plugs or pots 2 to 3 feet on center G F A

Juncus effusus.

Juncus polyanthemos.

Juncus polyanthemos.

Leymus arenarius 'Glaucus'.

Juncus polyanthemos (Australian gray rush) B A

Native to marshy habitats, mostly near the Australian coast. Clumping gray foliage is evergreen in milder climates and attains a height and spread of 4 feet. Prefers full sun and is surprisingly drought tolerant. Plant from plugs or pots 4 to 5 feet on center. Zones 8 to 10.

Juncus tenuis (pathway rush) G F

Short, green clumping rush, useful for naturalizing in moist soils and growing 6 to 12 inches. It tolerates foot traffic and can be mowed. Plant from seed, or plugs or pots 1 to 2 feet on center.

Koeleria macrantha (june grass) G F A NL

Circumpolar in the northern hemisphere. This cool-season grass is beginning to show up as a natural lawn. Though its use is largely untested, it deserves more experimentation. Probably best in coastal or western high-elevation applications. For lawns, best applied as seed; plugs would be too clumpy. It will brown somewhat in summer and green up again in the fall. Overwatering encourages turf diseases. As a meadow grass, it is a great late spring-flowering grass. Zones 3 to 9.

Leymus (wild rye)

Widespread in temperate Eurasia and North America. The wild ryes are a tough group of grasses; many are native to western U.S. coastal dunes. Most are cool-season, but interior species and those from colder climates go winter dormant. Most are tolerant of drought, and saline and alkaline conditions. Zones 3 to 10.

Leymus arenarius (European dune grass) G F A

Leymus arenarius 'Findhorn'. A nice compact small-leaved form of European dune grass collected by David Amme in Scotland, to 1 foot. Zones 5 to 9 G F A

Leymus arenarius 'Glaucus'. Northern Europe. A warm-season dune grass, growing 2 to 3 feet high, with metallic blue foliage that creeps aggressively from underground rhizomes. Takes any soil including dune sand and first-exposure seacoast. Tan flowers are carried 2 to 3 feet above the foliage. Best in full sun. Tolerates wind and can be an effective groundcover in tough sites. Plant from pots 18 to 24 inches on center. Zones 3 to 9 G F A

Leymus cinereus (Great Basin wild rye) G F B A

Native to the western United States, ranging into the cold interior and high elevations of the West. Good tall background grass in sweeps and drifts, bringing dramatic, even tropical effects to western meadows. Slowly spreading gray-green, often silver, foliage grows 3 to 5 feet high with spikes of tan flowers 3 to 5 feet above. Prefers full sun to light shade. Evergreen in mild climates; cold interior climates cause winter dormancy. Tolerates extreme heat with adequate moisture and is more cold tolerant than coastal species. Tolerates drought and a wide variety of soils. Plant from plugs or pots 2 to 3 feet on center. Zones 5 to 9.

Leymus condensatus (giant wild rye, canyon wild rye) G B A

Western United States. This slowly spreading evergreen grass grows on moist slopes and steep ravines in southern California chaparral. Tolerant of heavy soils or dune sand, this is one tough grass. Foliage grows 4 to 5 feet, and tan vertical flowers grow 3 to 4 feet above leaves. Glossy green foliage takes wind and makes a fine backdrop for coastal meadows. Best in full sun. Extremely drought tolerant, though it will be shorter on dry sites. Plant from seed or pots 3 to 4 feet on center. Zones 8 to 10.

Leymus condensatus 'Canyon Prince'. A more compact blue-leaved form, 3 to 4 feet high. Plant from pots 2 to 3 feet on center. Zones 7 to 9 G A

Leymus mollis (American dune grass, Pacific dune grass) G F A

Northern United States. This dune grass, largely replaced in many coastal environs by the more aggressive *Ammophila arenaria*, spreads from rhizomes to form large colonies on sandy shores. Evergreen in mild climates, this species is a softer blue than *Leymus arenarius*, with a more loose open habit. Though it's native to dune sand, it tolerates clay soils and is drought tolerant when established. Best in full sun. Plant from pots or bareroot divisions 1 to 2 feet on center; bareroot divisions must be planted to their crown and kept moist until established. Valuable for dune stabilization and as a groundcover in coastal gardens. Zones 7 to 9.

Leymus triticoides (creeping wild rye) G F

Western United States. This cool-season grass is one of the most durable sod-forming base grasses for western meadows, besting just about any other native western grass by providing

Leymus condensatus 'Canyon Prince'.

Leymus triticoides.

Luzula sylvatica 'Aurea'.

woodland shade. Excellent in combination with sedges (whose charms are likewise overlooked by most gardeners) where tree root competition is a challenge. Plants do best in woodland settings with moisture and good drainage. Many equally worthy North American native species are just now finding their way into the U.S. nursery trade. Plant from plugs or pots 12 to 18 inches on center. Zones 3 to 9.

Luzula nivea. Silvery gray-green foliage with showy white flowers. Foliage 6 to 8 inches, with flowers 8 to 10 inches above **F** **A**

Luzula sylvatica. Rich green leaves, 6 to 12 inches, flowers brown, 12 to 16 inches above **G** **F** **A**

Luzula sylvatica 'Aurea'. A golden-leaved form **G** **F** **A**

Luzula sylvatica 'Hohe Tatra'. A wide-leaved variety **G** **F** **A**

Luzula sylvatica 'Marginata'. A gilt-edged form **G** **F** **A**

Melica (melic)

Native to temperate regions of the world. Often overlooked in perennial borders, these mostly cool-season grasses are at their best in a meadow setting. Melics start growing early in the season, bloom in the spring, and are dormant—even brown—in the summer. But their delicate silky to fluffy flowers are irresistibly touchable and ethereal in their luminosity. Most thrive in fertile well-drained soils, but some species can tolerate seasonally dry soils. Most are easy from seed. Scatter melics throughout the meadow for light- and breeze-catching accents. Useful as specimens or in drifts. Most are best with cool-night, dry summers. Zones 5 to 9.

Melica altissima (Siberian melic) **F** **A**

Native to Russia. Vertical plants, 3 to 4 feet, with ribbony green foliage and fluffy flowers. Plant from seed, pots, or plugs.

Melica altissima 'Alba'. White flowerheads, fading to cream **F** **A**

Melica altissima 'Atropurpurea'. Flowers open purple and fade to tan **F** **A**

Melica californica (California melic) **G** **F** **A**
Melica imperfecta (smallflower melic) **G** **F** **A**

Both species grow on dry shady slopes in California hills and valleys. They are the first native grasses to green up and the first to go to sleep in summer: both are golden brown by June.

the most amount of green for the least amount of water. The slender green to blue-green foliage ranges in nature from 18 inches to 3 feet, depending on soil moisture and clonal traits (and depend upon it, shorter, taller, bluer, and greener clones are coming soon to a nursery near you). With moist fertile soil it can be an aggressive grower; in less than ideal settings, it is a tough, dependable groundcover. Tolerates a wide variety of soils and conditions from dune sand with first-exposure seacoast, to heavy clay in hot inland valleys. Good in bioswales. Tolerates saline and alkaline conditions. Easily planted from pots or plugs 18 to 24 inches on center. Slow from seed. Creeping wild rye is too aggressive for small gardens but extremely useful for large-scale plantings. Zones 6 to 9.

Leymus triticoides 'Elkhorn Green'. A fine compact green form, to 2 feet **G** **F**

Leymus triticoides 'Gray Dawn'. A silvery form, to 3 feet **G** **F**

Luzula (wood rush)

Native throughout the northern hemisphere. The wood rushes, a much-underused group of plants, are essential components for shady meadows. The two most often planted are *Luzula sylvatica* (sylvan wood rush) and *Luzula nivea* (snowy wood rush). Both make great early spring flowering accents for shady settings. The wood rushes tend to have soft hairs on their leaves, which sparkle with dew or glow with frost. They prefer part shade or shade, and many are drought tolerant in dry

Good on dry meadow margins and as accents. Their silky flowers are slender spikes, emerging green and drying to tan. Tolerates heavy rocky soils. Best planted from seed.

Melica ciliata (hairy melic, silky spike melic) G F A

Eurasia, North Africa. This showy flowering grass is a star performer in meadows with arching flower stems of creamy white fluffy flowers. Growing 18 to 24 inches high, this low spring bloomer is stunning backlit. Plants are often short-lived, so sprinkle them throughout the meadow and let them self-sow. Plant from seed, pots, or plugs. Zones 6 to 9.

Melinis nerviglumis (ruby grass, pink crystals) F A

This South African native is a clumping evergreen grass with soft-to-the-touch blue-green foliage growing to a height of 6 to 12 inches with another 6 to 12 inches of ruby-pink flowers that dry to tan. Tolerates a wide variety of soils and drought tolerant as well. Good drainage is essential where summers are humid. Plant from pots or plugs 12 to 18 inches on center. Not particularly long-lived and has great use as an annual grass in cold climates. Drought tolerant as well. Zones 9 and 10.

Melinis nerviglumis.

Melinis repens (Natal ruby grass) F A

This free-flowering self-sowing grass escaped onto roadsides and open fields in California and Florida. Still, showy pink cloudlike blossoms make it a useful flowering accent in hot humid and dry gardens. Tender to frost, it is killed by the first hard freeze in cold climates, where it makes a fine annual, spilling and flopping throughout the meadow. Blue-green foliage makes loose billowy mounds, 2 to 3 feet high and wide. Ruby-pink flowers bloom throughout the summer and are showy on the plant well into fall. Tolerates almost any soil, even coastal conditions. Best in full sun and grows poorly in too much shade. Plant from pots or plugs 18 to 24 inches on center. Natal ruby grass does naturalize, but it's controllable in most garden settings. Zones 9 and 10.

Milium effusum 'Aureum'.

Milium effusum (wood millet) F A

Native to the northern hemisphere. This cool-season species, a frequent component of woods and pasture in northern tier states, is rarely offered by nurseries and pretty much goes dormant by summer. Rich green ribbony leaves to 1 foot are

Miscanthus sinensis 'Morning Light'.

topped by dainty see-through flowers 1 to 2 feet above the foliage. Best planted from seed 12 to 18 inches on center. Zones 5 to 9.

Milium effusum 'Aureum'. Golden yellow leaves, fading to greenish yellow in the summer **F** **A**

Miscanthus floridulus (tall evergreen miscanthus) **B** **A**

Yet another grass with a confusing botanical past. This superb background grass forms tall columnar evergreen foliage topped by showy pink-red flowers in the fall. It should not be confused with *Miscanthus ×giganteus*, which is winter dormant and blooms silver-white in fall. This species grows 6 to 8 feet high with glossy green foliage that forms a tall arching clump. Its leaves, 1 to 2 inches wide, give a tropical effect. Broad leaf blades tatter in windy sites; protected plants will be neater in appearance. Plant from pots 4 to 7 feet apart or closer for hedging. Try this with big bold tropicals like cannas and philodendrons. Zones 7 to 9.

Miscanthus junceus (Okavango Delta grass) **B** **A**

Native to Africa. Our plants were grown from seed collected in Africa by a friend who was sitting on an elephant! This rush-like evergreen miscanthus makes a bold statement in tropical, desert, and Mediterranean gardens. Its gray-green cylindrical leaves grow in a column, 12 to 15 feet tall, topped by showy fluffy flowers. Drought tolerant (though it will be shorter in dry sites), but grows in water, too: in nature, this plant is under water three months of the year and baked dry for the other nine. Tolerates a wide variety of soils. Plant from pots 4 to 8 feet on center. A good container plant as well. Zones 9 and 10.

Miscanthus sinensis (maiden grass) **G** **F** **B** **A**

A very popular species of flowering grass, with available selections too numerous to list. Smaller varieties are useful specimens, or planted in drifts as low backdrop; those over 5 feet make good background grasses. Most of the smaller forms are warm-season grasses and can add fall color to the lower plane of the meadow. Narrow-leaved forms tend to grow better in hot climates. All are best in full sun with adequate moisture. These grasses sulk in the hot humid lower south, low deserts, and mild Mediterranean climates lacking sufficient winter chill. All have showy flowers.

Plant from pots 3 to 5 feet on center. Some miscanthus are reseeding in Mid-Atlantic and southern states. Zones 5 to 9.

Miscanthus sinensis 'Adagio'. A Kurt Bluemel selection with good separation of foliage and flower, 4 to 5 feet **G** **F** **A**

Miscanthus sinensis 'Gold Bar'. Horizontal variegation (perhaps the best of the yellow-banded varieties), columnar **F** **A**

Miscanthus sinensis 'Little Kitten'. A miniature, to 4 feet **G** **F** **A**

Miscanthus sinensis 'Little Zebra'. A compact form of *M. s.* 'Zebrinus' with horizontal yellow banding, 4 to 5 feet **F** **A**

Miscanthus sinensis 'Morning Light'. A very popular selection of a very popular grass, with fine-textured white variegated foliage that reads silver in the meadow. Grows well even in mild climates. One of the best grasses for winter color in mild climate. Height, 4 to 5 feet **F** **B** **A**

Miscanthus sinensis 'Yaku Jima'. Fine-textured green foliage, 4 to 5 feet **F** **B** **A**

Miscanthus sinensis 'Zebrinus'. Leaves emerge green with only occasional yellow bands, but as the season progresses, the yellow banding becomes more pronounced. By high summer, its yellow bands make the plant radiant when backlit **F** **B** **A**

Miscanthus transmorrisonensis
(Taiwanese miscanthus, evergreen miscanthus) **B** **A**

This clumping glossy background grass has arching foliage to 3 feet high and is topped by showy flowers that arch 3 feet above and out from the leaves. A mature plant can have a flower spread 5 to 6 feet high and wide. Because the flowers are held out from the foliage, they sway in even the slightest breeze. Prefers full sun and regular water but will take some drought once established. Evergreen in mild climates, it takes coastal conditions as well. Plant from plugs or pots 4 to 6 feet on center. Stunning en masse, flowering year-round in mild climates. Not invasive. Zones 6 to 9.

Molinia caerulea (purple moor grass) **F** **A**

Native to Eurasia. These mostly small flowering grasses make amazing flowering accents in meadow settings. Transparent and translucent, few grass flowers are as magical as the moor grasses, and this is reflected in the names of the cultivars, which try to describe their haunting beauty. All have brilliant fall color, usually yellow-orange; after the show, they completely collapse to

Miscanthus transmorrisonensis.

Molinia caerulea.

the ground, offering the briefest of winter interest. They are tolerant of a wide variety of soils, but they do need a pronounced winter chill to thrive. Best in full sun to light shade with regular water. Plant in groups or drifts, or scatter individuals throughout the meadow, from plugs or pots 18 to 30 inches on center. Here are some of the best forms.

Molinia caerulea 'Dauerstrahl' (Enduring Ray). 2 to 4 feet, upright, arching, grayish green [F] [A]

Molinia caerulea 'Hedebraut' (Heather Bride). 2 to 4 feet, upright, arching, grayish green. [F] [A]

Molinia caerulea 'Moor Hexe' (Moor Witch). 2 to 4 feet, columnar, grayish green [F] [A]

Molinia caerulea 'Strahlenquelle' (Source of Rays). 2 to 3 feet, arching, mounding [F] [A]

Molinia caerulea 'Variegata'. Brilliant yellow with creamy white stripes, 2 to 3 feet [F] [A]

Muhlenbergia (muhly grass)

This versatile genus of grasses offers beautiful flowering accents for hot climate gardens; taller species make fine background grasses and good medium height groundcovers as well. Most are evergreen in mild climates, heat and drought tolerant, and easy to grow, tolerating a wide variety of soil conditions. Zones 6 to 9.

Muhlenbergia capillaris (purple muhly) [G] [F] [A]

Two distinct forms of this showy flowering grass are offered by U.S. nurseries, so make sure you know which one you have. Florida nurseries and many southeastern nurseries grow the straight species, which can reach 3½ to 4 feet to the top of the purple-pink flowers; it is taller, and more elongated and arching, than the Texas form (the one offered by most western nurseries), which is never taller than 3 feet. *Muhlenbergia capillaris* var. *filipes* (as the Texas form is sometimes known) is also more cold hardy than Florida clones. New collections of plants are being made in New England and elsewhere, so be on the lookout for local genotypes that may be better adapted to your particular climate. In all forms, fine-textured gray-green foliage is covered in September by masses of purple flowers that turn gold when mature. Tolerates a wide variety of soils and is heat and drought tolerant even thriving in the low desert. Scatter throughout the meadow or plant in groups or masses, especially where grasses can be backlit. Plant from plugs or pots 3 to 4 feet on center. Selections are indistinguishable from the species, with one notable exception.

Muhlenbergia capillaris 'White Cloud'. A spectacular white-flowering clone [G] [F] [A]

Muhlenbergia dubia (pine muhly) [G] [F] [A]

Native to Texas. This superb large-scale groundcover, a recent addition to the western nursery trade, is getting wide praise for its dependable gray-green foliage in meadow settings. A tidy muhly, resembling a compact *Muhlenbergia rigens*, it grows to 3 feet in dense clumps. The silvery gray slender flowers are showy and neat on the plant from summer to fall, drying to tan. It is drought tolerant and grows in a wide variety of soils. Pine muhly is best in full sun in dry summer climates and would need excellent drainage in the Pacific Northwest. Plant from pots or plugs 2 to 4 feet on center. Zones 7 to 9.

Muhlenbergia dumosa (bamboo muhly) [G] [F] [A]

Native to Arizona, Texas, and Mexico. This ferny foliaged evergreen grass is native to rocky slopes in hot, dry climates where scarce rains are funneled to them. Well grown, this grass looks like an airy bamboo with bright green foliage that grows in arching clumps 4 to 5 feet high and wide. Small fuzzy flowers cover the plant in late spring, turning it the color of root beer foam. Tolerates heat and low desert conditions with adequate moisture. Drought tolerant but looks scruffy grown too dry. Grows in most soils and is best in full sun to light shade. Plant from pots or plugs 3 to 5 feet on center. The softness of bamboo muhly is a great foil to the harsh spikes and spininess of many desert plants. Plants are blasted dormant at 25°F. Zones 8 to 10.

Muhlenbergia emersleyi (bull muhly) [G] [F] [A]

Silver-gray foliage is topped by silvery pinkish plumes, reminiscent of a pennisetum, to 3 feet. Tough like most muhlys, it is also a sturdy groundcover. Plant from pots 3 to 4 feet on center. Zones 7 to 9.

Muhlenbergia involuta (Edwards Plateau muhly) [G] [F] [A]

Gray-green foliage with silky silvery white plumes, 3 to 4 feet. Very showy flowers, and it makes great groundcover as well. Plant from pots 3 to 4 feet on center.

Muhlenbergia dubia.

Muhlenbergia lindheimeri.

Muhlenbergia lindheimeri (Lindheimer's muhly) G F B A

This fine-textured grass makes an excellent 4- to 5-foot ever-green (in all but the coldest climates) backdrop in the meadow. Growing in dense clumps, its soft blue leaves are topped in early fall by silvery flowers, which dry to an attractive tan; foliage is usually 3 to 4 feet in height, with flowers held 18 to 24 inches above the leaves. Tolerates low desert heat, drought, and a wide variety of soils. Prefers sun to light shade; not at its best in high humidity or tropical conditions. Plant from plugs or pots 4 to 5 feet on center. The color of this muhly is handsome combined with other blue and silver grasses.

Muhlenbergia pubescens (soft muhly) G F A

Native to Mexico. Gray-green foliage is covered with silver-white hairs that are soft to touch. Purple flowers turn tan. Heat and drought tolerant. Needs good drainage. Plus or pots 2 to 3 feet on center. Zones 8 and 9.

Muhlenbergia rigens (deer grass, basket grass) G F B A

Native to the American Southwest. In moist swales or on fast-draining slopes, deer grass is a go-to grass for meadow mak-

Muhlenbergia rigens.

ing where summers are hot and dry, and it is indispensable as an evergreen background for meadows throughout the West. Called deer grass not because deer eat it, but because in large stands in nature, deer love to bed down in it. Gray-green foliage grows 3 to 4 feet in dense clumps and is topped by slender 2- to 3-foot flower spikes. Showy flowers emerge in late spring and remain attractive for most of the season. Extremely drought tolerant, although considerably shorter on dry sites. Tolerates first-exposure seacoast and almost any soil, including dune sand. Plant from plugs or pots 3 to 5 feet on center. This tough grass—whether as a single plant or in large masses—is stunning backlit. Zones 7 to 9.

Nassella (needle grass)

Their silky needle-like awns give these amazing flowering grasses their common name. The California species, while beautiful in their native settings, can be hard to manage in the Mediterranean meadow. To thrive, they must be allowed to dry out in the summer (brown is a color too!), a hazard in fire-prone western meadows; and their dormant foliage is fragile, easily flattened by foot and animal traffic. Still, properly sited and grown, they make beautiful flowering accents. Tolerates heat, drought, and a wide variety of soils. Best planted from seed. Zones 8 and 9.

Nassella cernua (nodding stipa). Native to California. Height, 2 to 3 feet, with nodding seedheads. *Nassella lepida* (foothill needle grass), to 3 feet, is similar G F A
Nassella pulchra (purple needle grass). Native to California. Height, 3 to 4 feet, with long awn. Purple on emergence, drying to gold G F A

Nassella tenuissima (Mexican feather grass, angel hair grass) G F A

The flowers of this tough native grass are like spun gold, glowing and swaying like no other. Bright, fine-textured iridescent green foliage is completely covered by mid summer with the silky golden awns of flowerheads. By the end of summer (depending on how much rain has fallen), seedheads need to be "combed" out of the clumps; otherwise, plants may look like they've had a bad hair day. In western meadows, they tolerate a wide variety of soils. Where summers are humid, plants need excellent drainage to thrive. Best in full sun to light shade.

Naturalizes freely: avoid planting where seedlings can spread to natural ecologies. Plant from pots 18 to 24 inches on center.

Panicum (panic grass)

Panic grasses are fantastic meadow components; tall species serve as background grasses, and medium-sized species and varieties offer great flowering accents in the meadow. All are warm-season grasses, and most add fall color and winter interest to the meadow as well. Most prefer full sun (they'll flop in too much shade), grow shorter in dry climates, and need plenty of water to thrive. They tolerate a wide variety of soils, including seacoast conditions. Zones 4 to 9.

Panicum amarum (coastal switch grass) G F B A

Native to the U.S. seashore from Connecticut to Mexico, undoubtedly with numerous genotypes and clones. Variably colored foliage, from gray-green to blue, grows 3 to 5 feet high and wide. Flowers in mid summer are fountain-like, evocative of water. Fall color is mostly golden yellow. Usually grows in dune sand but will tolerate heavy clay. Plant from plugs or pots 3 to 4 feet on center. Often considered only for dune stabilization, coastal switch grass deserves a role in meadow gardens as well. Zones 5 to 9.

Panicum amarum 'Dewey Blue' is a beautiful blue form selected by Rick Darke G F B A

Panicum bulbosum (Arizona panic grass) G F A

The shortest (at 1 to 2 feet) and showiest of the panic grasses, with gray-green foliage and showy cloudlike blossoms carried another 18 to 24 inches above the foliage, usually topping out at 3 feet overall height. Brilliant yellow fall color. Tolerates heat, drought, and a wide variety of soils. Self-sows, but this trait can be used to advantage in tough situations, where its low luminous flowers are welcome. Plant from pots 2 to 3 feet on center. Zones 6 to 9.

Panicum clandestinum (deertongue) G F A

A warm-season native American grass with bamboo-like foliage that grows in a sprawling clump 3 to 4 feet high. Small flowers bloom throughout the light green leaves, which turn yellow in fall. Grows in sun or shade. Best with regular water. Plant from pots 2 to 3 feet on center. A way underused shady meadow component: great in woodland meadows and naturalistic settings, and also a good filler.

Panicum virgatum (switch grass) G F B A

An indispensable species of native American grass, whose forms vary greatly in color of foliage, habit, and height. Use them scattered throughout the meadow or in drifts or groups; they are great along the water's edge. Switch grasses are light to moderate self-sowers, and named varieties do not usually come true from seed. You may need to weed out seedlings to keep plantings pure. Regardless, switch grass placed where it's backlit by early or late light is a true joy to behold. Most bloom mid summer, and many have good fall color. Plant from pots 3 to 4 feet on center.

Panicum virgatum 'Amber Wave'. Blue-gray foliage, turning red-purple in fall, to 4 feet G F B A

Panicum virgatum 'Hänse Herms'. Green foliage, reddish in fall, to 4 feet G F B A

Panicum virgatum 'Heavy Metal'. Good upright form. Metallic blue foliage, yellowish in fall. A Kurt Bluemel selection. Height, 4 to 5 feet G F B A

Panicum virgatum 'Northwind'. A good blue variety with yellowish fall color, and rust resistance in humid climates. A Roy Diblik, Northwind Perennial Farm introduction. Height, 4 to 6 feet G F B A

Panicum virgatum 'Prairie Sky'. Perhaps the bluest of the switch grasses. Foliage flops in rainy periods or in soil that is too rich. Yellow fall color. Introduced by Roger Gettig. Height, 4 to 5 feet G F B A

Panicum virgatum 'Rehbraun' (Russet) and *P. v.* 'Rostralbüsch' (Red Ray Bush). Two nearly indistinguishable clones, with green foliage turning red in fall. Both to 4 feet G F B A

Panicum virgatum 'Shenandoah'. Green foliage turning rich red in fall—the best of current red switch grasses, to 4 feet G F B A

Panicum virgatum 'Heavy Metal'.

G Groundcovers F Fillers B Backgrounds A Accents NL Natural Lawns

Paspalum quadrifarium.

Paspalum quadrifarium (crown grass) [G] [F] [B] [A]

Native to Paraguay and Uruguay. This clumping aqua-blue evergreen background grass grows 3 to 4 feet high and wide. Tolerates clay, sand, and coastal conditions. Best in full sun, but will handle medium shade. Strong tendency to naturalize in the Southwest; it is better behaved in hot humid climates. Noticeable flowers are slender and black on emergence; they dry to a nice tan color but are better removed to prevent reseeding. Plant from plugs or pots 3 to 5 feet on center. Reseeding can be a problem in some settings. Zones 9 and 10.

Pennisetum (fountain grass)

Native to Africa and Asia. Some of the showiest flowering grasses belong to this widely variable genus. Some fountain grasses are petite miniatures; others are among the tallest of ornamental grasses. Some are hardy to zone 4, others are nearly tropical and are used as annuals in colder climates. Some species can be wickedly weedy, and others well behaved. It's best to ask local grass growers which ones can be problematic in your climate. Nomenclature is confused, so always know the source of your plants and be aware that older plants have many synonyms. Some fountain grasses tolerate heat and drought. Most want full sun (in too much shade, they grow and flower poorly) and tolerate any soil, as long as they get adequate moisture, and even coastal conditions.

Pennisetum advena 'Rubrum' (purple fountain grass) [G] [F] [B] [A]

The most popular of the purple-foliaged fountain grasses, growing 4 to 5 feet high and wide. It is seed sterile. Showy flowers. Plants are killed at 28°F. Plant from pots 3 to 4 feet on center. Zones 9 and 10.

Pennisetum advena 'Eaton Canyon' (dwarf purple fountain grass, red riding hood). A fine compact form of common purple fountain grass, to 3 feet. Foliage is slightly less purple and more tender to frost. Plants are evergreen in mild climates. Plant from pots 2 to 3 feet on center. Seed sterile [G] [F] [A]

Pennisetum advena 'Green Form'. A reversion of the common purple form, green with bronzy tints to foliage and flower. Plant from pots 3 to 4 feet on center. Seed sterile [G] [F] [B] [A]

Pennisetum advena 'Little Pinkie'. A green sport of dwarf purple fountain grass with bronzy green foliage to 3 feet. Plant from pots 2 to 3 feet on center. Seed sterile [G] [F] [A]

Pennisetum advena 'Rubrum'.

Pennisetum alopecuroides (Chinese fountain grass) G F A

Native to Southeast Asia. This warm-season grass and its cultivars need plenty of winter chill to thrive. They perform poorly in heat and humidity, and in dry Mediterranean and desert climates. Many forms naturalize but are usually not problematic. A few can be weedy. The straight species has cream to tan flowers and good green foliage, 3 to 4 feet high and wide. Plant from pots or plugs 3 to 4 feet on center. Zones 6 to 9.

Pennisetum alopecuroides 'Hameln'. Compact, 2 to 3 feet, with dark green foliage and good orange-yellow fall color. Plant from pots 2 to 3 feet on center G F A

Pennisetum alopecuroides 'Little Bunny'. A miniature form to 18 inches with tan flowers and green foliage F A

Pennisetum alopecuroides 'Moudry' and *P. a.* 'National Arboretum'. Nearly identical forms, and therefore often confused by nurserymen—essentially they are the same plant: black flowering fountain grass. Both have rich lustrous green foliage, 2 feet high by 3 feet wide, topped by black flowers 18 to 24 inches above the leaves. Flowers emerge purplish black and are stunning backlit. Fall color is orangey brown, and flowers are handsome, even when foliage is dormant. These are among the few *Pennisetum alopecuroides* selections that thrive with little winter chill. They tolerate a wide variety of soils and self-sow wickedly, invading nearby lawns happily. In western meadows, plants will only naturalize in irrigated situations (they are probably the best varieties for southern California). Still, they are dramatic when well sited G F A

Pennisetum 'Fairy Tails' (Fairy Tails fountain grass) G F A

This sterile hybrid of unknown parentage, introduced from Greenlee Nursery, always attracts attention when it is in flower. A handsome clumping blue-green grass, 3 to 4 feet high and wide, it differs from most pennisetums in that its slender foxtail flowers are carried straight up on sturdy stems, with a good separation of foliage and flower. Flowers emerge pink, aging to tan, and are both showy and long lasting. Tolerates a wide variety of soils and conditions, including coastal conditions. Best in full sun with regular water, becoming more drought tolerant once established. Will survive extreme desert heat with adequate water. Does not reseed. Plant from pots 3 to 4 feet on center. Evergreen in mild climates but becomes fully dormant at 25°F. Zones 5 to 9.

Pennisetum alopecuroides.

Pennisetum alopecuroides 'Moudry'.

Pennisetum massaicum 'Red Bunny Tails'.

Pennisetum glaucum 'Purple Majesty' (purple pearl millet) B A

A striking annual for accents and tropical effects. Columnar plants grow quickly to 4 to 6 feet with ribbony purple-black foliage topped by thick purply seedheads. Showy flowers emerge covered by yellow stamens. Grows in any soil. Best in full sun with regular water. Plant from pots 3 to 4 feet on center. Birds love the seeds.

Pennisetum incomptum (spreading fountain grass) G F A

Native to China. Aggressively spreading from rhizomes and seed, this warm-season grass has blue-green foliage and vertical flower stems with showy flowers, to 4 feet. Potentially invasive, but sometimes you need that quality in a grass. Not for small gardens, but useful for contained sites or problem sites. Plant from pots 2 to 3 feet on center. Zones 4 to 9.

Pennisetum macrostachyum 'Burgundy Giant' (large purple fountain grass) B A

A good choice for a tall tropical evergreen background, this selection needs heat, humidity, and moisture to thrive. Large ribbony purple foliage grows 4 to 6 feet high. Tender to frost, it makes a great annual for colder climates. Plant from pots 4 to 5 feet on center.

Pennisetum massaicum 'Red Bunny Tails' G F A

A good flowering base grass for West Coast meadows. This clumping grass has glossy medium green foliage that blushes red in the fall. Foliage, evergreen in mild climates, is 18 to 24 inches tall, with flowers 12 to 18 inches above. The showy rabbittail-like seedheads are reddish black on emergence, just begging to be touched, and a favorite with kids. Best in full sun to light shade. Not particular about soils and tolerates coastal conditions. Plant from plugs 12 to 18 inches on center.

Pennisetum 'Oceanside' (giant fountain grass) B A

Origin unknown. This evergreen fountain grass grows in an upright column on almost woody stems 8 to 15 feet high! Leaves, 6 to 8 inches long, clothe the length of the branched, blue-white glaucous canes, 1 to 1½ inches thick; cattail-like flowers, 6 to 8 inches long, top the foliage. Our plant came from a single plant now naturalized in Oceanside near San Diego,

California. Tolerates seemingly any soil and both wet and dry conditions. Plant from pots or divisions 4 to 8 feet on center. Makes a truly tall tropical backdrop and a good windbreak. Zones 9 and 10.

Pennisetum orientale (oriental fountain grass) F A

Native to India and Pakistan. This warm-season grass has long-lasting showy light pink flowers that mature to a cream color and are attractive on the plant well into the fall. Gray-green fine-textured foliage grows 3 feet high and wide. Fall color is briefly yellowish; winter skeleton is not quite as attractive as other warm-season fountain grasses. Still, a fine flowering accent in meadow settings. Best in full sun to light shade. Tolerates a wide variety of soils and performs well in mild-climate western meadows. Plant from plugs or pots 2 to 3 feet on center. Does not reseed. Zones 6 to 9.

Pennisetum orientale 'Karley Rose'. Taller than the type, to 4 feet, and with pointy, pinker blossoms F A

Pennisetum orientale 'Tall Tails'. A Greenlee Nursery introduction, this sprawling fountain grass has pendulous fluffy flowers up to 8 inches long on tall lax stems that can reach up to 6 feet. Bright green warm-season foliage makes a large mound of glossy leaves that turn orangey yellow in the fall. Flowers are showy on the plant from early summer into fall. Tolerates any soil with adequate moisture and takes desert heat. Also good by the coast. Plant from pots 4 to 5 feet on center. Extremely floriferous. Some self-seeding F B A

Pennisetum purpureum (elephant grass) F B A

This large evergreen background grass—a must for big tropical foliar effects—grows in dense clumps, 5 to 6 feet high and wide, with 2- to 3-inch-wide bright green leaves. Our plant, a nonflowering form, came from a Florida research program breeding forage grasses for the Sudan; it is now being grown by the San Diego Zoo for elephant chow! Tolerates a wide variety of soils and is best in full sun or light shade. Drought tolerant when established, it prefers adequate moisture to keep the foliage looking good. Plant from pots or divisions 4 to 6 feet on center. Give this one some room! Zones 9 and 10.

Pennisetum purpureum 'Prince' and *P. p.* 'Princess'. These purple-foliaged fountain grass selections, introduced by Allan

Pennisetum orientale 'Karley Rose'.

Pennisetum orientale 'Tall Tails'.

Pennisetum spathiolatum.

Armitage, make columns of rich purple, including flowers, from 5 to 8 feet high and 2 to 3 feet high, respectively. They are mostly used as annuals in cold climates, where plants are killed by the first hard freeze. Plants begin growth with green foliage that grows increasingly purple as the season progresses. Best in full sun. They tolerate a wide variety of soils as long as moisture is adequate. Avoid planting where plants are subjected to hot, dry winds. Good by the coast. Prefer humid climates; may not flower in cold climates. Plant from pots 3 to 5 feet on center B A

Pennisetum setaceum (tender fountain grass) G F A

Native to tropical Africa and southwestern Asia. This popular warm-season grass is excellent for tropical effects in cold climates, where it behaves like an annual, but is perennial in mild and desert climates above 28°F. Fine-textured bright green foliage grows in dense mounds 3 to 4 feet high and wide; plants grown in humid climates can reach 5 feet if well grown. Flowers, which can grow up to 15 inches long, are pinkish purple, drying to tan at maturity. Evergreen and ever-blooming if well watered in southern California gardens, where it reseeds readily. Rarely a threat to pristine ecology, it thrives on disturbed coastal slopes and on roadsides. Properly sited, it makes a fine component in dry southwestern meadows. Tolerates any soil and is best in full sun or light shade. Plant from pots or plugs 3 to 4 feet on center. Zones 9 and 10.

Pennisetum spathiolatum (slender veldt grass) G F A

This evergreen clumping base grass has low mounding foliage to 18 inches and slender golden flowers held erect on wiry stems 2 to 3 feet above the foliage. A dramatic and versatile meadow grass, it is best in coastal and southwestern meadows. Largely untested in the South, but it has gotten great reviews in the Southwest from Napa to Phoenix. The slender flowers are see-through, and its verticality is excellent for creating brush-strokes in the meadow. Best in full sun to light shade, drought tolerant, and not particular about soils. Plant from plugs or pots 2 to 3 feet on center. This species is great in combination with *Festuca mairei*; the two textures and colors are similar, and their flowers work well together. Zones 7 to 9.

Pennisetum villosum (feathertop) G F A

Native to tropical Africa. This slowly creeping warm-season grass with showy flowers has been planted as an ornamental grass since the early 20th century. Considered a noxious weed in many U.S. states (though, curiously, rarely restricted) and invasive by many native plant authorities in southern California, it is nonetheless sold, grown, and cherished by many gardeners as a great flowering accent in the meadow. Creeping glossy gray-green foliage is covered by fluffy flowers that emerge creamy green and mature to pure white. Tolerates any soil and is best in full sun. Drought and heat tolerant. Easy from seed and self-sows readily. Plant from pots 2 to 3 feet on center. Feathertop is stunning backlit, and its strong growth is valuable in urban settings where self-sowing is not a problem. As it is tender to frost, it poses no threat to the environment where temperatures go below freezing. Zones 8 and 9.

Phalaris arundinacea (ribbon grass, reed canary grass) G F A

Europe, North America. This grass grows around the world throughout the northern hemisphere. European and native North American genotypes are virtually indistinguishable and probably have by now interbred and shared genetic material. Despised by many restorationists, this aggressive colony-forming warm-season grass is probably here to stay. In many gardens, it is a given: gardeners must decide whether to eradicate it or let it be. Elimination can be very problematic, requiring multiple chemical applications and/or burning in mid June. With aggressive rhizomatous grasses, you must pick your battle: if you can't eradicate it, cutting midseason will rejuvenate the plants and keep them looking better into the winter season.

Reed canary grass is rarely planted other than for "pasture improvement"; careful consideration should be given going forward before settling on this species for this purpose, however, as there are usually better, less invasive or native species that can accomplish the same goal. Reed canary grass grows 4 to 5 feet high with showy golden flowers in the summer. Medium green foliage dies back in hot summer climates. It takes a wide variety of soils and prefers full sun and moist soil. Nurseries rarely sell the straight species as plants; only seed is available. More usually, the variegated clones are sold by specialty grass nurseries. The colored-leaved forms are good in masses and drifts, especially on the water's edge; they are great accents and while still aggres-

sively creeping, they are much shorter than the species. Most colored forms have pink new growth in the spring. Plant from seed or plugs 2 to 3 feet on center. Zones 4 to 9.

Phalaris arundinacea 'Feesey' (strawberries and cream). Mostly pure white with green striping, strong pink new growth, 2 to 3 feet G F A

Phalaris arundinacea 'Luteopicta'. Pale yellow with green stripes, 2 to 3 feet G F A

Phalaris arundinacea 'Picta' (gardener's garters). Old favorite with white variegation, 2 to 3 feet. Can be invasive G F A

Phalaris arundinacea 'Woods Dwarf'. Fine-textured white variegated form, similar to 'Picta' but smaller, to 18 inches G F A

Phleum pratense (Italian timothy) G F A

Native to southern Europe. The first ornamental timothy available to meadow gardeners. This is one of the showiest of the shorter flowering grasses. Attractive clumping gray-green foliage grows 6 to 8 inches high and is topped by classic timothy flowers, vertical spikes, 8 to 12 inches tall, which emerge in late spring. Flowers are showy on the plant into fall, having dried to a tanny gold. Evergreen in mild climates. Best in full sun to light shade. Tolerates a wide variety of soils. Plant from pots 12 to 18 inches on center. Italian timothy is great in low meadows and along pathway edges. Zones 8 and 9.

Phragmites australis (common reed) B A

Cosmopolitan. Arguably one of the most successful grasses on the planet: chances are if you've got phragmites on your site, you'll always have phragmites on your site. An aggressively colonizing tall grass of wetlands, it's found worldwide in fresh or brackish water. While botanists debate its "native" pedigree, and whether "native" and European species have interbred, common reed is ubiquitous and most likely here to stay. Most gardeners do not plant it, they just inherit it, and in many cases, eradication strategies are futile. Chemicals are usually effective only in small gardens, where reinfestation is controllable. Despite its fearsome reputation, common reed can be managed at meadow edges.

Gray-green warm-season foliage is held on thick upright canes 8 to 18 feet high. Flowers in the summer are gold, becoming silver, and are showy and persistent on the plant. The dormant skeleton is dramatic in winter light. The typical species is rarely grown by nurseries; more often it comes with your site. Controlling is often not an option, so working with it makes more sense. Two variegated forms are available and, properly sited, can be useful tall background subjects or accents; they work well as container subjects, submerged in the water or contained on the water's edge. Both are shorter than the species. Plant from pots 3 to 5 feet on center. All plants take full sun to light shade, withstanding both coastal conditions and hot interior climates, and spread aggressively in moist soils, so site with caution. Root barriers or pots without drain holes may be necessary to contain the plants (check out "The Wicked Ones" in Chapter 7 for more on working with invasive grasses). Eventually, this often-maligned grass may serve in biofilters and help clean polluted water. Zones 3 to 10.

Phragmites australis 'Candy Stripe'. White variegation B A
Phragmites australis 'Variegatus'. Golden yellow variegation B A

Poa arachnifera (Texas bluegrass) G F A NL

An endangered species in most of its range in Texas and the Great Plains. This creeping, sod-forming cool-season base grass is one of the most drought tolerant dark green grasses there is. Its showy flowers are as silky as spider webs on emergence but dry less attractively than most grass seedheads. Many gardeners tidy up plantings by removing spent heads. Typically grows 12 to 18 inches; maintain a lower height by occasional cutting and keeping it on the drier side. It grows best in full sun but handles a surprising amount of shade. Perhaps too aggressive for small meadows, it is better behaved in shadier situations. Tolerates a wide variety of soils. Plant from pots or plugs 12 to 18 inches on center. Zones 4 to 9.

Poa compressa (Canadian bluegrass) G F NL

Native to Europe. This cool-season grass, which creeps from underground stems, is found through the northern tier of the United States, where it is often naturalized in pastures. It has soft bluish green foliage and a showy silvery flower. Untested and unused by most meadow gardeners, this tough grass deserves more experimentation: it tolerates a wide range of soils and conditions, is surprisingly drought tolerant, and is low growing by nature. Plant from pots or plugs 12 to 18 inches on center. Zones 3 to 9.

Pogonatherum paniceum (little bamboo grass) F A

Southeast Asia. This compact clumping grass has bamboo-like foliage that grows in neat mounds 2 feet high and wide. Tolerates a wide variety of soils. It prefers regular water and full sun to light shade. Inconspicuous flowers cover the plant with a fuzzy haze, and cool temperatures bring reddish tones to the leaves (plants are killed below 28°F). Great for low bamboo-like effects where running bamboos would be problematic. Plant from plugs or pots 2 to 3 feet on center. Zones 9 and 10.

Pogonatherum paniceum 'Variegatum'. Slight golden variegation F A

Reineckia carnea G F

China. This grasslike member of the lily family is an excellent grasslike groundcover for shady meadows in mild climates. Glossy bright green foliage, 1 to 2 feet tall, slowly spreads to form a colony. Showy pink flowers, which are slightly fragrant, are mostly hidden in the foliage; showy orange berries are easier to spot. Tolerates a wide variety of soils and even competition from tree roots. Good with ferns and sedges. Best in shade with regular water. Plant from plugs or pots 6 to 12 inches on center. Zones 8 to 10.

Rhynchospora latifolia (star grass) F A

Southern U.S. native, also known as white-top sedge, star sedge, and umbrella grass. The bright green foliage of this slowly spreading evergreen sedge grows 18 to 24 inches tall, and its showy flower bracts look like white stars. Found in moist sandy swales in acidic soils throughout the Southeast, star grass grows in shallow water and is at its best in wet meadows, in full sun to light shade. Plant from pots 12 to 18 inches on center. Zones 8 to 10.

Saccharum officinarum (sugar cane) B A

The source of sugar, this tall clumping evergreen grass makes a great tropical background. Usually growing 6 to 8 feet high and wide, plants have bright green leaves 2 to 3 inches wide and 2 to 3 feet long on arching woody canes. Grows in sand or clay, but needs regular water to look its best. Best in full sun; it flops in too much shade. Temperatures below 28°F can kill plants. Plant from pots 3 to 6 feet on center. Zones 9 and 10.

Saccharum officinarum 'Pele's Smoke'. Purple-leaved and purple-stemmed—a fine cultivar B A

Rhynchospora latifolia.

Saccharum officinarum 'Pele's Smoke'.

Schizachyrium scoparium (little bluestem) G F A

One of North America's most important native grasses, occurring throughout most of the continental United States. Its all-around ease of growth and versatility make this warm-season grass a great addition to meadow gardens big and small, as a groundcover, a flowering accent, and a fall and winter accent. Compact clumps of green to blue-green to blue foliage grow 6 to 12 inches high and wide. Slender vertical flowerheads, 18 to 24 inches above the leaves, emerge in summer and are showy and light-catching well into fall. Fall colors are intense, from orange and copper to red and even purple. Winter skeletons are sturdy and effective in the garden well into the depths of winter. It tolerates a wide variety of climates and soils; in fact, it thrives in poor soil conditions and resents soils that are too rich and fertile. Nevertheless, consider growing local clones whenever possible. It is best in full sun and flops in too much shade. Plant from seed or pots. Zones 3 to 10.

Schizachyrium scoparium 'Blaze'. A seed strain noted for its reddish fall and winter color G F A

Schizachyrium scoparium 'The Blues'. Compact upright form with metallic blue foliage G F A

Schoenoplectus californicus (tule) B A

Southern and western United States to South America. Green or gray-green, growing to 10 feet or more. This species and *Schoenoplectus acutus* (hardstem bulrush) were utilized by western Indians to make baskets, boats, and shelters. Aggressively spreading. Plant with caution—this plant is best contained. Plugs or pots 1 to 3 feet on center. Zones 7 to 9.

Sesleria autumnalis.

Sesleria heufleriana.

Schoenoplectus tabernaemontani (great bulrush, clubrush) F A

Height, 4 to 7 feet. Usually only the variegated forms of this species are offered; most of these prefer some winter chill to thrive. Plant from plugs or pots 12 to 18 inches on center. Zones 5 to 9.

Schoenoplectus tabernaemontani 'Albescens' (white bulrush, variegated bulrush). Stunning white linear variegation that makes the whole plant appear ghostly white. Grows to 5 feet. Plant from plugs or pots 12 to 18 inches on center F A

Schoenoplectus tabernaemontani 'Zebrinus' (zebra bulrush). Bright golden yellow banding on dark green stems. Usually less vigorous than other forms. Grows to 4 feet. Plant from pots 3 to 5 feet on center. Plant from plugs 12 to 18 inches on center F A

Sesleria (moor grass)

Perhaps no other genus of true grasses offers as many beautiful choices for meadow plantings. My personal favorite, *Sesleria autumnalis*, looks just as good in San Diego as it does in Minneapolis. Amazingly adaptive, moor grasses grow well in all but low desert and hot southeastern climates. They range in color from blue-green to yellow-green and are perfect for small meadow gardens, as all are tidy and well behaved. Zones 4 to 9.

Sesleria autumnalis (autumn moor grass) G F

Native to southern Europe. This soft yellow-green clumping grass is among the finest of base meadow grasses. Its chartreuse evergreen foliage grows 12 to 18 inches in neat clumps. The simple slender flowers emerge silvery white and dry to a nice tan color. Never messy and always attractive, autumn moor grass looks great year-round. It's best in sun or light shade. Prefers regular water in dry climates; drought tolerant in northern tier states. Plant from plugs 8 to 12 inches on center. Autumn moor grass used en masse is stunning when backlit.

Sesleria caerulea (blue moor grass) G F

Similar to *Sesleria autumnalis* but not as heat tolerant, with shorter blue-green foliage that grows 6 to 8 inches high and wide. The chalky white undersides of the leaves give blue moor grass a two-tone effect. Sweet little spring blooms fade quickly and disappear into the foliage. Plant from plugs or pots 6 to 8 inches on center. Makes a great blue-green groundcover that combines well with silver foliage.

Sesleria 'Greenlee's Hybrid' G F

A nice compact moor grass that appears to be a cross of *Sesleria caerulea* and *Sesleria autumnalis* with a height of 6 to 8 inches and coloring a blend of the two. Better in hot inland climates than *Sesleria caerulea*. Plant from plugs 6 to 8 inches on center.

Sesleria heufleriana (blue-green moor grass) G F

Similar to *Sesleria caerulea* only taller and wider, at 12 to 16 inches, with a cool, slightly less blue blue-green color. Plant from plugs or pots 12 to 18 inches on center. A superior year-round base meadow grass.

Sesleria nitida (gray moor grass) G F A

Native to Italy. While most seslerias have subtle flowers, *Sesleria nitida* has showy black flowers that bloom in early spring. Rich gray leaves grow 12 to 18 inches and are sharp and prickly. Best in full sun, it tolerates drought and a wide variety of soils. Plant from pots or plugs 12 to 18 inches on center. Makes a fine silvery gray groundcover as well as a flowering accent. Remember, the foliage is sharply pointed.

Setaria palmifolia (palm grass) B A

This clumping tropical background grass has bright green pleated leaves that resemble palm fronds. The dense clumps can easily be 5 feet high and 6 feet wide in moist soils. Although it prefers regular water, it is fairly drought tolerant once established. Reseeds readily, but seedlings are easily edited. Grows in sun or considerable shade. Tolerates a wide variety of soils. Foliage is damaged at 32°F, so protect the clumps in colder areas. Plant from plugs or pots 4 to 5 feet on center. Palm grass looks great on the water's edge. Zones 9 and 10.

Setaria palmifolia 'Dwarf'. A compact plant, growing 3 to 4 feet tall A

Sorghastrum nutans (Indian grass) G B A

North America. This widespread species, one of the major components of the tall grass prairie that once covered much of North America, is a clumping warm-season grass, growing 5 to 8 feet. Its rich green to blue-green foliage is topped by showy

Setaria palmifolia.

Spartina bakeri.

golden flowers. Many metallic blue forms have been recently made available, but the green forms are beautiful as well. Tolerates a wide variety of soils. It is best in full sun with adequate moisture. The extensive range of Indian grass means it's wise to consider local clones whenever possible. Plants prefer full sun and flop in too much shade; they will grow shorter in hotter, drier climates. Plant from pots 3 to 4 feet on center. Great in drifts and masses. Zones 3 to 9.

Sorghastrum nutans 'Indian Steel'. A good blue form G B A
Sorghastrum nutans 'Sioux Blue'. A good upright glaucous blue form G B A

Spartina bakeri (Florida cord grass, sand cord grass) G B A

This well-mannered evergreen clumping grass is one of the best tall background grasses for mild climates. Its fine-textured medium green foliage grows in dense mounds, 4 to 6 feet high and wide. Columnar at first, it spreads with age. Best in full sun or light shade. Flowers are noticeable but not showy, and tidy on the plant. Grows in sand or clay and takes coastal conditions as well. Tolerates windy sites and drought once established. Plant from plugs or pots 3 to 6 feet on center. Works well on the water's edge. Not invasive. Zones 8 to 10.

Spartina pectinata (prairie cord grass) G B

Native to freshwater marshes and wet prairies across most of the northern tier of North America. One of the best grasses for winter effects, this species will give cattails a run for their money and usually can compete with them, adding diversity to monostands. Aggressively spreading by rhizomes, this tall warm-season grass will dominate wet environs and can cover large areas with ease. Not for small gardens. Arching, sharp-edged foliage is rich green becoming yellow-orange in the fall. Its graceful form evokes motion, even completely still. Good winter skeleton is persistent, even in snowy climates. Grows in most soils; best in full sun to light shade. Plant from plugs or pots 3 to 4 feet on center. Zones 3 to 10.

Spartina pectinata 'Aureomarginata'. Nice golden yellow edges that catch the light. Plants are shorter and easier to control, and will also grow with average soil moisture G B A

Sporobolus airoides (alkali sacaton, alkali dropseed) G A

Western United States, found in seasonally wet areas that are baked dry, with little or no summer rain. A tough grass and a lovely native flowering accent for difficult sites, tolerating extreme heat, drought, salinity, and alkalinity, even of southwestern climates. The beauty of this warm-season grass belies its versatility. Gray-green foliage grows in dense clumps 1 to 2 feet high and wide. Flowers, which emerge greenish pink and dry to a beautiful golden brown, are held another 1 to 2 feet above the foliage. Yellow-orange fall color carries the plant into its tan winter skeleton. Best in full sun. Grows smaller in drier sites. Needs moisture to look its best in western meadows. Plant from seed, plugs, or pots 2 to 3 feet on center. Zones 4 to 9.

Sporobolus heterolepis (prairie dropseed) G A

Native to North America's prairies from Quebec to Colorado. Among the most elegant of all prairie grasses. The flowers are uniquely fragrant as they open (most people detect coriander or buttered popcorn); the scent disappears as flowers mature. Slow growing but worth the wait. Bright green foliage, 2 to 3 feet high and wide, stunning fall color. Good planted en masse and in drifts. Plant from seed, pots, or plugs 2 to 3 feet on center.

Sporobolus heterolepis 'Tara'. A good dwarf form G A

Sporobolus wrightii.

Stipa gigantea.

Sporobolus wrightii (giant sacaton, Wright's dropseed) G B A

Native from Arizona and Texas to Mexico—one of the West's great native grasses and the new darling of southwestern meadows. Handsome gray-green foliage can make dense arching clumps 3 to 6 feet high and wide; pinkish green flowering plumes that dry to a beautiful golden color are held 3 to 4 feet above the leaves. Extremely drought tolerant and resistant to saline and alkaline conditions. Performs well on the seacoast, too. Tolerates even low desert conditions. Plant from plugs or pots 4 to 6 feet on center. Dramatic semi-evergreen background grass, as a specimen or en masse. Zones 5 to 9.

Sporobolus wrightii 'Los Lunas Form'. A particularly robust
  introduction by David Salmon of High Country Gardens,
  bred as a windbreak for high-country agriculture G B A

Stipa gigantea (giant feather grass, giant oat) G B A

Native to southwestern Europe, North Africa. This evergreen Mediterranean grass is among the most dramatic of all the flowering grasses. Gray-green foliage, 2 to 3 feet in height, grows in dense clumps that are topped by golden yellow flowers 5 to 6 feet above the foliage. Emerging in late spring to early summer, the plants are stunning backlit. The tall columnar fountains of flowers are see-through and are surreal in late and early light; they look good well into summer. Plants must have good drainage but will tolerate a wide variety of soils and coastal conditions. Hard to grow where summers combine heat and humidity. Good in full sun and drought tolerant once established. Spectacular as a specimen or in drifts and sweeps. Plant from pots or plugs 3 to 5 feet on center. Zones 5 to 9.

Thysanolaena latifolia.

Tripsacum dactyloides.

Thysanolaena latifolia (tiger grass) G B A

This truly tropical grass makes a dramatic evergreen background, with distinctive bamboo-like foliage and large showy flowers that are long lasting and attractive on the plant. The huge arching clumps have almost woody stems, 10 to 12 feet high and wide. Foliage is damaged at 32°F, so protect the crown in colder climates. Tolerates a wide variety of soils but needs regular water to thrive. Large leaves tatter in windy sites, so it's best to protect this grass from hot, dry, or coastal winds. Plant from pots 6 to 8 feet on center. Zones 9 and 10.

Tripsacum dactyloides (eastern gamagrass) G B A

This wide-bladed clumping background grass grows 3 to 4½ feet high and wide, with grayish green leaves (evergreen in mild climates) and a curious flower, briefly showy, a nice accent as the seedheads mature. Very versatile, growing in almost all soil, tolerating boggy conditions as well as drought. Grows in sun or medium shade. Plant from plugs, pots, or divisions 3 to 5 feet on center. Try combining this with tall ferns. Surprisingly good on shady slopes. Zones 5 to 10.

Tripsacum dactyloides 'Cajun Dwarf'. Compact warm-season selection that came to us from Tim Kiphart. It's the only tripsacum we have that goes dormant even in our mild southern California climate. Grows in dense clumps 2 to 3 feet high and wide, with orange-yellow fall color. Tolerates any soil but looks best with light shade and regular water. Will tolerate full sun with adequate moisture. Plant from pots 2 to 3 feet on center. Good in drifts and moist swales. Zones 6 to 10 G F A

Tripsacum floridanum.

Tripsacum floridanum (Florida gamagrass, dwarf Fakahatchee grass) G F A

This clumping evergreen blue-green grass is a fine ground-cover choice for southern and southwestern meadows, growing 3 feet high and wide in tight, neat clumps. The flowers are insignificant and tidy, slender tan-colored spikes that add interest to the plant. Grows in full sun and moderate shade, in sand or clay, and tolerates coastal conditions. Plant from plugs or pots 2 to 3 feet on center. Zones 8 to 10.

Typha (cattail, reedmace)

Cattails are another warm-season grasslike plant, forming dense colonies that can be, in many situations, impossible to control. As with *Phragmites* and other aggressive wetland genera, dense stands of cattails often come with wetland sites. It can take up to two years of repeated chemical applications to effectively eliminate plants, and keeping them eliminated is almost always a never-ending battle. Spreading aggressively from both rhizomes and seeds, cattails can easily take over a pond edge;

Typha latifolia.

Typha latifolia. The most common species, 6 to 10 feet, with fat, wide leaves. *Typha latifolia* 'Variegata', with white striped foliage, is less aggressive G B A

Typha laxmannii. The most beautiful of the compact cattails, 3 to 5 feet G B A

Typha minima. Compact form, 2 to 2½ feet tall, with fat round seedheads. A weak grower in mild climates and prefers a winter chill to thrive G A

Vetiveria zizanioides (vetiver, khus khus) G B A

Native to India. This clumping semitropical evergreen background grass has been cultivated by man for thousands of years for its fragrant oils, which come from its roots (vetiver oil is one of the oldest perfume and medicinal bases known); and its leaves are used for baskets, screens, and mats. Recently, vetiver has been used to control erosion on steep tropical slopes to help restore damaged rainforest: its roots grow 6 feet or more into the soil. Best in full sun to part shade. Good in costal conditions as well. Tolerant of sand, clay, drought, and heat, vetiver will even grow in the low desert, in upright columns 4 to 8 feet high. The glossy bronzy green leaves have no scent at all; they are, however, sometimes braided to create a "coif" of grasses that is both sculptural and whimsical. Most plants in the U.S. nursery trade are non-flowering clones. The architecturally striking foliage has leaf tips that bend backward at the tip and curl like a party favor in winter—truly one of the best grasses for winter color in mild climates. In colder climates it will blush red with a hard freeze. Plant from plugs, pots, or divisions 1 to 4 feet on center. Zones 9 and 10.

Vetiveria zizanioides 'Silver Rockets'. Grows 5 to 8 feet high, with narrower, more silvery foliage topped by showy 3-foot silvery flowers G B A

yet, like other feared genera, they can be beautiful and have significant wildlife value. And children love cattails. Still, these are extremely invasive plants and should not be introduced to the meadow without thought as to how you will control their spread.

Distinctive, flat gray-green foliage is topped by classic cigar-shaped cattails that burst open in the fall and winter to distribute thousands of seeds that float in the wind. Golden fall color is replaced by brown winter skeletons. Cattails thrive in constantly wet soil, growing in marshes or in water to a depth of 2 feet, but they will tolerate almost any soil as long as it stays moist. Plants grow in full sun to light shade. The U.S. nursery trade usually offers more refined, shorter ornamental species, which are more easily controlled in northern latitudes; here is a selection of available cattails (though most sites with *Typha latifolia* and its southern and western cousin, *Typha domingensis*, inherit these plants). Plant from pots 2 to 5 feet on center. Zones 3 to 10.

Typha angustifolia. One of the better smaller cattails, growing 4 to 6 feet. Slender, more graceful foliage than *Typha latifolia* and *Typha domingensis* G B A

Typha domingensis. Taller than *Typha latifolia*, to 12 feet. More common in southern and western marshes G B A

Vetiveria zizanioides.

CHAPTER 7

MAKING A MEADOW

I like to get the plants on the site and move them around, then think about how they'll grow together.

If you intend to use a landscape contractor to install your meadow, find out as much as you can about their work. Ask for references, then call.

(next page) Because making meadows is fairly new to American gardeners, you'll probably have to search to find all the plants you'll want. Remember: once the base grasses have been planted, you can add the other plants over time.

THE SUCCESS OF YOUR MEADOW GARDEN depends on many factors: selecting the right plants for your soil and your design purposes, properly preparing your site before planting begins, and selecting the right method and time of year to plant. Failure on any one of these counts can mean the difference between a beautiful meadow garden or an unsatisfactory mess. Take some time to make sure you understand what's ahead of you. The information in this chapter should help your site be a joy to plant and an inspiration to observe, as it grows into a fully established meadow. Pay attention to detail at the start, and meadow making can go smoothly and plants settle in quickly.

Who's going to plant your meadow?

If you are going to do most of the work yourself, make sure you have considered all the factors involved in meadow construction. Do you really understand the time it will take? Do you have all the tools required to do the job? Will you have the resources to plant all your grasses and accents in a timely fashion? Even small meadow gardens require many plants to achieve good groundcover and get the required results. Plants arrive in containers of various size, from small plant plugs of just a few inches each, through 4-inch pots, right up to larger 1-gallon sizes and beyond for accent or feature plants. All these have to go into prepared ground as soon as possible after they arrive on site.

Seed used for sowing a meadow should be as weed-free as possible. Also, always look for the highest percentage of pure, live seed.

Another major factor to consider is that getting the types of grasses you will need for your meadow may involve dealing with wholesale and specialty grass nurseries who do not sell directly to the public. To get the best prices on your meadow grasses and other plants, you may need to work with a licensed landscape contractor or horticultural professional who is able to deal with the nurseries that are the source of the plants required.

If you are not going to plant your meadow yourself, you will need a good contractor. Most gardeners are aware that using a licensed, bonded, and insured landscape contractor is the best way to start a new garden. Before you get involved in a working relationship with a landscape contractor, find out what, if any, trade associations and professional bodies they belong to. Ask how many years they have been in business and check out their portfolios of completed projects. This is all made so much easier now, as many landscape contractors have Web sites. But the most important thing is to visit some actual sites: see the work they've accomplished and talk to their clients while there.

As with using other trades and professionals, nothing beats hearing how things went from previous clients—the things that went smoothly, and the hitches, both large and small. Let's face it, all home and garden projects have some glitches along the way, even when the results are great! Find out if they showed up when they said they would—nothing becomes more painful than contractors who are not reliable. Did they keep a clean site? Did they protect existing plantings and other areas not to be changed? Did they return phone calls and e-mails in a timely manner? Ask if the company can handle multiple trades or specialties—for example, groundwork including regrading, drainage, and other excavation, soil preparation, soil improvement, aeration, irrigation system design and installation. Look way ahead and find out about maintenance—some contractors do this work, but others do not. Companies that do have the expertise, with multiple trades in-house, can often save valuable time and money, as they will not have to coordinate multiple contractors, juggling many work and materials' delivery schedules. Remember that good contractors stay busy; you will have to contract with them well in advance of work beginning.

Since the notion of making meadows is relatively new, even nursery and landscape professionals who have been in the business for many years may be inexperienced at planting meadows. Fortunately, most specialty grass nurseries that grow and produce meadow grasses will consult on the grasses they sell. It is often a good idea to have a nurseryman or horticultural consultant visit the site prior to planting. And a second visit when the plants are delivered means that someone familiar with planting and growing meadow grasses is really involved in your project. This can save a lot of time and money in the long run. It's also a good idea to retain a nursery or horticultural consultant to review the project after it is completed, to make sure the new meadow is being properly maintained.

Arranging for the grasses

Meadow grasses are sold by seed, divisions, transplants, and rooted pots. Seed is usually available year-round. Inventories will be high in summer and fall, when most seed is harvested—exact timing varies with type of grass. And harvest time is when seed is the freshest it can be. Be sure to order seed that is as weed-free as possible—you do not want to import fresh weeds to a cleared site! Always look out for the highest percentage of pure live seed, and the lowest percentage of weeds. Seed must always be properly stored, to maintain quality and keep germination rates as high as possible. This means either applying seed as soon as possible or storing it in rodent-proof containers in a cool, dry place until your site is ready to plant.

Seed can be sown by hand broadcasting, hand-operated spreaders, or larger mechanical farm implements or drills. Hydroseeding, another extremely popular method of seed application, is very useful in large areas and on steep, hilly sites. It involves special equipment that mixes the seed in a tank with various paper fibers and water to make a slurry, which can then be sprayed onto the site. The fiber acts as a mulch, protecting the seeds from drying out and reducing weeds. Hydroseeded meadows tend to be uniform in their distribution of component plants, although differences across the site in soil types, moisture content, terrain, and light levels will affect which of the seeded plants thrive best in any given part of the new meadow. For more naturalistic effects, consider hand broadcasting some of the components, to have more control and vary the relative concentrations of some plants. This can be done just before the hydroseed mix is sprayed on.

Meadows planted from seed take longer to establish—usually at least two years, more often three. Depending on the components, the first season will usually be a year in which plants get started; grasses will grow, but many, especially perennial grasses, will need a second season to show their true character. This is why adding flowering plants that will perform in the first season is a good idea—it helps a meadow look good as early as possible. While seeding can appear to be the least expensive way to plant a meadow, the true cost might not be readily apparent. For best results, a weed-free environment has to be maintained for two years (weeds compete with selected meadow plants for water, nutrients, light, and space), and the costs related to this can be more than you might imagine.

Meadows planted from divisions, transplants, and rooted pots generally are established in the first season. They are essentially mature in 60 to 120 days, depending on the region and time of year. In addition to this faster rate of maturity, pre-emergent herbicides (chemicals that inhibit the growth of plants from seed) can be used to help new plantings establish with less weeding. There are both organic and inorganic forms of pre-emergents; most work only on inhibiting the germination of seeds, and do not affect newly planted grasses and meadow plants.

Many good filler grasses are sold as seed, and some meadow grasses can be grown from seed in a greenhouse setting, but their seed is either very expensive or not readily available to sow directly into a landscape. And some of the most desirable meadow

A simple hand-operated spreader works fine for sowing seed. People seem to have forgotten that you don't always need fancy equipment or hydroseeders to sow seed.

Field divisions, or transplants, are shipped bareroot to keep the shipping weight down. Bareroot plants should always be heeled in immediately upon arrival.

grasses, like the sedges that make such excellent natural lawns, are not usually offered as seed and can only be planted as plugs. Some plants (like *Pennisetum* 'Fairy Tails') are seed sterile hybrids or clones and can only be planted from plugs or divisions. It's best to count on a procurement strategy that involves both seed and plants.

Many meadow grasses are grown in the ground or in nursery beds and are "harvested" when the plants are ordered. The terms "division" or "transplant" are often used interchangeably (and indeed, sometimes it makes no difference); but here I shall define divisions as bareroot pieces of grass plants with root shoots and stems but no soil on the roots—literally, bareroots. Transplants, also called field divisions, usually come with some soil on the roots, though some—to confuse matters further—are shipped sans soil or bareroot. With most species, it makes no difference if soil is on the rootball or not, as long as the grasses are kept cool and moist, and planted in a timely fashion. Some genera of grasses do not transplant well—*Stipa* and *Nassella*, with their fragile root systems, are prime examples of those that dislike disturbance. Still, the vast majority of meadow grasses are easily planted from division or transplants, when properly done. Timing is important: many grasses are difficult to dig and transplant in the heat of summer.

Transplanted grasses should always have their foliage and roots cut back to an appropriate proportion. On average, the amount cut back is usually one-half to one-third, depending on the size of the division. Divisions can vary greatly in size, and specialty grass nurseries can propagate grasses from single or two-shoot propagules. Most divisions sold for landscape purposes are three- to five-shoot clumps at a minimum. Usually, both the roots and the foliage are cut at the time of division to encourage new growth in both.

Bareroots, transplants, and divisions are available only in late winter, spring, and fall, depending on the grass; once the heat of summer is on, it becomes a riskier proposition to dig and divide many grasses, and many nurseries will not ship grasses to customers in hot weather. This all works out just fine, as most grasses are best transplanted in spring and fall (mid-winter divisions in southern tier states are a possible exception to this rule). Unless the plant is a tropical grass, actively growing during hot summer months, divisions and transplants in landscape settings should not be attempted during summer heat. Another factor to be considered, as you make your best laid plans, is that any change in "normal" weather patterns—unseasonably hot, dry fall weather, for example—means that your supplier will postpone the digging and dividing or transplanting of your grasses (and most other plant material). It's good to doublecheck with your nursery suppliers to see how your crop is coming along, so that other arrangements can be put in place if needed.

Groundcover grasses are often needed in large quantities, so it is best to place your orders as soon as possible. And because these base grasses are relatively new on the scene, availability can be a problem, so it's best to contract early, especially for large amounts, to ensure they'll be there when you need them. Remember, not all grasses are available at all times of the year, especially in the small, economical sizes. Failure to order your plants in advance can result not only in not having the plants that you want for your meadow when you need them but also in having to pay more for them, or having to buy larger, more expensive, plants.

Contract growing is often the best way to ensure both availability and the best price. Most specialty meadow grass suppliers will grow on contract for specific dates, sizes, and quantities. Usually, they require nonrefundable deposits of 30 to 50 percent. Be aware that many nurseries will charge a maintenance fee to hold your crop past its due date, and charge you a restocking fee on plants not taken. Most reputable specialty growers will make their policies clear at the time of making the contract, but be sure to read the fine print of any contract before signing.

Grasses rooted in pots come in many sizes, with nurseries now producing material ranging from trays of thimble-sized units right up to 15-gallon (or more) tubs of grass specimens. Smaller pots are sometimes referred to as liners, a word that derives from old nursery phraseology, "lining out stock." Traditionally, liners were individual pots, 2½ inches wide by 2 to 4 inches deep, but with the advent of molded plastic, the term "liner" covers trays with units of various root depths (36, 64, 72 are typical counts of liner trays). Be aware that some liners are for nursery production only—plants are too small to be planted directly into the landscape. If you are going to plant your grasses from liners, know the dimensions of the liner and approximately how many grass shoots are in each unit. Healthy liners are suitable for most meadow installations and usually are

(left) Potted grasses come in a wide variety of sizes, from tiny liners to multi-gallon specimens. Many groundcover grasses are planted from small pots because they grow quickly and considerable money can be saved by planting smaller sizes. Background and accent grasses may be available only in larger pots.

(right) Liner trays typically hold from 36 to 72 plants. Be careful with liner plants—some may be too small to plant directly in the garden and may be intended for nursery production only.

the lowest price and therefore the best value for your budget. Many grasses are available as liners only at certain times of the year—usually winter, spring, or fall—unless they are contract-grown specifically for a project.

Most groundcover grasses are grown in plugs, liners, 4-inch pots, and 1-gallon cans. I plant from smaller sized pots whenever possible: smaller plants get their roots out into the native soil on site more quickly, and they are also faster to plant—shallower planting holes save time and money. Plants with larger rootballs, in addition to being more costly to buy, are more expensive to plant. They have a greater volume of nursery soil around their root systems, requiring deeper planting holes, and nursery soil is, of course, not the soil the plants will eventually have to grow in. This difference can lead to slower plant establishment and potential rotting or drying out, as nursery soils tend to be different from native soils. It is also important to note that a liner, depending on the time of year in which planting takes place, is often only a few weeks behind the 4-inch pot in growth. In turn, a 4-inch pot is not that far behind a 1-gallon can, which in turn is not that far behind a 5-gallon can. The cost of a liner could be three to five times less than a 1-gallon can, and not only that, it will establish quicker and be a healthier plant in the long run.

Specimen grasses are often available in larger sized pots or tubs, and provided they are properly planted, they should grow just fine. Just remember that most grasses planted from pots grow quickly. Rooted plants from pots can often be planted in the heat of summer, where seeding, divisions, and transplants might be ill advised, as long as the newly planted plants can be kept moist. But this may require round-the-clock monitoring of irrigation demands.

The wicked ones

The most important factor in the process of making a meadow is site preparation, and the most important part of that process is getting your site weed-free. Failure to acknowledge and deal with noxious perennial weeds at the outset will greatly diminish your meadow's chances of success. Before any grading or soil moving begins, you must know what weeds are on the site, near the site, and have the potential to show up on the site. To identify what weeds are on your property, consulting a trained professional may be the best option, saving you time and money in the longer term.

Weeds are everywhere—in the soil, in the air, in the water. Sadly, most people do not clearly know or understand the nature of weeds or the concepts of disturbance ecology. Exposing soil to the surrounding ecology can result in more problems than benefits. Cultivation without knowing your weeds can do more harm than good. Every time you turn the soil, you create an entry point for weeds. Grading or tilling weed-infested soil will sometimes make more weeds, depending on whether the weeds are annuals (seed) or perennials (stolons and rhizomes). Often, mulching bare soil is a much better way to keep weeds from growing than tilling.

Bare soil looks empty, but usually it is a seed bank, full of weeds that are invisible as they wait to germinate—which they do as soon as the soil temperature warms up, rain or water is applied, and daylight encourages plant growth. It is best to do weed control before you do any grading, as—depending on what weeds are present—all you will be doing is spreading more inoculum over the site. Topsoil brought onto a site might be contaminated with weeds and weed seeds. Always know the source of any soil brought to your site; unless obtained from a quality supplier, soil can contain noxious perennial weeds that will not show themselves until later. Field grown material and specimen trees are notorious sources of contamination.

A weed is often defined as a plant out of place—by this criteria, corn is a weed in a wheat field. But that said, what many people consider to be a "weed" in their garden may not be a "weed" in your meadow—which is why some of the first gardeners to plant meadows got into difficulties with neighbors and city authorities. For example, consider *Oxalis* species, some of which are considered weeds in traditional, closely mown lawns. Low to the ground, they may be considered unsightly imperfections in conventional lawns, but in a meadow, the same plants will not be out of place, particu-

The site for your meadow should be weed-free, properly graded, and have adequate moisture.

Clover—considered a weed in traditional lawns—isn't always out of place in a meadow. Because it's a legume, clover helps add nitrogen to the soil. Some clovers can be managed, and more native clovers are showing up in nurseries.

larly the more ornamental wood sorrels. And the same is true of other "weed" plants—red clover (*Trifolium pratense*) associates well with meadow grasses and has been used by such renowned designers as Christopher Lloyd and Piet Oudolf.

But no matter how charitably you try to view them, some plants are weeds by just about every standard there is. Here is a summary of the worst potential weed threats—the Wicked Ones, as I call them. Note that the vast majority are either perennial grasses, or plants that reseed themselves prolifically, or have underground stems that defy elimination by almost any means. They are horticultural bullies and should be eliminated whenever possible. If you don't know these plants, you should hire a professional who does. Failure to eliminate these weeds is the number one cause of meadow failures.

This meadow of lupines is being invaded by Johnson grass (*Sorghum halepense*). Sometimes weeds can be managed and actually work as groundcover grasses.

Acroptilon repens (Russian knotweed)

Eurasia. This troublesome spreading weed grows 1 to 3 feet high and can be difficult to eliminate. Seed banks can reinfect areas unless successive grow-kill cycles are employed. Zones 3 to 10.

Ambrosia (ragweed)

North America. Spreading thugs that misbehave if allowed to prosper. Plants spread from seed and runners. Spray with herbicide to control. Zones 3 to 10.

Arctium minus (burdock)

Europe. A deep-rooted biennial that spreads from seed and grows 4 to 5 feet tall. Applications of herbicide are necessary to eliminate this weed. Zones 3 to 9.

Bromus inermis (smooth brome)

Eurasia. Among the worst weedy grasses, often a highway erosion control species. Although used as a pasture grass, prairie expert Neil Diboll (who has dubbed it "*Bromus enormous*" on account of its aggressive spreading) considers it a problem grass. Zones 3 to 10.

Centaurea solstitialis (yellow star thistle)

Eurasia, Mediterranean. This annual thistle has sharp prickly foliage and spreads prolifically from seed. It should be eliminated whenever and wherever it appears. Repeat herbicide applications are best. Zones 5 to 10.

Cirsium arvense (Canada thistle)

Native U.S. thistles rarely cause problems. Canada thistle is an entirely different creature, growing upward of 4 to 5 feet tall. It should be eliminated whenever possible. This wicked invader spreads from seeds and rhizomes to create dense colonies that are difficult to eradicate, even in the best of conditions. Zones 3 to 10.

Convolvulus arvensis (morning glory, bindweed)

This creeping vine-like plant, with gray-green foliage and showy white flowers, spreads aggressively from seed and underground rhizomes. Repeat herbicide applications are a must to eliminate. Zones 3 to 10.

Cynodon dactylon (Bermuda grass)

Eurasia, Africa. This is enemy number one of meadow gardens in the southern half of the United States. Gray-green foliage creeps from aboveground stolons, underground rhizomes, and seed. Hybrid forms, planted as lawns, are finer textured and seed-sterile but still creep from stolons and rhizomes. Unmowed, the grass can grow up to 18 inches high, and stolons can climb a chain link fence. Coastal Bermuda grass, a form planted for forage in the hot humid South, can grow up to 4 feet high.

Bermuda is a warm-season grass that does not mix well with mostly cool-season meadow grasses. Many gardeners mistake it for crab grass (*Digitaria*). Over time, most older lawns in the southern tier states become infected with Bermuda, as lawn care services often spread this grass from garden to garden.

The key to elimination is to stimulate growth before and during grow-kill cycles. You cannot kill Bermuda grass that is not actively growing. Do not move infested soil around your project until it is killed completely. If you do, you may end up spreading the infestation. Under some circumstances it may be impossible to control Bermuda grass. If it is in your neighbor's lawn, it may return and dominate your site, so diligence is required. Zones 6 to 10.

Cyperus esculentus (nutgrass)

This moisture-loving creeping sedge, which spreads from underground runners and seed, is often present in wet meadows. Its underground tubers, or "nutlets," resprout with a tenacity that is almost unrivalled. There are now specific herbicides to combat this weed, so it's best to use these whenever possible. Dense infestations may be impossible to eliminate, and working with this sedge may prove more successful in the long run. Zones 3 to 10.

Digitaria (crab grass)

Annual weeds, resembling Bermuda grass but nowhere near as dangerous. Still, best removed from proposed meadows.

Lonicera japonica (Japanese honeysuckle)

Asia. Sweet fragrance is insufficient reason to live with Japanese honeysuckle. Its twining habit and vigorous growth will swallow a meadow in short order. Spray with herbicide wherever it appears.

Pennisetum clandestinum (kikuyu)

Asia. This creeping warm-season grass spreads from seed and stolons. It is often a lawn grass or a component of weedy lawns in the South and West. Easier to eliminate than Bermuda grass because it does not spread from underground rhizomes, it is still difficult to manage and is best eliminated from meadow plantings. Zones 8 to 10.

Polygonum (knotweed)

Eurasia. Many knotweeds are problematic and are best dealt with, as they can dominate meadows and become real pests. Repeat herbicide applications are the most effective means of control. Zones 3 to 10.

Rubus (blackberry)

Eurasia. Newly planted meadows are easily swallowed up by the rampantly spreading thorny canes of blackberries or brambles. Keep them out or off to the side of the meadow whenever possible, or consult local authorities for less invasive, better-behaved varieties for your area. Zones 3 to 10.

Securigera varia (crown vetch)

Eurasia. This persistent low-growing vine, commonly planted for erosion control, spreads by underground rhizomes and seed. It is pernicious and difficult to eliminate. Avoid its use and discourage local agencies form using it, as there are many native groundcovers that pose no threat to the environment which could be used instead. Zones 3 to 9.

Solidago canadensis (Canada goldenrod)

North American native. While there are many well-behaved species and varieties of goldenrod, this one is a thug and should be removed and avoided at all costs. Spreads from seed and rhizomes. Repeat herbicide applications are the most effective means of control.

Sorghum halepense (Johnson grass)

Native to southern Europe. This slowly creeping warm-season grass grows 4 to 6 feet tall and spreads readily from seed and rhizomes. Usually found in moist soils in ditches and drainage swales. Thuggish in nature and tough to eliminate. Repeat herbicide applications are a must to get rid of it. Zones 5 to 10.

Toxicodendron (poison ivy, poison oak)

These plants spread by seed and rhizomes, and their toxic sap is a dangerous skin irritant that causes severe dermatitis on contact in most people. While species are native and have wildlife value, they can spread throughout a meadow, making maintenance difficult. Repeat herbicide application when plants are actively growing is required in order to control and eradicate.

Methods of controlling weeds can be a controversial ecological topic. Many people are against chemical use in any way, shape, or form, in their homes and in their gardens. Each gardener must decide where their sympathies lie. But consider the following—the basics of weed control, as they relate to my experiences of site preparation—before you decide what is right for you and your situation.

Organic weed control

No single one of the various organic methods of weed control are effective on all weeds in every situation. Barrier methods, for example, can be very effective at dealing with some weeds but prove inefficient against others. Acetic acid (vinegar) in high concentrations will kill many cool-season turf grasses in the northern tier states, but it will not kill Bermuda or like grasses in southern latitudes. Topsoil is sometimes removed, but this soil has to be taken somewhere, which may be costly and offset any "green" benefits. I personally do not like to strip topsoil from a site as it can open up yet another can of worms (disturbance ecology, again).

Sometimes weeds can be controlled by "baking" the soil. In soil baking, the soil is covered with black plastic tarp for a year or more; the covered soil heats up when the sun hits the plastic and this—in addition to light starvation—will kill weeds. But this happens only when soil temperatures get over 100°F for a prolonged period of time, and in my experience this method only cleans the first few inches of soil. It is not a guaranteed method of ridding a site of all weeds, particularly not the really noxious types.

Covering the soil with newspaper, another type of organic weed control, likewise works best in warm weather, on mostly annual weeds; use a minimum 2-inch thick layer of old newspapers, and weigh them down so they do not blow away. Leave in place for two to 15 months. You can also use an old carpet to cover areas of soil for periods of a year or more, so that weed growth is inhibited through lack of light.

Tilling (turning the soil over by hand or mechanical means) works on many annual weeds, but, again, it actually propagates some perennial weeds. By chopping through their underground stems, you make more plants, which makes cycles of tilling necessary: every two to three weeks over spring and into the summer for at least two years. To eliminate tough perennial weeds, you may need to till every two weeks so that new growth does not have time to get re-established.

Though it is not an option for suburban gardeners, burning the area in late winter will certainly eliminate some weeds. Never use fire on your property in this way without proper permits. Dangerous times with high winds, high temperatures, and low humidity must be avoided. Weed torches burn hydrocarbons, so burning may not be as "green" a method of weed control as you might think. While fire is an historically indispensable tool for managing prairie, most meadows are founded on cool-season grasses. Burning has a limited application in meadow gardening and can be ineffective in eradicating many noxious weeds.

Mowing can eliminate many annual weeds, especially if it is done after the weeds have spent most of their energy growing and are about to set seed for the next generation. Successive mowings usually do not adversely affect perennial meadow grasses and flowers. Use a weedeater with a string trimmer or blade. Alternatively, there are special "weed mowers," which mow at heights of 6 to 8 inches. The mown material can be left on the ground to become mulch, or, with taller weeds, you may want to rake and remove it.

Old lawns can be removed by sod cutters, but if they contain noxious perennial weed grasses and other unwanted plants, this will not solve your problem. Unless you are absolutely sure your lawn does not contain creeping rhizomatous weeds, sod cutting will almost always leave some problem weeds behind. Don't forget, there is also the expense of hauling away the old lawn.

Chemical weed control

The proper use, and I stress the *proper* use, of certain chemicals may actually cause less pollution and leave less of a carbon footprint. It basically depends on exactly which weeds you are trying to kill. Weed control chemicals, properly used, may be the last chemicals you'll ever need for your meadow, with little or no consequences to the environment. Think it over. Once a site is clean, spot weeding can be handled easily. Remember, meadows are far better for the environment than conventional lawns.

The best way to eliminate weed growth on a planned meadow site or old lawn is with at least three grow-kill cycles. In each cycle, you first encourage weeds to grow and then kill them with glyphosate chemical weed killers, such as Roundup™. Repeat until the site is exhausted of weed seeds and other unwanted plants. Always be sure to follow the directions on the label of any chemical you use; the instructions are there by law, for a good reason. When properly applied, glyphosate weed killers do not affect people or pets; they are metabolized by green plant tissue to become toxic to the target plants. Nor do they adversely affect the health of your soil.

It is crucial that all targeted plants are actively growing, as they have to be taking up liquid and nutrients into their systems in order for the chemicals to work. This means that you must eliminate all weeds during their active growing season—usually spring, summer, and early fall, when the soil is warmer. You cannot kill warm-season-growing weeds effectively in the middle of winter. Depending on where you live, getting plants to be actively growing may mean that first you must fertilize and water the very plants you intend to kill! The old, bad lawn you want to convert into a vibrant meadow may be drought dormant and look dead, but as soon as it is watered and fertilized, dry grass and weeds will perk up and start growing again. You want this to happen before you plant your meadow, not after.

Dry soils and older lawns that are dry should be watered for two to three weeks prior to each spraying. If temporary irrigation is needed, the solutions are simple and inexpensive: a water timer can be installed at a hose bib; attach a sprinkler to the hose and set timer for 20 to 30 minutes. Older weeds and lawns should be mowed to 3 to 5 inches and fertilized with a 16-6-8 mix at 5 to 8 pounds per 1,000 square feet. This will get the weeds growing, and, with luck, get weed seeds to germinate and begin to grow, too. Ideally you want to spray the targeted plants before they flower and set a new generation of seed.

Spray weed killers only on windless days, wearing proper protective gear. It will usually take seven to ten days for their effects to show. Once the weeds are dead, you can either remove them or mow the crispy growth stubble as close to the ground as possible. I have created many meadows without removing the dead stubble, which eventually decomposes, adding organic matter to the soil. After the first or second grow-kill cycle, 1 to 3 inches of bark mulch can be applied over the shorn stubble to prevent further weed growth until the grow-kill cycles have been completed. Bark mulch also prevents planting sites from becoming muddy while grow-kill cycles continue.

Continue to look for weeds; their seed will continue to blow into the site whether mulched or not. Often noxious weeds will come in with new nursery plants when they arrive, with underground stems that are unseen and just waiting to grow. To be safe, subject any added topsoil to thorough grow-kill cycles.

Finally, sometimes it's nice to put up a sign educating people that a new meadow is on its way. Something that explains why you haven't planted anything for two or three months!

GROW-KILL CYCLE ESSENTIALS

» The more actively growing the plant, the better the kill.

» Get the old lawn and all soil really moist before treatments.

» Kill your lawn well before the first frosts are possible.

» Always follow directions on the labels of all chemicals used.

» The more grow-kill cycles, the more likely your plantings will be weed-free.

» A new meadow full of weeds can mean starting the whole process over again. It's much better to kill all the weeds first.

» Be careful when importing topsoil. Make sure it is weed-free or better yet, apply grow-kill cycles to it as well.

No weed control

Still, there are situations where weed control is not feasible. Usually this is because the area you have chosen to re-create as meadow cannot be sprayed or is surrounded by so much contaminant that reinfestation is inevitable. In such cases, you might consider another option. Learn to live with the weeds! Adding grasses and accent plants that match the aggression of existing hard-to-eliminate weeds just might be smarter than struggling to eliminate what can never be eliminated. You may still face an uphill battle—a Darwinian survival of the fittest—to get the equally strong-growing and taller components established, but by creating a place for the weeds, so that they are in "place," they won't be weeds anymore. It's a case of "If you can't beat them, join them."

Grading and soil preparation

Once all weeds have been killed, it is time to turn to other key aspects of site preparation. Grading has to do with the moving of soil around the site to establish the final lay of the land. If desired, mounds or depressions can be created at this time. Mounding is usually an aesthetic decision, not a practical one. Remember that moisture will drain off a rise and flow to a depression. If you want to use grasses that require good drainage, it makes sense to locate these on a rise so proper drainage is achieved; similarly, low spots or depressions in the landscape can be a plus if you are trying to work moisture-loving grasses onto a level site. Grading is a very subjective process and is best done by contractors with proper equipment and knowledge of how water moves across your site.

Concepts of soil preparation have undergone major changes in recent years as the issues of gardening and ecology have come together. Many ecologists would say tradi-

Grading is both an art and a science. Improper grading can result in wet and dry spots and lead to problems down the line.

tional garden "soil preparation" is a myth and actually harmful to the environment. If you harvest peat moss from a peat bog in Canada and ship it thousands of miles to clay soil in California and then rototill it into the top 6 inches of your site, are you really improving the soil? Might it not be a better strategy to plant plants that thrive in whatever soil you have, where their roots will penetrate deep into the existing soil on site? Damaging one ecology to "improve" another with a temporary boost is silly and hard on the planet.

Does traditional soil preparation help the establishment of meadows? Yes. But can meadows be made without traditional soil preparation? Again, yes. Breaking up the soil by tilling will speed the planting of small plant plugs, but it is not necessary to do so. Proper plant selection and fertilization will help meadows be more successful than any Cadillac version of soil preparation. Often the addition of large amounts of organic matter depletes soil nitrogen initially, as soil bacteria consume nitrogen to digest the rich feast. It is a fundamental principle of meadow establishment that grasses love nitrogen. If you want grass to grow, give it nitrogen, water well and consistently.

This country of ours is too vast and varied in soils and climates to give any magic formula, but suffice to say, additional nitrogen—whether granular, or liquid, organic or inorganic—makes grass grow and will help your meadow get established. "Organic" fertilizers tend to be low in nitrogen, so they may need to be applied more frequently. It's best to avoid weed and feed mixes (fertilizers with weed control chemicals added to them). Finally, always fertilize only when needed—mostly to get plants established. If you are unfamiliar with fertilizers, it's best to get professional help.

Mulch or shredded bark spread on the surface of the meadow site to be planted is far more beneficial than mulch tilled into the soil. Surface mulch conserves moisture, inhibits weed growth, and helps keep the newly establishing meadow looking tidy. It keeps mud to a minimum and is essential in meadow plantings where kids and dogs will traffic the area. Since most meadows are planted from smaller pots or plugs, often the bark mulch can be applied before planting so that mud, weeds, and soil compaction is mitigated.

Almost any kind of mulch will work in your meadow. Ecologically, whatever is locally generated is best for the planet. Whether they're of pine, eucalyptus, shredded plywood, or any combination, wood chips do not adversely affect the growth of most grasses. You can always brush 1 to 3 inches of mulch aside to plant plugs or 4-inch pots, with little excess soil generated to "dirty" the mulch. You can apply surface bark mulch after planting, but small plants and plugs may get trampled while doing so. You can always apply a thin layer of wood mulch, plant plugs and plants, then finish with a "clean" top-up layer afterward. You can also mulch with layers of gravel, aggregate, or sand.

With your site weed-free, graded, tilled, and mulched, you are ready to plant your meadow.

Spacing

Plant spacing is not an exact science—nature doesn't worry about it. But for gardeners, many variables factor into successful plant spacing. A lot depends on the desired overall effect: space the plants at a particular distance on center and one effect is achieved; spread the same plants further apart, and you get an entirely different result. There are general rules, but in meadow gardening, rules are meant to be broken and much is subjective.

You must know both your plants and your site to determine the right spacing for your meadow. Plants grow differently in different soils—slower in clay, faster in sand. They grow shorter at the top of a slope, bigger at the bottom; since soils are drier on slope tops, you might want to plant grasses there closer on center than grasses toward the bottom of the slope. As a basic rule, if you intend to plant flowering perennials and bulbs between your meadow grasses, then your grasses need more space between them. With creeping grasses in particular, budget may be a deciding factor on plant spacing. Since creeping grasses will fill in eventually, you may space them further apart and save some money. However, if budget is of no concern, you can space the plants as close as you see fit.

In general, plants should be spaced somewhat proportionally to their height and width. For example, plants growing 3 feet high by 4 feet wide should be spaced 3 to 5 feet apart. Meadow plants are usually sited in staggered rows—that is, in the second row, the plants are spaced midway between those in the previous row. In most meadow planting, it's OK to vary the plant spacing and type, as meadows in nature are never geometrically precise. In fact, it's better not to be too precise, as discrepancies are less apt to show. Again, for a faster fill-in, plant more closely on center, but realize that, depending on the varieties, you may need to thin the plantings as they grow, adding additional and sometimes unnecessary costs. But this strategy can be particularly effective on larger scale projects, where work is being scheduled in phases. Plants thinned from early stages of planting can be used for the next phases; in addition to being a cost-saving move, the plants will benefit from being grown at the site.

With clumping grasses, take into consideration the eventual height and spread of selected plants. Clumping grasses planted too close on center can appear crowded and messy; too far apart, and they'll look clumpy, awkward, and disjointed. For more uniform, less lumpy effects, plant clumpers closer on center than their eventual spread. Some species may need to be thinned if they are planted too close on center, or the plantings may overgrow and patch out. You may want to purposely spread clumping grasses out, if you want to leave space in between the clumps for flowers, bulbs, and perennial accents. If you space the grass clumps too far apart and don't plant something to fill in between the clumps, nature will do it for you, usually with weeds.

To work out how many plants you'll need for a particular spacing, see the accompanying box. Remember, it is better to have a bit too many plants than too few. Overage in plants may come in useful for replacing failures, if necessary.

Spacing isn't an exact science. Grasses should be more widely spaced if you're going to add lots of flowering perennials in between.

CALCULATING PLANT ORDERS

Measure the area of the new meadow

9 square feet = 1 square yard

43,560 square feet = 1 acre

100 square feet = 10 × 10 feet

1,000 square feet = approx. 32 × 32 feet, or 50 × 20 feet

5,000 square feet = 50 × 100 feet

10,000 square feet = 100 × 100 feet

**Multiply the number of square feet by the number of plants
you will use per square foot (spacing)**

Spaced on center	Plants per square foot
6 inches	4
8 inches	2.25
10 inches	1.44
12 inches	1
18 inches	0.44
24 inches	0.25
36 inches	0.10

**Seeding rates (native grasses on their own or blended with wildflowers)
are usually calculated by the amount of pure live seed (PLS) in each batch**

1 pound PLS per 4,000 square feet

10 pounds PLS per acre

Timing

The best times to plant meadows are spring and fall. Depending on where you live, it is possible to plant in winter or summer; it just means that you will have to make some adjustments to your process. Previously, weed control was problematic in the cool of winter; but if weeds are under control, planting meadows in the winter can work just fine, especially in the South and Southwest. Plant availability may be an issue, and certainly many plants will grow more slowly in cooler winter temperatures, but as spring arrives, their growth will speed up and they will establish just fine.

It's foolish to even think about planting a meadow in summer in the hot desert climes of the Southwest. Elsewhere, summer planting can be attempted but presents its own set of challenges. Plant availability again may be an issue, but the biggest potential problem is keeping new plantings from drying out. If moisture can be maintained through automatic irrigation or diligent hand watering, it becomes possible to plant in summer months. As a general rule, cutting grass foliage back after planting is good

horticultural practice, as it reduces water demands and helps grasses establish. Even so, constant overhead irrigation may be needed initially until roots have established. This might mean programming multiple start times on your sprinkler system—another time when a bit of professional expertise might help. A professional may also spray grass foli-age with Wilt-Pruf™ or an antidesiccant, which reduces transpiration or water loss. As with all chemicals, always read the label and follow the makers' directions.

Spring and fall are the optimum times for most garden plantings, and meadows are no exception. In spring, newly planted meadows have time to establish before the heat of summer. Frost tender grasses can be planted in the spring after the threat of frost has passed and will quickly grow and provide interest until the first frost. In fall, there is usually enough residual warmth to get grasses rooted and settled—ready to sit through

Spring and autumn are the best times to plant a meadow. They're good times to accessorize as well. Many bulbs, for instance, are available only in autumn. Also, autumn-planted meadows really take off the following spring.

winter and blast off in the spring when soils warm up and days lengthen. Some experts particularly recommend fall plantings in heavy clay soils, as young seedlings can get well established before there is any chance for soil to dry out and harden—both restrict the downward growth of young roots.

Depending on where you live, certain meadow components are best seeded in the fall, which works well with a spring planting scenario: the bulk of the meadow is planted, left to grow over summer, and then overseeded with grass fillers and flowers in the fall. In the West, fall seeding of wildflowers is preferred for most species, especially favorite perennials such as lupines and poppies. Adopting a fall seeding method can even accommodate the application of pre-emergent herbicides—most will leach out of the soil well before fall seeding takes place.

Early spring seeding is effective throughout much of the country. In northern tier states, many meadow grasses and wildflowers are warm-season growing, and their seed is best sown in the spring. Even in northern regions, cool-season grasses do better when planted in the early spring and fall, when soil and air temperatures are most favorable. By June, most seeding operations should be finished. When fall comes around, seeding cool-season meadow components can resume.

Shipping and delivery

Meadow plants are shipped in a variety of ways, whatever form they are supplied in— pots, bareroots, and so forth—by truck or in boxes through freight services like FedEx and UPS. Once temperatures warm in spring, many nurseries begin to ship plants in earnest. In the southern tier states and the West, nursery stock is usually available throughout the year. But in the northern tier states, plant shipping is all about spring. Early in the season, when temperatures are still relatively cool, plants can withstand three to five days in transit with little ill effects. But as spring turns into summer, plants can suffer if they spend too much time in dark boxes, or on the tarmac dispatch area of some anonymous shipper. Two-day service is recommended whenever possible, as plants will suffer if shipping is delayed. Always be aware of your nursery's policy on plant shipping—they vary from grower to grower. Gardeners should realize that wholesalers rarely guarantee plants: they assume they are supplying fellow professionals and usually only guarantee that their plants are true to name. It's wise to make any damage claims immediately, if plants arrive in anything but good condition.

Once they have arrived, place plant deliveries in a cool, shady place and open them immediately. Meadow grasses should be planted as early as possible after their arrival, so planting should be scheduled as close to delivery times as possible. If you are ordering large quantities of very small plants, it might be wise to break up the shipment into quantities that can be readily planted by the available labor. Also, it helps to have plants shipped early in the week; otherwise, an unexpected delivery problem could result in your plants sitting in a box all weekend. Aim for your plants to spend as little time as possible out of the ground, in packaging.

If new plants cannot be planted immediately, or very soon after delivery, they should always be taken out of boxes or packaging and heeled in—that is, expose their foliage to air and daylight and cover their roots with moist soil or mulch in a slightly shady space, where they will not receive too much direct sun. New grass starts or bareroots can usually be held for weeks, once heeled in and properly watered, although this extra step may add additional labor costs to your project.

Often, your plants may be delivered by semi-truck. In warm months, or when crossing hot climates, plants should always be shipped in refrigerated trucks. Depending on where you live and where your nursery source is located, your plants may need to be inspected and be accompanied by a phytosanitary certificate. This means the nursery must treat the plants with chemicals to ensure no pests or diseases come along with the plants. Always check to make sure you are dealing with reputable nurseries that are not trying to bypass the rules, or you may find yourself in serious trouble with agricultural authorities, facing fines or the seizing and destruction of all your plants.

When plants arrive from a mail-order nursery, open the box immediately and put them in a cool, shady place.

Brightly colored irrigation marker flags can help you place each variety in the intended spot. Marker paint, gypsum, or lime can also be used to mark out groups and drifts.

Laying out the plants

Meadow plantings can be problematic to lay out. Many designers prefer to position the plants in the field. Others like to create detailed plans. These often complex plans may require considerable skill to translate into field placement. Complex plantings and larger spaces require some coordination in order to arrange layers of different grass and meadow accents heights, and plan where different plant shapes and masses are required to realize the design. Spraying marker paint on the ground and using colored irrigation marker flags are both indispensable tools for large meadow plantings. It's often easier to place and plant one variety at a time so as not to confuse untrained laborers, who may not be able to tell one grass variety from another. One way to avoid confusion is to lay out and plant a sample small area, which is then duplicated across the site.

A groundcover pick is a good tool for planting small grasses. Bulb-planting drills and small power augers can be useful as well.

Mulch needs to be spread carefully to avoid smothering newly planted grasses. Sometimes you can spread the mulch first then scoot it away to plant small plugs.

I am able to visualize on-site. Often, I will place and plant the base grasses first, then add the accent plants later. Another useful planting strategy is to plant only grasses first, particularly if broadleaf weeds such as thistle are a potential problem. This way, you can use a selective broadleaf weedkiller and not affect the new grass plants. Wait until after the grasses are established, and then add whatever broadleaf planting and accents you require. Broadleaf herbicide can either be discontinued completely or used for spot treatments only in problem areas.

Getting plants into the ground

Most small plants are easily planted using groundcover picks or trowels. Plugs and 4-inch pots can be planted easily this way in all but the heaviest soils. In heavy clay, a small shovel may be required for even the smaller plant sizes. It helps to have moist rather than wet soil to plant into. Avoid planting in saturated soil, particularly clay soil, as it can become compacted during planting. Avoid planting in bone-dry soil, as this can slow the planting process and wick the moisture out of the small root systems of new plants. Always water new plants immediately. I always water new plantings in by hand and don't rely on sprinkler irrigation for the first watering. A thorough first watering closes the air pockets around the fine roots of newly planted plants.

Another way to plant small grass starts is to use a gas or electric drill motor, with a 3- to 4-foot-long drill bit extension and a 3- to 4-inch drill bit, such as is sometimes used for planting bulbs. Though noisy, it can save a lot of backbreaking labor. Ear protection for the person operating the drill is a must.

If bark mulch is applied prior to planting, scoot the mulch aside to create a clearing, to make sure that young plants are planted in soil, not just in the surface layer of bark. If bark is added after planting, be careful not to smother the new plants with it. If you are going to use pre-emergent herbicides, this is best done before spreading bark mulch so that the spray has direct contact with the soil surface. Likewise, if fertilizer was not added during soil preparation, spread granular or apply liquid fertilizer before mulch is laid down. Fertilizer can be added after mulch has been spread but will need watering in well, so that it can work its way down into the soil around plant roots. Always water fertilizers in immediately after application to prevent burning the foliage or roots of new plants.

When planting, match the crown of the plant with the existing soil level. Plant too low, and plants may rot at the crown. Plant too high, and exposed roots will dry out and die. Although some rhizomatous species are "bulletproof" and will grow even if planted upside down, I do not recommend doing so. On slopes or in hot climates, it helps to make a small basin or berm of soil around the base of each plant to catch and hold overhead water where it is most needed. The larger the plant, the more important this becomes—use this method when planting larger grasses.

Now that your plants are in the ground and watered in, your new meadow is on its way.

CHAPTER 8

ESTABLISHING AND MAINTAINING A MEADOW

Most meadows and natural lawns need only one or two cuts per year, and once established don't need constant watering and fertilizing.

This newly planted meadow is filling in. New grass plantings shouldn't be subjected to drought stress. Until they're established, even drought tolerant grasses need constant moisture.

A NEWLY PLANTED MEADOW GARDEN is a fragile thing. Grasses are extremely perishable plants until they have gotten their roots in the ground sufficiently to stand on their own. Diligence in the first few weeks after planting will pay off in spades.

Watering is critical, and meadows in areas of low precipitation are harder to establish and preserve than those in areas receiving regular rainfall. Young grass plants cannot be allowed to dry out. If this happens even once, it may have disastrous results. Save for washing small young plants away, it is nearly impossible to overwater new grass plantings in their first few weeks of life in the garden. If drying winds are fierce, water must be applied as needed by the plants.

Sometimes, in late season plantings or if temperatures rise high during or right after new plantings, grass foliage may be damaged, but the plants themselves will be fine.

Should this scenario arise, damaged foliage should be cut off and new fresh foliage will grow from the base of the plant and take its place. Damaged foliage will never repair itself. If heatwaves can be foreseen, cutting foliage in advance can help new plants soldier through sweltering conditions.

As new grasses begin to send out roots into the surrounding soil, the plants will start to acquire more strength and become more able to stand on their own. A gentle tug on newly establishing plugs will indicate that plants are rooting out and getting established. Very little new foliage will be generated during this period. Most growth will be in root production, out of sight. Foliage or shoot growth above ground will happen later. This is particularly true in cooler periods, when there may be little to no foliage growth until soil and air temperatures increase in line with the increased day lengths of spring.

Warm-season grasses and meadow accents may root in fall plantings but seemingly just sit there. These plants are biding their time till spring arrives. No amount of water or fertilizer will make them grow visibly—just be patient. Again, depending on where you live and what time of year you plant, meadows planted from divisions, transplants, and rooted pots usually establish in 60 to 120 days; they fill in in six or seven months and look good the first season. Seed takes much longer; meadows planted solely from seed can take two or three seasons to assume their mature character. Overseeding to add accents or fillers is usually effective in improving the look of a seeded meadow in its first season.

Weeding, feeding, and mowing/cutting are the three building blocks of meadow establishment. Don't let weeds get ahead of you, and feed new grass plantings proactively, not reactively. If you want grasses to thicken and spread, cut them or mow them, as mowing promotes tillering, the production of side shoots. For the same reasons we take fruit off young fruit trees, we cut grasses to thicken them and get them established. I recommend using fertilizer every four weeks with a formula of 16-6-8 or equivalent at 5 to 8 pounds per 1,000 square feet until the meadow has filled in. Once this has happened, you may never have to fertilize again.

Getting newly seeded meadows established can be much more difficult than plugged or planted meadows. When seedlings are just 3 to 4 inches high, it can be nearly impossible for an untrained gardener to know the difference between the "good guys" and the "bad guys." By the time there is a problem, it might be too late to fix. Newly seeded meadows must be monitored so that they are not pushed to do what they cannot. Put simply, you have to give them time. Cool-season grasses grow when it is cool, so don't expect them to put on lots of growth in the heat of summer. Be patient—they'll start growing again when temperatures drop down in the fall. I am often asked to look at "failed" seeded meadows only to report to my clients that they need only to be patient, wait until next year.

Fertilization of newly seeded meadows should be approached judiciously, as seedlings are easily burned by overapplications of fertilizers. It is better strategy to use mild fertilizer mixes more often than to "push" a newly seeded meadow too hard. Established meadows don't need to be fertilized: overfertilized grasses will create foliage more susceptible to drought and disease.

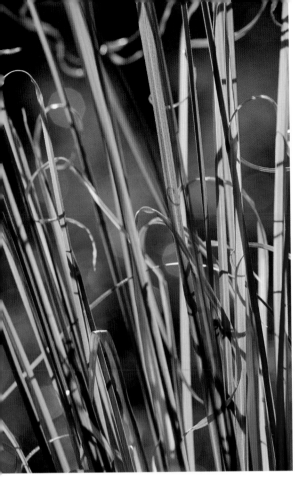

You may want to leave certain grasses uncut if they have striking autumn or winter coloration, like this specimen of vetiver (*Vetiveria zizanioides*).

(next page top) In this late winter/early spring shot of my old garden, the new shoots are just beginning to show underneath the dormant foliage. When this dormant foliage is cut, more sunlight will warm the ground, making the grasses shoot even faster.

(bottom) We call this the Big Chop. It looks pretty scary at this point, but the meadow comes charging back almost immediately. This is a good time to edit and add accents.

Mowing young meadow lawn plantings every four to eight weeks will help get plants established. Be careful not to cut new seedlings too close to the ground. Never cut newly seeded meadows lower than half their height, and never mow them before mature foliage has emerged—usually between 30 to 60 days.

Editing meadows

Once planted, the meadow's dynamic changes over time. After all, nature is organic, and meadow design decisions, too, are ongoing. I like to watch out for subtle shifts in meadow planting, perhaps heightening seasonality by adding meadow accents, adding layers of depth to the overall tapestry. We must be flexible with our gardens, in our gardening, and in managing an original design concept. Inevitably, nature will add a twist to even the best laid plans: certain plants will tend to dominate over time and will require thinning out or removal if they are not to take over and crowd out other desirable plants. However, deciding which plants are desirable is up to you. As time goes on in your meadow, your own sense of seeing and being will develop as well, influencing your decisions as you come to appreciate different qualities that emerge. Your annual "buzz" may well peter out, but while it lasts, allow for it in your maintenance schedule. Embrace opportunities to divide larger older plants and expand meadows into other areas. Or give them away—spread the joy of meadow plants!

Like all other kinds of gardens, meadows require maintenance to look their best and thrive throughout the years, but properly planted, they are relatively easy to maintain. Depending on their complexity, meadows may be low or high maintenance—it all depends on how your meadow was created and what components are in it. No garden stays the same over time—plants thrive and grow or die, they flower and set seed, their life cycles changing with the seasons and passing of time. For me, part of the joy of meadow gardening is watching these changes occur. I've always felt the best meadow gardens are a little like Mickey Mouse as the Sorcerer's Apprentice in *Fantasia*—we're never totally in control of the situation. Nature and time rule in the meadow. Big chill freezes, heatwaves, storms, wild weather, floods, droughts, combined with bugs, both good and bad, will all affect how meadows grow.

Cutting meadows

In nature, most grass ecologies are either grazed by animals or burned. In our gardens, cutting or mowing is used to imitate these processes. We know that prairies want to be burned, and need to be burned or mowed to stay healthy. Most meadow grasses need to be cut down at least once a year, and prairie-like meadows especially enjoy an annual cut.

The exact timing of your cut may vary depending on what grasses you have and what accents you have added to the meadow. In the southern tier states and the Southwest, for example, a fall or winter cutting can be done whenever you want to see fresh new foliage. Warm-season grasses that are winter dormant can add wonderful winter effects—cutting in fall would deprive you of this particular joy.

It's best not to cut dense, clumping grasses and cool-season grasses too hard the first year. Cut conservatively until you know what works best for your meadow in your climate.

Some gardeners prefer a "tidy" winter meadow. This is more of an aesthetic or stylistic decision rather than a horticultural one. True, the plants can be cut back at any time, but some people prefer seeing the beauty of nature in their meadow's winter dormancy rather than looking at sheared clumps of plants through the cooler season. Another natural aspect of meadow gardening is how the ecology you have created becomes colonized by wildlife over time. Leaving seedheads and top growth on plants through fall and winter not only looks beautiful to my mind and to many others, it also provides rich food sources and habitats for wildlife. In my own garden, I prefer to make the Big Chop at the end of winter right before spring. In California, this is usually late January, early February—but timing will depend on where your meadow is. In colder climates, the Big Chop may come in March.

Most meadows are best cut in late winter to early spring, just as the new season's growth is about to emerge. The signal that it's time to cut is when you notice new growth starting to push out from the base of the clump. The exact time will vary from year to year, depending on temperatures and the weather. Cutting sooner usually doesn't hurt plants: if temperatures are cool, plants will take their time growing out and the worst is that you'll be looking at chopped plants longer than you might like. Cutting later, after new growth has begun, usually won't harm plants either. New foliage, once cut back, will just grow out again, so don't worry about being late: most meadows want to be cut.

Most grasses should be cut to at least one-third to one-quarter their height. The majority of warm-season grasses can be cut as close to the ground as you can effectively cut them, but cool-season grasses resent too close a cut, so keep in mind which is which. Dense clumping grasses are also sensitive in this way, so don't cut them too close to the ground.

Many cool-season grasses can be cut throughout the growing season. You may want to cut off old flower spikes, if they are unsightly. Whether you do or do not is up to you; it won't affect the health of the grass. Often, cutting cool-season grasses a second or even a third time will produce a flush of new foliage that keeps plants looking better longer into the winter. Sophisticated meadow gardens are synchronized to accommodate the mowing or cutting back of the grasses. Careful coordination of the plants can keep downtime to a minimum. For example, early spring bulbs can be used to add color and interest while grasses regrow after an early season chop. As the bulbs finish, the grasses emerge and swallow the senescing bulb foliage. Flowers that rebloom after they have been cut make good meadow components. Obviously the more different kinds of flowers and accents you add to your meadow, the more likely you will have to cut some flowers along with the grass. Usually, the cutting back is good for flowers too—cut them and take them inside.

After cutting your grasses, you will be left with the cut foliage. Some people prefer to leave a layer of chaff in between the clumps of cut grass. Over time, this foliage will compost and return nutrients to the soil. As mulch, it will conserve moisture and deter weeds. Each individual gardener will decide whether to leave chaff on the ground or clean up the site completely and use another type of decorative mulch. Often there may

be seeds of meadow grasses and accents in the chaff, and spreading the chaff will spread seeds. Depending on your goals, this can be a good thing, or a bad thing. Obviously there are ecological ramifications, but one person's "natural look" is another person's "messy." Try to choose a style that works for you and the planet. Chaff and dormant grasses can be made into art and enjoyed as art. Try braiding your grasses or laying out chaff in patterns. I know some mischievous gardeners who spray paint dormant grass clumps and make them outrageous colors and enjoy them as art. Have some fun!

Meadows can be cut by a variety of methods, depending on their size and what's in them. Using hedge shears and loppers works well for cutting back most small meadows. Sure, it can be hard work, but you may do it only once or twice a year. Many grasses have lots of silica in the stems that will dull cutting tools with amazing speed. Keep your tools really sharp, as dull clippers will tear the leaf blades, not cut them off clean. Getting down on your hands and knees is a great way to get to know your meadow up close. While cutting back the meadow, you can contemplate minor changes or additions.

Power tools are a must for a larger area. Weed eaters, mowers, and power hedge trimmers can make short work of large planting. String trimmers may not be efficient at cutting large grasses, and so a weed eater with a blade (plastic or metal) may be used. Some mowers are specially built for mowing tall grasses and have wheels, which can be raised to mow tall-growing grasses high.

A good time to make additions or changes is after you've cut back your meadow. You can keep an eye on new plants, giving them the extra attention they need to get established.

(left) In this meadow, a layer of chaff has been left to serve as mulch.

(right) These clumps of vetiver (*Vetiveria zizanioides*) have been tied for ornamental winter effect. Winter grasses are magical—it's a shame to cut them back too soon. I've had gardening friends even spray paint dormant grasses. Why not? Have fun, make art.

Watering meadows

Irrigation is necessary maintenance for many meadows. Established meadows should thrive on once-a-week watering in the hottest part of the summer—a regime that few lawn grasses can equal. In periods of drought, the meadow may go brown and dormant; supplemental irrigation may be required to "green it up." The trick is getting the most amount of green for the least amount of water.

In climates with summer rain, meadows may not need additional irrigation, but in regions with little or no summer rain, some irrigation is needed to keep grasses green and also keep the meadows fire-safe. Unless they are growing in permanently moist soil, no grasses stay green year-round without adding water or receiving summer rain. Planting grasses that stay green with little additional water is better for the environment, and economically smarter, as water availability and costs are increasingly a problem throughout the country.

Water can be applied by drip or overhead spray. Tall meadows can block sprinkler sprays, so heads may need to be elevated as the season progresses. Large area sprinklers may need to be positioned so their spray can arc up over tall grasses. It's best to work with trained irrigation specialists when designing a sprinkler system; a professional will know which sprinklers are best for your soil. Drip irrigation is efficient but can be problematic if you later decide to include additional plants. It's easy to lose track of where pipes are, and severed drip lines are best repaired by a professional.

However it is delivered, watering should be thorough and deep, to encourage deep rooting and drought tolerance. Always put the water down at a rate the soil can absorb.

— — —

Meadow maintenance, in my opinion, involves watching what is happening and reacting to it. My internal dialogue goes something like this: "I planted that sedge over here, and now it's showing up over there. Well, maybe that's not a bad thing—maybe it showed up 'there' for a reason." Invariably, you put plants where you want them, but they end up where they want to be. Such is the never-ending fascination of the meadow.

Meadow gardening is more about editing than trying to "control" the process. As some meadow components thrive, others will fade away. These subtle processes may be transitory—here this year, different next year—or permanent, perhaps with one species gaining too much of the upper hand and becoming overdominant in your meadow. It is OK to learn by doing. If you learn to "read" your meadow, meadow gardening will be a constant source of joy and inspiration.

Loppers work well for cutting small grasses between paving stones.

(next page top) For larger grasses, or larger areas, a power trimmer is the best choice. You can also use a weed eater with a blade or a groundcover or weed mower.

(bottom) Once grasses are established, deep, infrequent irrigation is best to keep meadows healthy and to conserve water.

RESOURCES

Nurseries

The following nurseries specialize in supplying grasses that I find useful in my work of designing and planting meadows. Terms of business are indicated, along with whether the nursery offers mail order. Many of these nurseries have catalogs available either online or as hard copy. No endorsement of businesses included in this section is intended, nor is any criticism implied of any source not mentioned.

AAA Ornamentals
8S953 Jericho Road
P.O. Box 277
Big Rock, IL 60511
630-556-4507
Retail; mail order

Amber Wave Gardens
1460 Hillandale Road
Benton Harbor, MI 49022
www.amberwavegardens.com
Retail; no mail order

Annie's Annuals
740 Market Avenue
Richmond, CA 94801
www.anniesannuals.com
888-266-4370
Wholesale and retail; mail order

Berkeley Horticultural Nursery
1310 McGee Avenue
Berkeley, CA 94703
510-526-4704
www.berkeleyhort.com
Retail; no mail order

Bernado Beach Native Plant Farm
Star Route 7, Box 145
Veguita, NM 87062
bernadobeachnatives.com
505-345-6248
Wholesale and retail; no mail order

Bluestem Nursery
4101 Curry Road
Arlington, TX 76001
800-356-9164
www.bluestemnursery.com
Wholesale and retail; no mail order

Carroll Gardens
P.O. Box 310
444 E Main Street
Westminster, MD 21157
www.carrollgardens.com
Retail; mail order

Comstock Seed
917 Highway 88
Gardnerville, NV 89460
www.comstockseed.com
Wholesale and retail; no mail order

Country What Not Gardens
7129 E. 500 N.
Rochester, IN 46975
574-353-7915
www.countrywhatnotgardens.com
Retail; mail order

Curtis and Curtis
Star Route, Box 8A
4500 N Prince
Clovis, NM 88101
505-762-4759
www.curtisseed.com
Wholesale and retail; no mail order

Daryll's Nursery
15770 W Ellendale Road
Dallas, OR 97338
503-623-0251
www.daryllsnursery.com
Retail; no mail order

Digging Dog Nursery
P.O. Box 471
Albion, CA 95410
707-937-1130
www.diggingdog.com
Retail; mail order

Earthly Pursuits
2901 Kuntz Road
Windsor Mill, MD 21244
410-496-2523
www.earthlypursuits.net
Retail outlet for Kurt Bluemel, Inc.; mail order

Elkhorn Native Plant Nursery
1957B Highway 1
Moss Landing, CA 95039
www.elkhornnursery.com
831-763-1270
Wholesale and retail; no mail order

El Nativo Growers
200 S Peckham Road
Azusa, CA 91702
626-969-8449
www.elnativogrowers.com
Wholesale and retail; no mail order

Emerisa Gardens
555 Irwin Lane
Santa Rosa, CA 95401-5657
707-525-9644
www.emerisa.com
Wholesale and retail; no mail order

Ernst Conservation Seeds
9006 Mercer Pike
Meadville, PA 16335
800-873-3321, or 814-336-2404
www.ernstseed.com
Retail; mail order

Glasshouse Works
P.O. Box 97
Church Street
Stewart, OH 45778-0097
740-662-2142
www.glasshouseworks.com
Retail; mail order

Granite Seed
1697 W 2100 North
Lehi, UT 84043
www.graniteseed.com
801-768-4422
Wholesale and retail; no mail order

Greenlee Nursery
P.O. Box 885
Chino, CA 91708
909-342-6201
www.greenleenursery.com
Wholesale and retail; mail order

Hedgerow Farms
21905 County Road 88
Winters, CA 95694
530-662-8647
www.hedgerowfarms.com
Wholesale and retail; no mail order

High Country Gardens
2902 Rufina Street
Santa Fe, NM 87507-2929
www.highcountrygardens.com
800-925-9387
Retail; mail order

Jelitto Perennial Seeds
125 Chenoweth Lane #301
Louisville, KY 40207
www.jelitto.com
502-895-0807
Wholesale and retail; mail order

Larner Seeds
P.O. Box 407
Bolinas, CA 94924
415-868-9407
www.larnerseeds.com
Wholesale and retail; no mail order

Milaeger's Gardens
4838 Douglas Avenue
Racine, WI 53402-2498
800-669-1229
Retail; no mail order

Mostly Native Nursery
P.O. Box 258
27235 Highway 1
Tomales, CA 94971
707-878-2009
www.mostlynatives.com
Retail; no mail order

The Native Plant Nursery
P.O. Box 7841
Ann Arbor, MI 48107
734-677-3260
www.nativeplant.com
Wholesale and retail; no mail order

The Natives
2929 JB Carter Road
Davenport, FL 33837
863-422-6664
www.thenatives.net
Retail; no mail order

Nature Hills Nursery, Inc.
3334 North 88th Plaza
Omaha, NE 68134
402-934-8116
www.naturehills.com
Wholesale and retail; no mail order

Nearly Native Nursery
776 McBride Road
Fayetteville, GA 30215
770-460-6284
www.nearlynativenursery.com
Retail; mail order

North American Prairies Company
11754 Jarvis Avenue
Annandale, MN 56379
320-274-5316
www.northamericanprairies.com
Retail; no mail order

Northeast Nursery Garden Center
234 Newbury Street
Peabody, MA 01960
978-535-6550
Wholesale and retail; no mail order

Northwind Perennial Farm
7047 Hospital Road
Burlington, WI 53105
www.northwindperennialfarm.com
Wholesale and retail; no mail order

Plant Delights Nursery
9241 Sauls Road
Raleigh, NC 27603
919-772-4794
www.plantdelights.com
Retail; mail order

Plants of the Southwest
3095 Agua Fria Street
Santa Fe, NM 87507
800-788-7333
www.plantsofthesouthwest.com
Retail; mail order

Prairie Moon Nursery
32115 Prairie Lane
Winona, MN 55987
507-452-1362
www.prairiemoon.com
Retail; mail order

Prairie Nursery
P.O. Box 306
Westfield, WI 53964
800-476-9453
www.prairienursery.com
Retail; mail order

Prairie Seed Source
P.O. Box 83
North Lake, WI 53064-0083
www.prairiebob.com
Retail; mail order

Southwestern Native Seeds
P.O. Box 50503
Tucson, AZ 85703
www.southwesternnativeseeds.com
Retail; mail order

Stock Seed Farms
28008 Mill Road
Murdock, NE 68407
www.stockseed.com
800-759-1520
Retail; mail order

Theodore Payne Foundation
10459 Tuxford Street
Sun Valley, CA 91352-2126
818-768-1802
www.theodorepayne.org
Retail; mail order

Triple Oaks Nursery
P.O. Box 385
2359 Delsea Drive
Franklinville, NJ 08322
856-694-4272
www.tripleoaks.com
Retail; no mail order

Twombly Nursery
163 Barn Hill Road
Monroe, CT 06468
203-261-2133
www.twomblynursery.com
Retail; mail order

Western Native Seed
P.O. Box 188
Coaldale, CO 81222
719-942-3935
www.westernnativeseed.com
Retail; mail order

Wild Earth Native Plant Nursery
P.O. Box 7258
Freehold, NJ 07728
732-308-9777
Retail; no mail order

Wild Seed
P.O. Box 27751
Tempe, AZ 85285
602-276-3536
Retail; no mail order

Wildseed Farms
100 Legacy Drive
P.O. Box 3000
Fredericksburg, TX 78624
800-848-0078
www.wildseedfarms.com
Retail; mail order

Wildtype Design
900 N Every Road
Mason, MI 48854
517-244-1142
www.wildtypeplants.com
Retail; no mail order

Yucca Do Nursery
P.O. Box 907
Hempstead, TX 77445
www.yuccado.com
979-826-4580
Retail; no mail order

Organizations

California Native Grasslands Association
P.O. Box 72405
Davis, CA 95617
530-759-8458
The mission of the CNGA is to promote, preserve, and restore the diversity of California's native grasses and grassland ecosystems through education, advocacy, research, and stewardship.

California Native Plant Society
2707 K Street #1
Sacramento, CA 95816-5113
916-447-2677
The CNPS is a nonprofit organization dedicated to the understanding and appreciation of California's native plants and the conservation of them and their natural habitats through education, science, advocacy, horticulture, and land stewardship.

California Society for Ecological Restoration
2701 20th Street
Bakersfield, CA 93301-3334
661-634-9228
SERCAL is a nonprofit membership-based organization dedicated to the purpose of bringing about the recovery of damaged California ecosystems. To this end, the organization's activities are focused on the presentation of conferences, symposia, workshops, field trips, and other educational activities dealing with the many different aspects involved in restoration of California native habitats.

California Weed Science Society
P.O. Box 3073
Salinas, CA 93912-3073
831-442-0883
The CWSS provides information exchange on weed science and technology through an annual conference, publications, and other activities; advises stakeholders on matters pertaining to weeds; facilitates cooperation among individuals, agencies, and organizations; encourages careers in weed science; and promotes professional growth and interaction for its members in California.

The Ecological Conservation Organization
120 S. Cross Street
Little Rock, AR 72201
501-372-7895
ECO is an Arkansas-based and -operated environmental nonprofit organization, whose mission is simple: "Restore natural ecosystems through research, restoration, and advocacy."

Native Habitats
17287 Skyline Blvd. #102
Woodside, CA 94062-3780
Mission statement: "We participate in and support efforts to restore and preserve native ecosystems (urban, suburban, and wild) . . . for the sake of restoring ecological process and biodiversity . . . allowing native species, both flora and fauna, to survive and thrive."

Society for Ecological Restoration International
285 W. 18th Street #1
Tucson, AZ 85701
520-622-5485
The Global Restoration Network (GRN), a project of the society, offers the field of ecological restoration a new database and web-based portal to trustworthy and hard-to-find information on all aspects of restoration, from historic ecosystems and recent causes of degradation to in-depth case studies and proven restoration techniques. The overriding mission of the GRN is to link restoration projects, research, and practitioners in order to foster the creative exchange of experience, vision, and expertise.

MEADOWS TO VISIT

Visiting meadows in your own region is the perfect way to start to understand the type of meadow that might be created in your garden, and to see the plants that might naturally be grown in a created meadow. Many of our great national parks include areas of native grasslands (www.nps.gov) and the Nature Conservancy has a section on grasslands (www.nature.org/earth/grasslands). A list of botanic gardens and arboreta with native plant displays follows.

Arizona

The Arboretum at Flagstaff
4001 Woody Mountain Road
Flagstaff, AZ 86001
928-774-1442
www.thearb.org

Arizona-Sonora Desert Museum
2021 North Kinney Road
Tucson, AZ 85743
520-883-1380
www.desertmuseum.org

Desert Botanical Garden
1201 North Galvin Parkway
Phoenix, AZ 85008
480-941-1225
www.dbg.org

California

Davis Arboretum
University of California
One Shields Avenue
Davis, CA 95616
530-752-4880
arboretum.ucdavis.edu/

Quail Botanical Gardens
230 Quail Gardens Drive
Encinitas, CA 92024
760-436-3036
www.qbgardens.com

Rancho Santa Ana Botanic Garden
1500 N. College Avenue
Claremont, CA 91711
909-625-8767
www.rsabg.org

San Francisco Botanical Garden at Strybing Arboretum
9th Avenue and Lincoln Way
San Francisco, CA 94122
415-661-1316
www.sfbotanicalgarden.org

Santa Barbara Botanic Garden
1212 Mission Canyon Road
Santa Barbara, CA 93105
805-682-4726
www.sbbg.org

University of California Botanical Garden
200 Centennial Drive #5045
Berkeley, CA 94720
510-643-2755
botanicalgarden.berkeley.edu/

Colorado

Denver Botanic Gardens
909 York Street
Denver, CO 80206
720-865-3500
www.botanicgardens.org

Connecticut

The Connecticut College Arboretum
270 Mohegan Avenue
New London, CT 06320
860-439-5020
arboretum.conncoll.edu/

Delaware

Mt. Cuba Center, Inc.
P.O. Box 3570
Greenville, DE 19807-0570
302-239-4244
Mtcubacenter.org

District of Columbia

U.S. National Arboretum
3501 New York Avenue NE
Washington, DC 20002-1958
202-245-2726
www.usna.usda.gov/

Florida

Bok Tower Gardens
1151 Tower Boulevard
Lake Wales, FL 33853-3412
863-676-1408
www.boktower.org

Fairchild Tropical Botanic Garden
1091 Old Cutler Road
Coral Gables, FL 33156-4299
305-667-1651
www.fairchildgarden.org

Georgia

State Botanical Garden of Georgia
University of Georgia
2450 S Milledge Avenue
Athens, GA 30605
706-542-6195
www.uga.edu/botgarden

Hawaii

Harold L. Lyon Arboretum
University of Hawaii
3860 Manoa Road
Honolulu, HI 96822
808-988-0456
www.hawaii.edu/lyonarboretum

National Tropical Botanical Garden
3530 Papalina Road
Kalaheo, HI 96741
808-332-7324
www.ntbg.org

Waimea Arboretum and Botanical Gardens
Waimea Arboretum Foundation
59–864 Kamehameha Highway
Haleiwa, HI 96712
808-638-8655

Illinois

Chicago Botanic Garden
1000 Lake Cook Road
Glencoe, IL 60022
847-835-5440
www.chicago-botanic.org

Morton Arboretum
4100 Illinois Route 53
Lisle, IL 60532-1293
630-968-0074
www.mortonarb.org

Massachusetts

Arnold Arboretum
Harvard University
125 Arborway
Jamaica Plain, MA 02130-3500
617-524-1718
www.arboretum.harvard.edu

New England Wild Flower Society
Garden in the Woods
180 Hemenway Road
Framingham, MA 01701-2699
508-877-7630
www.newenglandwild.org

Minnesota

Minnesota Landscape Arboretum
University of Minnesota
3675 Arboretum Drive
Chaska, MN 55318
952-443-1400
www.arboretum.umn.edu

Mississippi

Crosby Arboretum
370 Ridge Road
Picayune, MS 39466
601-799-2311
www.crosbyarboretum.msstate.edu/

Missouri

Missouri Botanical Garden
P.O. Box 299
Saint Louis, MO 63166-0299
314-577-5100
www.mobot.org

Prairie State Park
128 NW 150th Lane
Mindenmines, MO 64769
417-843-6711
www.mostateparks.com/prairie.htm

Nebraska

Nebraska Statewide Arboretum
P.O. Box 830715
University of Nebraska
Lincoln, NE 68583-0715
402-472-2971
arboretum.unl.edu/

New Jersey

The Rutgers Gardens
Cook College, Rutgers University
112 Ryders Lane
New Brunswick, NJ 08901
732-932-8451
rutgersgardens.rutgers.edu/

New Mexico

Santa Fe Botanical Garden
1213 Mercantile Street, Box 23343
Santa Fe, NM 87502-3343
505-471-9103
www.santafebotanicalgarden.org

New York

Brooklyn Botanic Garden
1000 Washington Avenue
Brooklyn, NY 11225-1099
718-623-7200
www.bbg.org

New York Botanical Garden
200th Street and Kazimiroff Blvd.
Bronx, NY 10458-5126
718 817 8700
www.nybg.org

North Carolina

JC Raulston Arboretum
North Carolina State University
4301 Beryl Road
Raleigh, NC 28806-9315
919-515-3132
www.ncsu.edu/jcraulstonarboretum/

North Carolina Arboretum
100 Frederick Law Olmsted Way
Asheville, NC 28806-9315
828-665-2492
www.ncarboretum.org

North Carolina Botanical Garden
University of North Carolina
Chapel Hill, NC 27599-3375
919-962-0522
www.unc.edu/depts/ncbg

Ohio

Holden Arboretum
9500 Sperry Road
Kirtland, OH 44094-5172
440-946-4400
www.holdenarb.org

Oregon

Berry Botanic Garden
11505 SW Summerville Avenue
Portland, OR 97219-8309
503-636-4112
www.berrybot.org

Pennsylvania

Bowman's Hill Wildflower Preserve
P.O. Box 685
New Hope, PA 18938-0685
215-862-2924
www.bhwp.org

Longwood Gardens
1001 Longwood Road
Kennett Square, PA 19348
www.longwoodgardens.com

Morris Arboretum of the University of
Pennsylvania
100 Northwestern Avenue
Philadelphia, PA 19118
215-247-5777
www.upenn.edu/arboretum

Texas

Lady Bird Johnson Wildflower Center
The University of Texas at Austin
4801 La Crosse Avenue
Austin, TX 78739
512-232-0100
www.wildflower.org

Mercer Arboretum and Botanic Gardens
22306 Aldine-Westfield Road
Humble, TX 77338-1071
281-443-8731
www.cp4.hctx.net/mercer

San Antonio Botanical Gardens
555 Funston Place
San Antonio, TX 78209
210-207-3250
www.sabot.org

Utah

Red Butte Garden
University of Utah
300 Wakara Way
Salt Lake City, UT 84108
801-581-4747
www.redbuttegarden.org

Virginia

Norfolk Botanical Garden
6700 Azalea Garden Road
Norfolk, VA 23518-5337
757-441-5830
www.norfolkbotanicalgarden.org

Washington

Bellevue Botanical Garden
12001 Main Street
Bellevue, WA 98005
425-452-2750
www.bellevuebotanical.org

Wisconsin

University of Wisconsin Arboretum
1207 Seminole Highway
Madison, WI 53711-3726
608-263-7888
uwarboretum.org

BIBLIOGRAPHY

Bormann, F. Herbert, Diana Balmori, and Gordon T. Geballe. 1993. *Redesigning the American Lawn*. Yale University Press.

Burrell, C. Colston. 1997. *A Gardener's Encyclopedia of Wild Flowers*. Rodale Press.

Cullina, William. 2008. *Native Ferns, Moss, and Grasses*. Frances Tenenbaum/Houghton Mifflin.

Daniels, Stevie. 1995. *The Wild Lawn Handbook*. Macmillan.

Darke, Rick. 2007. *The Encyclopedia of Grasses for Livable Landscapes*. Timber Press.

Druse, Ken. 2004. *The Natural Habitat Garden*. Timber Press.

Foerster, Karl. 1988. *Einzug der Gräser und Farne in die Gärten*. Eugen Ulmer.

Gould, Frank W. 1988. *Grasses of the Southwestern United States*. The University of Arizona Press. First published 1940.

Greenlee, John. 1992. *The Encyclopedia of Ornamental Grasses*. Rodale Books.

Lloyd, Christopher. 2004. *Meadows*. Timber Press.

McClaren, M. P., and T. R. van Devender, eds. 1995. *The Desert Grassland*. The University of Arizona Press.

Oakes, A. J. 1990. *Ornamental Grasses and Grasslike Plants*. Van Nostrand Reinhold. First published 1915.

Phillips, Roger, and Martyn Rix. 1991. *The Random House Book of Perennials*, 2 vols. Random House.

Pollan, Michael. 1991. *Second Nature*. The Atlantic Monthly Press.

Robinson, William. 1994. *The Wild Garden*. Sagapress/Timber Press. First published 1870.

Rockwell, F. F., and Esther C. Grayson. 1956. *The Complete Book of Lawns*. American Garden Guild/Doubleday.

U.S. Department of Agriculture. 1971. *Common Weeds of the United States*. Dover.

Wasowski, Sally. 2002. *Gardening with Prairie Plants*. University of Minnesota Press.

Yarlett, Lewis L. 1996. *Common Grasses of Florida and the Southeast*. Florida Native Plant Society.

INDEX